FROM STOKE MANDEVILLE TO SOCHI: A HISTORY OF THE SUMMER AND WINTER PARALYMPIC GAMES

IAN BRITTAIN

FROM STOKE MANDEVILLE TO SOCHI: A HISTORY OF THE SUMMER AND WINTER PARALYMPIC GAMES

IAN BRITTAIN

First published in 2012 in Champaign, Illinois, USA
by Common Ground Publishing LLC
as part of the Sport and Society book series

Library of Congress Cataloging-in-Publication Data

Brittain, Ian.
 From Stoke Mandeville to Sochi : a history of the summer and winter paralympic games / Ian
Brittain.
     pages cm.
 Includes bibliographical references and index.
 ISBN 978-1-61229-412-4 (pbk : alk. paper) -- ISBN 978-1-61229-413-1 (pdf : alk. paper)
 1. Paralympics--History. 2. Sports for people with disabilities. 3. Athletes with disabilities. I. Title.

 GV722.5.P37B746 2014
 796.087--dc23

                          2013051208

Cover photo credit: the International Wheelchair and Amputee Sports Federation (IWAS)

Table of Contents

Acknowledgements

So many people have assisted me with this project over the last thirteen years that I simply do not have space to thank them all individually, but I would like to give you all a heartfelt thank you for your time, assistance and unstinting generosity. In thirteen years, only one organisation has refused to assist with my research or allow me access to their archives. I would particularly like to thank the International Wheelchair and Amputee Sports Federation for all their help. In their former guise as the International Stoke Mandeville Wheelchair Sports Federation, they were responsible for helping to found the Stoke Mandeville Games that went on to become the Paralympic Games, and they have been kind enough to provide a large portion of the images that appear throughout the book, especially in chapter one. Other organisations that have assisted greatly are the International Paralympic Committee and the Canadian Paralympic Committee. Numerous Paralympians and disability sports organisations from around the world have played a part in the formation of this book, and without their help, advice, and assistance, this book simply would not have been possible. Thank you again, one and all!

Photographic Credits/Acknowledgements

Rudi van den Abbeele
Pamela Barnard
Jane Blackburn
Stuart Braye
Dr Ian Brittain
Canadian Paralympic Committee
Kevin Davies
Deutsche Schützenbund
Brian Dickinson
Elizabeth Edmondson
Prof. Ted Fay
Lara Ferguson
Sally Haynes
Gershon Huberman
Peter Hull
Anne Ragnhild Kroken
Anne Marie Lannem
International Paralympic Committee
International Wheelchair and Amputee Sports Federation
Paul Lyall
Mark de Meyer
Paddy Moran
Inge Morisbak
Paul Noble
Jenny Orpwood

Valerie and John Robertson
Tony Sainsbury
John Sawkins
Mike Shelton
Dr Danielle Stewart
Trish Taylor
Rita Thompson
Steve Varden
Terry Willett

Medal Image Credits

Hans Anton Ålien
Jane Blackburn
Dr Ian Brittain
Kjarten N. Haugen
Bob Matthews
Margaret Maughan
Delphine van Opdorp
David Roberts
Valerie Robertson
Pertti Sankilampi
Matthew Stockford
Trish Taylor
United Kingdom Sports Association for People with Learning Difficulties
Karolina Wisniewska

Introduction

As someone who has spent over ten years travelling the world interviewing former Paralympic sportsmen and women and visiting various archives for organisations and venues that have been connected with Paralympic sport since its inception in order to try and gather materials and information the author regularly hears the same story – it has been thrown away! Families of deceased athletes from the early Games have thrown it out because they deemed it worthless, many former athletes who are still alive stated they had moved house to smaller accommodation and had thrown things away because of lack of space (including their Paralympic medals) and disability sports organisations have moved offices and thrown records out due to lack of storage space and the belief that they were of no value. The author has visited cities as far apart as Arnhem (hosts in 1980) and Toronto (hosts in 1976) to find nothing more than a small file of newspaper clippings left as the legacy of those Games and places like the Royal Perth Hospital, where the first Australian team at the Stoke Mandeville Games in 1957 originated to find little more.

This book then is an attempt to salvage some of this history and bring it together in one accessible and easy to read volume. From the outset I would like to make it very clear that this book is not meant to be an academic text. It has always been my intention that it should be a resource for anyone with an interest in the history of the summer or winter Paralympic Games. The idea was to bring together in one place all of the facts, figures and interesting stories that have occurred in the development of the Games from their roots at Stoke Mandeville hospital in the United Kingdom to the global mega-event they have become today. To my knowledge this is the first publication to bring together in one place all the available images of artefacts connected with the Games such as posters and winners medals – some of which have never been seen in print before. Although I have endeavoured to include all of the key relevant information available to me this is by no means a complete history, but more a starting point from which future researchers and historians may begin. It has taken the best part of thirteen years to collect the information contained in this book. I hope that in time it will inspire others to contribute to a more complete history in much the same way as has happened in the area of Olympic history.

Format

With the exception of the first and last chapters each chapter follows a standard pattern, hopefully making the book easy to search for a particular piece of information.

Accuracy of Data

For those of you unacquainted with the Paralympic Games, record keeping for the Games prior to 1988 in Seoul when the Games returned to being hosted by the same city as the Olympic Games was quite poor. There are various possible reasons for this, but the two main ones are likely have been a lack of time and resources to fully document a Games and also lack of belief that the Games would ever become of such importance that future generations might be interested in the documentation attached to them. This second reason has been reinforced greatly to me by the number of organisations, particularly national organisations, I have contacted or visited in the course of my research only to be told that any documentation had been thrown out due to lack of storage space and a belief that it was of no importance. I have, therefore, had to piece this history together from a wide variety of sources, some of which gave conflicting accounts. In these cases I have had to take an educated guess based upon the overall evidence. This is particularly true in the case of participation numbers at Games prior to Seoul. It should also be pointed out that in early 'Official Results Books' they often did not list the names of competitors in relay events or team sports, but just put the country name instead.

Missing Data

Following on from the section on the accuracy of data above and as stated in the introduction, what is contained in this book is not a complete history. I am still missing some posters for example. In addition many of the early 'Official Results Books' are incomplete. This has become apparent throughout the course of my research, especially when comparing results appearing in various newspapers with the official results. On finding such results I have always provided this information to the International Paralympic Committee (with accompanying evidence) in order that their results data-base can be up-dated. However, this is a slow process and so there may appear to be discrepancies between what appears in this book and what the IPC data-base shows.

Do you possess some missing data or think something is inaccurate?

If upon reading this book you believe you have some missing data or you think something contained in the book is inaccurate then you can e-mail me at **parahist@hotmail.co.uk**. In the case of perceived inaccuracies please try to ensure that you have corroborating evidence for your claims.

Chapter 1: The Birth of a Worldwide Mega-event: 1948–1959

Prior to 1948: The Introduction of Sport as a Form of Rehabilitation

Prior to World War II, the vast majority of those with spinal cord injuries died within three years following their injury. Indeed, Dr Ludwig Guttmann, the universally accepted founder of what is today known as the Paralympic movement, whilst a doctor in 1930s Germany encountered on a ward round a coal miner with a broken back. Guttmann was shocked to learn from the consultant that such cases were a waste of time as he would be dead within two weeks. This was usually from sepsis of the blood or kidney failure or both. However, after World War II sulfa drugs made spinal cord injury survivable. The other major issue for individuals with spinal injuries was the major depression caused by societal attitudes to them, which, at the time, automatically assigned them to the scrap heap of life as useless and worthless individuals.

Guttmann was a German – Jewish neurologist who fled Nazi occupied Germany with his family in 1939 and eventually settled in Oxford, England where he found work at Oxford University. In September 1943 the British Government commissioned Guttmann as the Director of the National Spinal Injuries Unit at the Ministry of Pensions Hospital, Stoke Mandeville, Aylesbury. This was mainly to take care of the numerous soldiers and civilians suffering from spinal injuries as a result of the war. Guttmann accepted under the condition that he would be totally independent and that he could apply his philosophy as far as the whole approach to the treatment of those patients was concerned, although many of his colleagues were apparently surprised by his enthusiasm for what they perceived as an utterly daunting task. "They could not understand how I could leave Oxford University to be engulfed in the hopeless and depressing task of looking after traumatic spinal paraplegics" (Goodman, 1986).

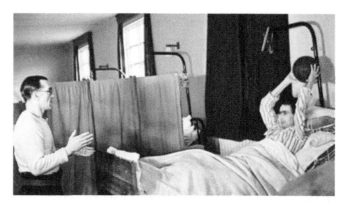

'Q' Hill, Remedial Gymnast, using a medicine ball to strengthen a patient's upper body

Prior to World War II there is little evidence of organised efforts to develop or promote sport for individuals with disabling conditions, especially those with spinal injuries who were considered to have no hope of surviving their injuries. Following the war, however, medical authorities were prompted to re-evaluate traditional methods of rehabilitation which were not satisfactorily responding to the medical and psychological needs of the large number of soldiers disabled in combat. According to McCann (1996), Guttmann 'recognised the physiological and psychological values of sport in the rehabilitation of paraplegic hospital inpatients' and so it was that sport was introduced as part of the total rehabilitation programme for patients in the spinal unit. The aim was not only to give hope and a sense of self-worth to the patients, but to change the attitudes of society towards the spinally injured by demonstrating to them that they could not only continue to be useful members of society, but could take part in activities and complete tasks most of the non-disabled society would struggle with.

Further strengthening of the upper body using rope climbing

According to Guttmann (1952) they 'started modestly and cautiously with darts, snooker, punch-ball and skittles' Sometime later, apparently after Guttmann and his remedial gymnast, Quartermaster 'Q' Hill had 'waged furious battle' in an empty ward to test it, the sport of wheelchair polo was introduced. This was perceived a short time later, however, as too rough for all concerned and was replaced by wheelchair netball. This later became what we now know as wheelchair basketball.

Punchball Wheelchair Polo

The next sport to be introduced into the programme at Stoke Mandeville was to play a key role in all areas of Guttmann's rehabilitation plans. That sport was archery. Guttmann (1952) claims that archery was 'of immense value in strengthening, in a very natural way, just those muscles of the upper limbs, shoulders and trunk, on which the paraplegic's well-balanced, upright position depends.'

Archery proved excellent for posture, balance and the upper body strength required by a paraplegic.

However, it was far more than just that. It was one of very few sports that, once proficient, paraplegics could compete on equal terms with their non-disabled counterparts. This led to visits of teams from Stoke Mandeville to a number of non-disabled archery clubs in later years, which were very helpful in breaking down the barriers between the public and the paraplegics. It also meant that once discharged from hospital the paraplegic had an access to society through their local archery club. According to Guttmann 'These experiments were the beginning of a systematic development of competitive sport for the paralysed as an essential part of their medical rehabilitation and social re-integration in the community of a country like Great Britain where sport in one form or another plays such an essential part in the lives of so many people'. As the next section will show archery was also the sport that got the whole disability sport movement started.

1948: The Grandson of Old Bill

For an event that would later go on to become the largest ever sporting event for people with disabilities and the second largest multi-sport event on the planet after the Olympic Games the event now known globally as the Paralympic Games had a rather inauspicious beginning. It began life as an archery demonstration between two teams of Paraplegics from the Ministry of Pensions Hospital at Stoke Mandeville and the Star and Garter Home for Injured War Veterans at Richmond in Surrey, that was held in conjunction with the presentation of a specially adapted bus to the patients of Stoke Mandeville by the British Legion and London Transport.

Perhaps more auspicious was the date chosen for the handover of the bus and the archery demonstration; Thursday 29th July 1948, the exact same day as the opening ceremony for the Games of the Fourteenth Olympiad at Wembley in London less than thirty five miles away. Given the low key nature of the archery event at Stoke Mandeville that day written accounts of the event itself are few and far between and what appears here has been gleaned from a variety of sources and carefully pieced together. A total of sixteen archers took part in the event with eight competing on each team. The team from the Star and Garter home were all male, whereas the team from Stoke Mandeville consisted of six males and two females. The names of twelve of the archers have been identified and are set out below:

Star and Garter Team

Joseph William Blackmore	Sgt. Royal Garrison Artillery
Dennis Henry Goodman	Pte. Royal Field Artillery
Charles Frederick Groves	Pte. Somerset Light Infantry
Gerrard Gilbert Grimshaw	Pte. 2nd East Yorkshire Regiment
William Foster	Sglr. Royal Garrison Artillery
Charles Horrobin	Sglr. Royal Garrison Artillery
Henry Tomlinson	Driver Royal Electrical and Mechanical Engineers
William Edwin "Peter" Twiss	Trooper. 148th Regiment, Royal Armoured Corps

Stoke Mandeville Team (Known Members)

Mr Leslie W. Johnson
Ms Joan "Bunty" Noon
Ms Robin Imray
Mr Roy Jennings

The Missing Four[1]

The four photos below show the four un-named members of the Stoke Mandeville archery team from the very first competition held on Thursday 29th July, 1948.

Competition commenced at 10.30am with shooting over a distance of 50 yards. The Stoke Mandeville team were all dressed in team strip of green shirts bearing the Stoke Mandeville team badge (A large SM with two crossed arrows underneath). The Star and Garter team were all dressed in white shirts. The competition was officiated over by Frank Bilson, Champion Archer of England, who had given up much of his own time to develop archery for wheelchair users and had actually given the Star and Garter team their very first lesson in archery. He had obviously taught them well because according to Peter Twiss of the Star and Garter team, in a report for the Star and Garter Magazine, it appears it was the Star and Garter's dominance over the longer distances that won the day. After the end of the 50 yard round the Star and Garter team held a lead of 121 points. The next round was shot over a distance of 40 yards and when the final arrow of the round had found its target the Star and Garter Team had extended their lead at the lunch break by a further 71 points giving them an overall lead of 192 points with one round remaining.

---

1. If anyone can put a name, preferably with photographic evidence, to anyone of these four then please e-mail parahist@hotmail.co.uk.

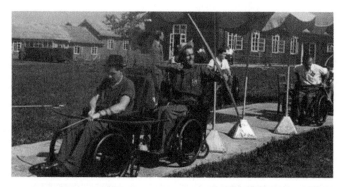

Roy Jennings (Stoke Mandeville) releases his arrow watched by his fiancée, Effie Wright.
'Old Bill', the specially adapted bus, can be seen in the background.

Following an informal lunch the hand-over ceremony for the specially adapted bus was held in brilliant sunshine. The bus itself was a double-decker with the top taken off, painted in the legion colours of blue and yellow and with a special ramp at the back to allow wheelchair users access. Once aboard the wheels could be secured. Mr A. Durrant, mechanical engineer for London Transport described the bus as the grandson of 'Old Bill', the famous bus of World War I.

'Old Bill', a specially adapted bus for use by Stoke Mandeville patients

The bus was presented on behalf of the British Legion and London Transport by Major Sir Brunel Cohen, himself a disabled ex-serviceman from World War I, to Mr H.A. Marquand MP, Minister for Pensions. The aim of the bus was not only to allow patients to travel around the country to various activities and events, but also to allow them to get back out into the community and enter more into the life of the town. Other dignitaries present at the handover ceremony included Mr Arthur Blenkinsop MP (Parliamentary Secretary to the Ministry of Pensions), Miss M.S. Cox (Deputy Secretary), Colonel Gordon Larking (National Chairman, British Legion), Major General Sir Richard Howard Vyse (National Vice-Chairman), Major W. Scott Evans (County British Legion Secretary), Professor P. Kilner, Major Ashby, Dr D.T. Prideaux (Director General, Medical Services) and Dr Ludwig Guttmann. Throughout the ceremony the band of the Royal Air Force played.

Following an opportunity for those present to inspect the new bus, the final round of the archery competition took place over a distance of 30 yards. Despite a valiant effort by the Stoke Mandeville archers the Star and Garter team were able to extend their overall lead by a further 39 points. The final scores after the three rounds had been completed were as follows:

Star and Garter   1821 points
Stoke Mandeville 1590 points

The Winning Star and Garter Team

1949: The Paraplegic 'Olympic Games' of the Future

Dr Guttmann's 'Grand Festival of Paraplegic Sport', as the second incarnation of the Games were described in The Cord, were held on Wednesday, 27th July 1949. Building upon much hard work done by Dr Guttmann, his staff and the impact of various Stoke Mandeville patients moving to other spinal units around the country and taking their new found enthusiasm for sport with them the number of teams entered rose to seven. These were as follows:

Stoke Mandeville
Stoke Mandeville Ladies
Stoke Mandeville Old Boys living at home
Chaseley Home, Eastbourne, Sussex
Lyme Green Settlement, Macclesfield, Cheshire
No. 3 Polish Hospital, Penley, Denbighshire
Star and Garter Home, Richmond, Surrey

A grand total of thirty seven individuals took part in these Games and with the exception of the archers from the Polish Hospital at Penley every competitor had, at some time, been a patient of Dr Guttmann. With the possible exception of the Polish competitors from Penley, who it is currently impossible to know whether they were British residents, these Games saw the participation of the first identifiable 'international' patient - Emanuel Kanakakis, competing for Chaseley, but actually a Greek citizen. In addition to a repeat of the previous year's archery competition 'net-ball' was added to the programme for these Games. This was a kind of hybrid of netball and basketball played in wheelchairs and using netball posts for goals. A total of six teams entered the archery competition and three teams were entered for the net-ball competition as follows:

Archery   **Net-ball**
Stoke Mandeville   Stoke Mandeville
Stoke Mandeville Ladies   Lyme Green
Stoke Mandeville Old Boys living at home   Chaseley
Chaseley
Star and Garter
Penley

At the close of competition all the athletes and guests were provided with tea in the Sister's Dining Room. Amongst the guests were Alderman J. Holland (Mayor of Aylesbury) and his wife, Sir Francis Prideaux (Director General of the Ministry of Pensions), Miss EE Warr (Matron, Royal Bucks Hospital), the Right Honourable AH Marquand (Minister of Pensions) and Miss M. Cox (Deputy Secretary of the Ministry of Pensions). It was Miss Cox who went on to present the prizes of Cups and medals to each of the winners, the medals themselves having been designed and made by the patients attending the precision engineering class at the hospital, some of whom, such as Betty Green, had taken part in the days sports activities.

Netball match between Stoke Mandeville and Chaseley

At the end of the day Dr Guttmann gave a speech in which he made the now famous claim that the Stoke Mandeville Games would one day become recognised as the paraplegic's equivalent of the Olympic Games. This certainly showed remarkable foresight given that he himself admits that, despite the widely accepted success of the day, the statement was met with very little shared optimism from those gathered in the audience. However the Minister for Pensions, the Right Honourable HA Marquand did state 'this is really Dr Guttmann's day. The splendid performance of these paraplegic patients this afternoon is testimony to his work in the treatment and rehabilitation of paralysed ex-servicemen'.

1950: Javelin Thrown into the Sporting Mix

The third Stoke Mandeville Games took place on Thursday 27th July, 1950. The number of competitors almost doubled from the previous year with 61 sportsmen and women taking part from ten competing institutions and organisations. Hexham, Southport and Wharncliffe competed at the Games for the first time and javelin throwing was added to the programme taking the total number of sports to three.

Competing Institutions and Organisations

Chaseley Home, Eastbourne, Sussex
Lyme Green Settlement, Macclesfield, Cheshire
National Spinal Injuries Unit, Stoke Mandeville
No. 3 Polish Hospital, Penley, Denbighshire
Star and Garter Home, Richmond, Surrey
Wharncliffe Hospital, Sheffield
Spinal Injuries Unit, General Hospital, Hexham, Northumberland
Stoke Mandeville 'Old Boys' living at Kytes Settlement, Watford
Spinal Injuries Unit, Promenade Hospital, Southport, Lancashire
Stoke Mandeville Old Boys living at home (including Duchess of Gloucester House)

Sports: Archery, Javelin, Netball

Dr Guttmann giving his opening address to the competitors

At the opening ceremony Dr Guttmann declared that he had travelled to various parts of the world over the previous year and that 'amongst the British medical and social achievements the introduction of sport for the disabled, and in particular the paralysed, has aroused the greatest interest and respect and even enthusiasm.' The increased size of the Games obviously necessitated a great deal of behind-the-scenes preparation and Dr Guttmann was quick to thank Dora Bell, Joan Scruton and Charlie Atkinson, who as well as helping prepare for the event, also did a number of vital jobs on the day such as checking archery scores (Joan) and refereeing all the netball games (Charlie).

Guests of Honour

The prize giving was attended by Sir Arton Wilson, Permanent Secretary to the Ministry of Pensions, his wife Lady Wilson, who distributed the prizes and Dr Rees, Director General of Medical Services of the Ministry of Pensions. Also in attendance on the day were the Beverley Sisters, who were in England for a short London season before returning to America. In the evening they sang to the patients in the wards. Dr Guttmann concluded the prize giving by stating that he hoped it might be possible to add swimming to the programme the following year and also that teams from abroad might be able to take part.

1951: First Signs of Internationalism

In 1951 the Games moved from a weekday to a weekend. This is possibly due to the increasing number of former patients who were successful in finding full-time work and, therefore, unable to attend the Games on a weekday. Therefore, this year the Games were held on Saturday 28th July. Once again the number of competitors taking part almost doubled from 61 the previous year to 121 this year.

Competing Organisations and Institutions

Chaseley Home, Eastbourne, Sussex
Star and Garter Home, Richmond, Surrey
Stoke Mandeville 'Old Boys' living at home
No. 3 Polish Hospital, Penley, Denbighshire
Lyme Green Settlement, Macclesfield, Cheshire
National Spinal Injuries Unit, Stoke Mandeville
Duchess of Gloucester House, Isleworth, Middlesex
Spinal Injuries Unit, General Hospital, Hexham, Northumberland
Stoke Mandeville 'Old Boys' living at Kytes Settlement, Watford
National Spinal Injuries Unit, Stoke Mandeville (Ladies' Team)
Spinal Injuries Unit, Promenade Hospital, Southport, Lancashire

DrGuttmann's wish that the Games should become international in nature took a small step towards reality with four individual international patients based at various units around the country coming to take part in the Games.

Individual International Patients

Emanuel Kanakakis (Greece/ Duchess of Gloucester House)
Pierre Ducher (France/ Star & Garter)
Charlene Todman (Australia/ Stoke Mandeville)
Un-named Southern Rhodesian patient

Snooker made its first appearance at the Games taking the total number of sports to four. In addition there were two demonstrations throughout the day. The first was for club swinging. This was done by twenty Stoke Mandeville paraplegics in time to music. This first started out as an exercise class taken by two physiotherapists, Miss Wylde and Miss Saint. An excellent exercise for deriving balance the class was worked up into a show of rhythmical precision and demonstrated to those present at the Games.

Sports: Archery, Javelin, Netball, Snooker
Demonstrations: Club Swinging, Table Tennis

The table tennis demonstration was carried out by four patients from the Star and Garter Home – Syd Taylor, Doug Traverse, Pierre Doucher and Charlie Groves. Although only a demonstration event it appears that the 'winners' of this demonstration were surprised to find at the prize giving ceremony that they too were to receive a prize for their efforts.

As had occurred every year since the Games began in 1948 music for the day was supplied by the Central Band of the R.A.F., based at nearby RAF Halton and conducted by Flight Lieutenant F.A. Gale, their Director of Music.

Members of the Central Band of the RAF admire a specially adapted motorbike for paraplegics.

Guests of Honour

Guests of honour at this year's Games were George Isaacs, the Minister for Pensions, who presented the prizes, and Sir Arton Wilson, the Permanent Secretary to the Ministry of Pensions who had also attended with his wife the previous year.

Dr Guttmann, Sir Arton Wilson and Mr George Isaacs try their hand at archery as
Charlene Todman (Australia) watches

In concluding the day Dr Guttmann thanked all the competitors for their splendid
performances, as they had given again a shining example of the modern
conception of rehabilitation.

1952: The Games Go Truly International

Finally, five years after they began, Dr Guttmann's dearest wish for the Games
came true when a team of four athletes, a physiotherapist (W.Simmers) and a
nursing sister (C.M van Nispen) arrived at Stoke Mandeville from the Doorn
Military Rehabilitation Centre, Aardenburg in the Netherlands and the Games
became truly international. The team was led by Dr J.E. van Gogh. This was
greatly aided by the assistance of the World Veterans' Federation (WVF) who
arranged and paid for the visit through their rehabilitation programme. Mr Kurt
Jannson, director of the WVF rehabilitation programme announced at the Games
that the WVF intended to make it possible for more teams from other countries to
attend the Games the following year, which would help 'make the idea of
Olympic Games for the disabled a "practical reality"' Interestingly, Mr W.M.
Van Lanschot, Secretary-Treasurer of the World Veterans' Federation, was also
President of the Dutch Disabled Veterans Association, which may explain the
choice of the Netherlands team as the first to be supported by the WVF. Unlike
previous years, however, there was only a very small increase in the overall
number of competitors from 121 the previous year to 130 this year. The Games
took place on Saturday 26th July 1952. In keeping with his vision Dr Guttmann, in
his opening speech, was quick to point out that the Olympic Games were in
progress in Helsinki and that he hoped that 'one day the paraplegic games would
be as international and as widely known in its own sphere as the Olympics'.

International Nations Represented: The Netherlands

Netherlands (Military Rehabilitation Centre, Aardenburg)

(Gerard van Opdorp, Renus Hoogendoorn, Fritz van Ommen, Arri Prins)

British Organisations and Institutions

Chaseley Home, Eastbourne, Sussex
Lyme Green Settlement, Macclesfield, Cheshire
National Spinal Injuries Unit, Stoke Mandeville
No. 3 Polish Hospital, Penley, Denbighshire
Stoke Mandeville 'Old Boys' living at home
Stoke Mandeville 'Old Girls' living at home
Duchess of Gloucester House, Isleworth, Middlesex
Spinal Injuries Unit, General Hospital, Hexham, Northumberland
Stoke Mandeville 'Old Boys' living at Kytes Settlement, Watford
National Spinal Injuries Unit, Stoke Mandeville (Ladies' Team)
Spinal Injuries Unit, Promenade Hospital, Southport, Lancashire
Star and Garter Home, Richmond, Surrey

With regard to sports table tennis was upgraded from demonstration sport the previous year to a full medal sport this year. Once again there was a club swinging demonstration.

Sports: Archery, Javelin, Netball, Snooker, Table Tennis
Demonstration: Club Swinging

Guests of Honour

Guests of honour at this year's Games were Sir George Schuster, Chairman of the Oxford Regional Hospitals Board, who presented the prizes and Mr Derick Heathcoat-Amory, Minister of Pensions, who gave a speech at the closing ceremony. In his speech the Minister stated that 'doctors may prescribe medicine and treatment, but it is the undefeatable spirit of the patients themselves, which really helps to produce results. He also paid tribute to the team from the Netherlands and welcomed the idea of teams coming from abroad to compete.

Gerard van Opdorp's medal from 1952

1953: Swimming Makes Its First Splash

The Games of this year were held over the evening of Friday 7th and the whole of Saturday 8th August. A specially designed flag for the Games was flown for the very first time. This first version of the flag had six white stars – one for each of the nations represented at the Games. In future years, every time a new nation was represented another star would be added to the flag. The flag was displayed above a sign that displayed the message the Games were meant to get across to the rest of society. In his message contained in the programme for the Games, Dr Guttmann reinforced the Olympic link once more stating 'Like the Olympic Games, which were started by a small group of people who believed in sport as a great medium for furthering true sportsmanship and understanding amongst human beings, our Stoke Mandeville Games will, we believe, unite paralysed men and women of different nations to take their rightful place in the field of sport'.

International Nations Represented (Number of Competitors)
Canada   (7) Finland* (3) France* (2) Israel* (3) Netherlands (10)
*Supported by WVF

New Flag and Message designed for the Games

Dr Guttmann apparently invited eight nations to take part in these Games. Of the eight only Austria, Belgium and the United States failed to attend. Of those that did attend many were assisted financially by the World Veterans' Federation.

British Organisations and Institutions

This year saw the participation of the first spinal injuries unit based outside of England – the Rookwood Centre in Cardiff, Wales, which had opened its doors in late 1952.

Chaseley Home, Eastbourne, Sussex
Lyme Green Settlement, Macclesfield, Cheshire
Stoke Mandeville 'Old Boys' living at home
Stoke Mandeville 'Old Girls' living at home
No. 3 Polish Hospital, Penley, Denbighshire
Star and Garter Home, Richmond, Surrey
Spinal Injuries Unit, General Hospital, Hexham, Northumberland
Stoke Mandeville 'Old Boys' living at Kytes Settlement, Watford
National Spinal Injuries Unit, Stoke Mandeville (Ladies' Team)
Spinal Injuries Unit, Promenade Hospital, Southport, Lancashire
Ministry of Health Spinal Injuries Unit, Rookwood, Cardiff
Duchess of Gloucester House, Isleworth, Middlesex
National Spinal Injuries Unit, Stoke Mandeville

Known Individual International Patients

In addition to the teams visiting from overseas there were a small number of known individual international patients resident at various units and centres who participated in the Games. However, reports on this are a little confusing. Paraplegia News, an American publication, states 'a South African and two Australians were also in the Paralympics', but a local newspaper (Bucks Advertiser & Aylesbury News) really confuses things when it states (in the same article) 'a South African and two Australians were also in the Paralympics' and then further down 'although Australia and South Africa were not represented by an official team one of his (Dr Guttmann's) patients was there who was also an Australian and there were two others who were South Africans'.

Tom Butler (Australia)
Emanual Kanakakis (Greece)
Un-named individual(s) (South Africa)

Sports: Archery, Javelin, Netball, Snooker , Swimming, Table Tennis

The official opening of the new swimming pool at the hospital by Mrs Dorothy Jean Walley, Chairperson of the Royal Bucks and Associated Hospitals Management Committee, on the Saturday allowed for the addition of yet another new sport to the competitive programme – swimming. The pool had been constructed by the Ministries of Pensions and Works, to a design of Dr Guttmann. It measured 42 feet in length, was four and a half feet deep and held fifty thousand gallons of water that were changed every ninety minutes.

Demonstrations: Club Swinging, Dartchery

Another sport, that was demonstrated on the Friday evening, was archery-darts or dartchery as its name was shortened to. This game began at the Chaseley home in Eastbourne, where a team of wheelchair archers would take on teams of non-disabled darts players from pubs and clubs in the area. The non-disabled darts players would play their normal game throwing at the normal board. The wheelchair archers would use a bow and arrow shooting at a board exactly three times the normal size at a distance of thirty feet. Out of seven matches played in October and November 1952 the Chaseley team won five, drew one and only lost one match. The only difficulty they had was finding a venue with enough space.

Guests of Honour

The guests of honour this year were Mr Derick Heathcoat-Amory, the Minister of Pensions, Miss Pat Hornsby-Smith, the Parliamentary Secretary to the Ministry of Health and Brigadier 'Jackie' Smythe, the Parliamentary Secretary to the Ministry of Pensions. At the prize giving ceremony Dr Guttmann read a message from the Prime Minister, Winston Churchill wishing all the competitors present a pleasant day. This was followed by a speech from the Minster of Pensions in which he stated that 'there was nothing the Ministry had been associated with that they were prouder of than the development of Stoke Mandeville'.

The Minister of Pensions giving his speech

Immediately prior to the playing of the national anthem at the close of the Games the Central Band of the RAF played, for the very first time, 'the Stoke Mandeville March' composed by Mr Pierre Haas, a paraplegic from Boulogne, in honour of all the paraplegics at Stoke Mandeville.

1954: The First Parade of Nations

The Games of 1954 were held on Friday 30th and Saturday 31st July. However, media and other written coverage of this year's Games appears to be quite sparse. In his opening address Dr Guttmann informed those present that a telegram had been sent to the Queen 'conveying on behalf of all participants their loyal greetings' to which the Queen had apparently responded with her thanks and had sent best wishes for the success of the Games.

Dr Guttmnn's opening speech (Note the 8 new stars on the flag)

This year also saw the addition of eight new stars on the Games flag, representing the participation of athletes from eight new countries since the Games became truly international in 1952. Some of these nations were represented by patients based at Stoke Mandeville e.g. Tom Butler, a paralysed farmer from Western Australia, whilst others were represented by small teams of athletes attending specifically for the Games. What is slightly strange about this is that Tom Butler had competed in the previous year's Games, but no mention of Australia as a nation had been made, nor had a star been added to the Games flag to represent their participation. It is likely, however, that this was done in an attempt to make the Games more newsworthy and increase interest in them.

International Nations Represented

Australia, Austria*, Belgium*, Canada *, Egypt*, Finland*, France*, Germany*, Israel*, Pakistan*, Portugal, Netherlands, Yugoslavia*
*Supported by WVF

British Organisations and Institutions

Chaseley Home, Eastbourne, Sussex
Star and Garter Home, Richmond, Surrey
Stoke Mandeville 'Old Boys'
No. 3 Polish Hospital, Penley, Denbighshire
Stoke Mandeville 'Old Girls'
Thistle Foundation, Edinburgh, Scotland
Lyme Green Settlement, Macclesfield, Cheshire
National Spinal Injuries Unit, Stoke Mandeville
National Spinal Injuries Unit, Stoke Mandeville (Ladies' Team)
Spinal Injuries Unit, General Hospital, Hexham, Northumberland
Spinal Injuries Unit, Promenade Hospital, Southport, Lancashire
Ministry of Health Spinal Injuries Unit, Rookwood, Cardiff, Wales
Duchess of Gloucester House, Isleworth, Middlesex

Dartchery was promoted to full sport status this year and in addition the sport of wheelchair fencing was demonstrated to those present by a patient from the Rookwood Centre in Wales and his non-disabled instructor, apparently watched by a large and appreciative audience.

Sports: Archery, Dartchery, Javelin, Netball, Snooker, Swimming, Table Tennis
Demonstrations: Club Swinging, Wheelchair Fencing

Fencing Demonstration

Guests of Honour

Guests of Honour at the 1954 Games were Iain Macleod, Minister of Health, Lord Burghley, British IOC member and President of the International Amateur Athletics Federation and Elliott Newcomb, Secretary General of the World Veteran's Federation. Also in attendance was the South Korean Minister of Social Affairs, Mr Koo Cha Hun, who was visiting Stoke Mandeville to learn more about the rehabilitation techniques used there. In keeping with his constant references to and use of Olympic practices Dr Guttmann introduced a 'Parade of Nations' this year, which commenced at 5.45pm on the Saturday evening. The participants paraded past a specially constructed saluting base occupied by Iain Macleod and Lord Burghley and completed the parade at the prize giving area, where each of the guests gave a speech before Lord Burghley presented the prizes.

The Minister of Pensions reported that the disappearance of the Ministry of Pensions the previous year, to be replaced by the Ministries of Health and National Insurance had raised concerns about what would happen to spinal injuries units such as those at Stoke Mandeville. He assured those present that in no way would the work of such units be interrupted. Mr Elliot Newcomb of the World Veteran's Federation, whose financial help made the International Stoke Mandeville Games possible, claimed that in the Stoke Mandeville Games had been found 'something that is common to all nations, something that crosses all national boundaries and can further better international relationships'. Before presenting the prizes Lord Burghley stated that it had been a remarkable day, underlining the enthusiasm and comradeship of those taking part and that the good name of Stoke Mandeville was spreading like wildfire all over the world.

The first 'Parade of Nations' at the Games

The day was concluded by a get-together and concert in the gymnasium in the evening at which Major Jan Linzel, from the Netherlands, presented the remaining prizes and medals.

1955: The Pan Am Jets Make Their First Landing

The Games this year were held on Friday 29th and Saturday 30th July, 1955. Eighteen nations were represented with the addition of visiting teams from Denmark, Norway and the USA and individual patients from Malaya (Abdul Wahid Bin Baba) and Turkey (Nas Huseyin). The eleven members of the American team were all employees of Pan American Airways who were sponsored by their employers. Dr Guttmann was apparently especially happy to have an American team present and this lead him to hope that the next year he might be able to get a team from Russia to attend. He felt that the presence of these two world sporting super-powers would give true recognition to the Games. A total of 280 competitors took part.

International Nations Represented

Australia, Austria*, Belgium*, Canada*, Denmark, Finland*, France*, Germany*, Israel*, Malaysia, Malta, Netherlands, Norway, South Africa, Turkey, USA, Yugoslavia*
*Supported by WVF

British Organisations and Institutions

The number of British organisations present this year was bolstered by the addition of two organisations representing mineworkers who had been injured in colliery accidents. These were the Northumberland and Cumberland Paraplegic Mineworkers' Club and the Miners' Rehabilitation Centre in Uddington, Scotland

> Chaseley Home, Eastbourne, Sussex
> Lyme Green Settlement, Macclesfield, Cheshire
> Stoke Mandeville 'Old Boys'
> Stoke Mandeville 'Old Girls'
> No. 3 Polish Hospital, Penley, Denbighshire
> Star and Garter Home, Richmond, Surrey
> National Spinal Injuries Unit, Stoke Mandeville
> Thistle Foundation, Edinburgh, Scotland
> National Spinal Injuries Unit, Stoke Mandeville (Ladies' Team)
> Northumberland and Cumberland Paraplegic Mineworkers' Club
> Spinal Injuries Unit, Promenade Hospital, Southport, Lancashire
> Miners' Rehabilitation Centre, Uddington, Lanarksire, Scotland
> Ministry of Health Spinal Injuries Unit, Rookwood, Cardiff, Wales
> Duchess of Gloucester House, Isleworth, Middlesex
> Spinal Injuries Unit, General Hospital, Hexham, Northumberland

There were no new sports on the programme in this year, although wheelchair fencing was up-graded to a full-medal sport. However, for the first time since the Games began they were not restricted to the front lawns of the hospital, but took place on a specially constructed and much larger sports ground at the rear of the hospital. For the first time, therefore, the archery competition was divided into two disciplines. There was a Windsor Round for the more experienced archers and the usual Columbia Round for those that had not reached quite such high standards of marksmanship.

Sports: Archery, Basketball, Dartchery, Javelin, Snooker, Swimming, Table Tennis, Wheelchair Fencing
Demonstrations: Club Swinging

Given the huge and rapid growth of the Games over the previous few years and the fact that it was becoming more and more difficult to find space to accommodate participants in the hospital wards as had been done in previous years, the biggest problem the organisers faced in putting on the Games of 1955 was finding space to house the ever increasing number of competitors. This apparently caused Dr Guttmann quite a few headaches and was finally overcome by the construction of two new large huts next to the sports ground. The huts, which were completed in less than three months, housed approximately eighty people and were paid for by the King Edward's Hospital Fund, the British Legion and the National Playing Fields Association. They were officially opened by Sir George Schuster, Chairman of the Regional Hospital Board.

A new feature added to the programme for this year's Games was the holding of a scientific meeting on the Friday, which was attended by approximately fifty surgeons and doctors from around the globe. This apparently proved so successful that it was decided to make it an annual event to be held in conjunction with the Games. In 1961 this body was officially constituted as the International Medical Society of Paraplegia (ISMP). In 1963 ISMP produced the first edition of a journal called *Paraplegia*, which still exists today under the name of *Spinal Cord*.

Guests of Honour

Guests of Honour for the 1955 Games included Dr Roger Bannister, who presented the prizes; Sir George Schuster, Chairman of the Regional Hospital Board; Brigadier J.G. Smyth, Parliamentary Secretary to the Minister of Pensions and National Insurance who took the salute during the wheelpast of nations; Major General C.W. Fladgate, Chairman of the World Veteran's Federation; Miss Avis Scott, a television personality and Mademoiselle Genevieve de Galard-Terraube. Mlle Galard-Terraube, who was a nurse in the French Royal Air Force and was at Stoke Mandeville with a team of French disabled servicemen and civilians, was nicknamed 'the Angel of Dien Bien Phu' by the media following her actions at the battle of that name in French Indochina.

The British Paraplegic Sports Endowment Fund

Slowly, but surely, the Games were becoming a victim of their own success. In the four years since the Games had become truly international in nature in 1952 they had grown from 130 participants from two nations to 280 participants from 18 nations. The increasing cost of putting the Games on, combined with the problems of housing all the athletes and officials, led to the announcement by Dr Guttmann at the Games of 1955 that the future of the Games was in danger. This was partly due to the fact that the small local Paraplegic Sports Fund had become insufficient to meet the rising costs of putting on the Games and this was exacerbated by the fact that the World Veteran's Federation had announced that they would be unable to continue the generous financial assistance they had previously given to help get the Games established. In addition, the Games had previously used vacant hospital wards to host visiting participants, but these were rapidly filling up with patients and so were unlikely to be available for future Games making accommodation a key issue.

The announcement by Dr Guttmann at the Games of 1955 that the future of the Games was in danger caused Mr J.C.A. Faure, a spectator at those Games and father of one of the physiotherapists at Stoke Mandeville, to approach Dr Guttmann in order to see what could be done to rectify the situation. Mr Faure, a successful businessman with Unilever and also President of the Principal Oil Seed, Oils and Fats Trade Association, had discussions with Dr Guttmann as to the best way forward and on 15th November 1955 a group of interested individuals gathered at Stoke Mandeville with a view to setting up a Paraplegics Sports Endowment Fund in order to put the future of the Stoke Mandeville Games on a firm financial footing. It should be noted that at this time there was only one version of the Games in existence that catered for a large number of national spinal units as well as a number of visiting international teams. In order to do this it was decided that a sum of not less than £60,000 would be required. As Dr Guttmann had previously done in inviting politicians and celebrities to distribute prizes at the Games, the first thing that was done to try and gain the confidence and support of the public for the new fund was to attract well-known personalities to associate themselves with the aims of the fund. As can be seen from the list below that list read like a page from Debrett's or Who's who?

Patron
The Marquess of Carisbrooke

Vice-Patrons
Earl and Countess Mountbatten of Burma
Field Marshall Sir and Lady Gerald W.R.
Templer
Air Chief Marshall Sir and Lady Dermot
A. Boyle

President
Sir Arthur E. Porritt

Vice Presidents
Rt Hon Lord Cohen of
Birkenhead
Rt Hon Lord Webb-Johnson
Sir Geoffrey Jefferson
Sir Selwyn Selwyn-Clarke
Sir Reginald Watson-Jones
Right Reverend Lord Bishop of
London
Viscount Leverhulme
W.J. Everard
Niels Max Jensen
Ralph Tadman

A management board was set up with Mr Faure as its Chairman, Dr Guttmann as the Vice-Chairman with the other members being co-opted from the now defunct Paraplegic Sports Fund, whose remaining funds were transferred to the newly titled British Paraplegic Sports Endowment Fund. The appeal was launched in March 1956 with an open letter published in The Times newspaper and signed by many of the eminent individuals named above. The Marquess of Carisbrooke also wrote directly to many large industrial and commercial organisations. The result of this appeal was that a total of £13,114 was raised by the end of September that year. By the end of September 1959 the appeal had raised £40,954.

However, in order to ensure the Games of 1956 could take place it was decided that it would be necessary to build a further two accommodation huts in addition to the two completed for the 1955 Games. It was estimated that this would cost approximately £6,000 and without knowing whether the appeal would be successful or not, Mr Faure and his business associates guaranteed the whole £6,000 in order that building work could begin immediately.

The Fund itself and the money it generated were used in a variety of ways. These include:

i.   New accommodation huts
ii.   Erection of temporary stands for spectators
iii.   Running costs of the Games themselves
iv.   Purchase of sports equipment for paraplegics who had left hospital and were now living at home
v.   Financing paraplegic teams and individuals to take part in sports events at home and abroad
vi.   Grants to The Cord, the journal for paraplegics

It is clear from this list that the organisers of the Stoke Mandeville Games considered the organisation of the Games to be a national activity to be paid for from national funds alongside activities that would help develop sport for wheelchair users within Britain.

1956: The Italians Add another Star to the Flag

The Games this year were held on Friday 27th and Saturday 28th July, 1956. Eighteen nations were represented with Italy taking part for the very first time. Dr Guttmann's wish, stated the previous year, that a team from Russia might attend was partially met when two Russian neuro-surgeon's, Professor V.D. Golovanov from Moscow and Professor V.M. Ougriumov from Leningrad attended the scientific congress held in conjunction with the Games. When asked if a Russian team might attend a future Games they were unable to say as sport and physical activity for paraplegics did not actually exist in Russia at that time. A total of 300 competitors took part in the Games. The Games cost £676 to put on and sale of programmes and admission fees raised £201 meaning the Games had a net cost of £475. The admission charge for the general public on the Saturday was one shilling.

International Nations Represented

Australia, Austria*, Belgium, Canada, Denmark*, Finland*, France, Germany*, Israel*, Italy, Malaysia, Netherlands, Norway*, Pakistan*, South Africa, USA, Yugoslavia*
*Supported by WVF

Italy, the newest team at the Games

Perhaps the most impressive participant at the Games, however, was Neville Cohen from South Africa. Neville had previously been a patient at Stoke Mandeville three years previously and had arrived in the UK in late April, having driven overland with a friend all the way from Johannesburg in South Africa. According to his autobiography by the time Neville applied to take part in the Games all of the accommodation was already full and so he pitched his tent underneath the window of Dr Guttmann's office.

The issue of accommodation had been raised as a major problem at the previous year's Games with £6,000 needing to be raised immediately to built two further accommodation huts in addition to the two completed for the Games of 1955. One of the needed huts was supplied and equipped as a result of a donation of £4,500 from the Royal Air Force Association. The money had been raised as a result of cinema collections at screenings of the film 'The Dam-Busters'. This hut was officially opened on the Saturday at 3pm by Air Chief Marshall Sir Geoffrey Bromet who uncovered a plaque surmounted by the RAF Association crest, which was affixed to the hut.

Air Chief Marshall Sir Geoffrey Bromet officially opens the RAFA accommodation hut

British Organisations and Institutions

Chaseley Home, Eastbourne, Sussex
Lyme Green Settlement, Macclesfield, Cheshire
Stoke Mandeville 'Old Boys' living at home
Stoke Mandeville 'Old Girls' living at home
Spinal Injuries Unit, Lodge Moor, Sheffield
Star and Garter Home, Richmond, Surrey
Thistle Foundation, Edinburgh, Scotland
Pinderfields Hospital, Wakefield
No. 3 Polish Hospital, Penley, Denbighshire
National Spinal Injuries Unit, Stoke Mandeville
Coal Industry Social Welfare Organisation, Derbyshire
Duchess of Gloucester House, Isleworth, Middlesex
Spinal Injuries Unit, General Hospital, Hexham, Northumberland
National Spinal Injuries Unit, Stoke Mandeville (Ladies' Team)
Northumberland and Cumberland Paraplegic Mineworkers' Club
Spinal Injuries Unit, Promenade Hospital, Southport, Lancashire
Miners' Rehabilitation Centre, Uddington, Lanarksire, Scotland
Spinal Injuries Unit, Edenhall Hospital, Musselburgh, Midlothian, Scotland
Ministry of Health Spinal Injuries Unit, Rookwood, Cardiff, Wales

In terms of sports there were no new additional sports, but an archery event for boys aged 12 years and under and a foil fencing competition for ladies were added to the programme.

Sports: Archery, Dartchery, Javelin, Snooker, Swimming, Table Tennis, Wheelchair Basketball, Wheelchair Fencing
Demonstrations: Club Swinging

Guests of Honour

Sir Arthur Porritt making his speech

Following on from the setting up of the Paraplegic Sports Endowment Fund in the wake of the 1955 Games it was perhaps apt that the guests of honour at this year's Games were made up primarily of the Fund's Patrons. These included Sir Gerald and Lady Templar and Sir Dermot and Lady Boyle, who were all Patrons of the Fund; Sir Arthur Porritt, President of the Fund and Lady Porritt and Sir Selwyn-Clarke, one of the Funds Vice Presidents. Sir Gerald Templar, the Chief of Imperial General Staff, took the salute at the wheel-past of nations and his wife, Lady Templar, handed out the prizes. Mr Curtis Campaigne, Secretary General of the World Veteran's Federation gave a speech on behalf of the visiting teams. Sir Arthur Porritt, the principal speaker on the day, apparently discarded the speech he had prepared beforehand declaring it quite inadequate to describe what he had witnessed that afternoon. Sir Arthur's presence at these Games was to play a major part in spurring Dr Guttmann even further down the path he had set of closer links with the Olympic Games as will be seen in the next section.

Olympic Recognition: The Award of the Sir Thomas Fearnley Cup

Sir Thomas Fearnley (1880-1950) was an IOC member for Norway from 1927 until 1948 and an honorary member from 1948 until his death in 1950. He was also President of the Norwegian Federation of Ship Owners. Just before his death he decided to offer a cup in his name, to become known as the Fearnley Cup, which was awarded annually by the IOC between 1950 and 1974 to a sports club for its outstanding merit in the name of Olympism. The original cup remains at Campagne de Mon-Repos in Lausanne, Switzerland, with the recipient receiving a miniature copy and a diploma.

Side and top view of the replica awarded to the Stoke Mandeville Games

Diploma that came with the Fearnley Cup

At the Stoke Mandeville Games of 1956 some of the prizes were presented by Sir (later Lord) Arthur Porritt, himself a surgeon and also an IOC member for Great Britain. At the Games he is reported as stating that 'The spirit of these Games goes beyond the Olympic Games spirit. You compete not only with skill and endurance but with courage and bravery too.' In fact the Games so impressed him that a few weeks later he wrote to Otto Mayer, Chancellor of the IOC, nominating the Games for the Fearnley Cup. He also assured Herr Mayer that he was certain that the nomination would be backed by Lord Burghley, Great Britain's other IOC member at the time, who had also presented prizes at the Stoke Mandeville Games of 1954. Otto Mayer replied less than a week later stating that he was uncertain about the eligibility of the Games as the cup was awarded for "meritorious achievement in the service of the Olympic Movement". However, he put the nomination forward anyway and at their session held in conjunction with the Olympic Games in Melbourne two months later the members voted to award the Fearnley Cup to the organiseers of the Stoke Mandeville Games. This was the first time the cup had ever been awarded to a British organisation or any kind of disability sport organisation anywhere. There may be some who would argue that the organisers of the Stoke Mandeville Games were an international organisation (which might possibly have made them ineligible for the Fearnley cup as it was for a 'sports club'), but at that time the Games were organised and paid for out of national funds that were almost totally raised from companies, organisations and charities within the United Kingdom. The organisation of the International Stoke Mandeville Games at that time was also almost entirely carried out by staff members and volunteers from Stoke Mandeville Hospital and the Spinal Injuries Centre. The International Stoke Mandeville Games Committee was not constituted until the Meeting of Trainers at the end of the 1959 International Games.

The replica cup and diploma were presented to Dr Guttmann by Sir Arthur Porritt in a special ceremony held on 30th January, 1957 at the British Olympic Association headquarters in London. Also present at the ceremony were the Secretary and the Appeals Secretary of the British Olympic Association along with Dr Guttmann's organising team for the Stoke Mandeville Games – Miss Dora Bell, Miss Joan Scruton, Mr Charlie Atkinson and Mr Thomas 'Q' Hill.

Sir Arthur Porritt presents the replica to Dr Guttmann

The award of the Fearnley Cup motivated Dr Guttmann to dream of far bigger things as is shown in the report of his opening speech at the 1957 Games when, with reference to the Fearnley Cup he is reported to have stated "I hope this is only the beginning of a closer connection between the Stoke Mandeville Games and the Olympic Games. In the past few years I have always emphasised that the Stoke Mandeville Games have become the equivalent of the Olympic Games." He apparently went on to say that after the splendid recognition by the Olympic Committee in awarding them the Fearnley Cup he hoped that the Olympic Games would soon be open to disabled sportsmen and women.

1957: Space is Getting Tight

Possibly driven by the publicity surrounding the award of the Fearnley Cup the participation in the Games of this year jumped from 280 competitors from 18 nations the previous year to 360 competitors from 24 nations this year. This increase in competitors also meant that some heats in events such as table tennis had to be held on Thursday 25th July, the same day as the annual Scientific Congress, followed by two full days of competition ending on Saturday 27th July. Teams competing for the very first time were Argentina, Ireland, Sweden and Switzerland. In addition, teams visiting especially for the Games for the first time, as opposed to being represented by patients based at Stoke Mandeville or other Spinal Units, were Australia, Greece and Malta. This also meant that for the first time ever in the history of the Games all continents of the globe were represented.

International Nations Represented

Argentina, Australia*, Austria*, Belgium*, Canada, Denmark, Finland*, France, Germany, Greece*, Ireland, Israel*, Italy, Malaysia, Malta*, Netherlands, Norway*, Pakistan*, Portugal,South Africa, Sweden, Switzerland, USA
*Supported by WVF

British Organisations and Institutions

Banstead Place, Dorincourt, Leatherhead
Lyme Green Settlement, Macclesfield, Cheshire
Chaseley Home, Eastbourne, Sussex
National Spinal Injuries Unit, Stoke Mandeville
Stoke Mandeville 'Old Boys' living at home
Stoke Mandeville 'Old Girls' living at home
Spinal Injuries Unit, Lodge Moor, Sheffield
Star and Garter Home, Richmond, Surrey
No. 3 Polish Hospital, Penley, Denbighshire
Team from Cheltenham
Thistle Foundation, Edinburgh, Scotland
Lodge Moor 'Old Boys'
Coal Industry Social Welfare Organisation, Derbyshire
Duchess of Gloucester House, Isleworth, Middlesex
Spinal Injuries Unit, General Hospital, Hexham, Northumberland
National Spinal Injuries Unit, Stoke Mandeville (Ladies' Team)
Northumberland and Cumberland Paraplegic Mineworkers' Club
Spinal Injuries Unit, Pinderfields Hospital, Wakefield
Spinal Injuries Unit, Promenade Hospital, Southport, Lancashire
Miners' Rehabilitation Centre, Uddington, Lanarksire, Scotland
Spinal Injuries Unit, Edenhall Hospital, Musselburgh, Midlothian, Scotland
Ministry of Health Spinal Injuries Unit, Rookwood, Cardiff, Wales

This year saw the introduction of shot put to the programme for the first time, which proved very popular drawing 49 entries. As with the javelin it was split into two classes (Cervical lesions and Thoracic lesions) to ensure fair competition.

Sports: Archery, Dartchery, Javelin, Shot Putt, Snooker, Swimming, Table Tennis, Wheelchair Basketball, Wheelchair Fencing
Demonstrations: Club Swinging

For the first time in the history of the Games the weather did not stay fair for the whole of the event. On the Saturday umbrellas were needed as the skies clouded over and the rain set in. It appears the competitors took it in their stride and continued to compete where possible. However, some events were delayed, the fencing had to be switched from pitch two to the gymnasium and the final round of the Columbia round of archery had to be cancelled, so only 48 arrows were shot.

The World Veteran's Federation, who had helped to finance the Games since 1952 by assisting in the travel costs of athletes coming from abroad, finally had to bring their financial involvement to an end in order to concentrate upon their commitments and projects in other fields of rehabilitation. This was, therefore, the last year they would be financially involved in the Games held at Stoke Mandeville having assisted Malta and Greece to send participants to this year's Games. In response to this several countries had set up their own sports funds in order to try and make themselves financially independent in the future.

For the second year running a special stand was erected adjacent to pitch one that allowed twice as many spectators to watch the events there in comfort. This was paid for by the Paraplegic Sports Endowment Fund, who also paid for the dismantling of two old cycle sheds next to the sports ground entrance. This allowed Mr Davies, the Unit's engineer, and his staff to erect a new archway entrance to the sports arena.

New archway entrance to the sports ground erected for the Games

Guests of Honour

The Guests of Honour at this year's Games were the Duchess of Gloucester, who officially opened the Games on the Friday; Sir Arthur Porritt, who took the salute during the wheel-past of nations and Miss Gillian Sheen, Olympic Gold Medallist in Fencing, who presented the prizes. Dr George Bedbrooke of Australia was due to give the closing address on behalf of visiting teams from abroad, but was delayed en route and so the speech was given by the captain of the Australian team, Bill 'Slim' O'Connell.

The Duchess of Gloucester giving her opening speech

Following a meeting of experts in the field of sport and the disabled convened by the World Veteran's Federation in Paris in May 1957 it was decided a technical meeting of experts should be convened to try and unify the rules of the various sports into one international set of rules for each sport that could be agreed and adhered to by all. The need for this had been further strengthened by the events that occurred during the incomplete lesion basketball final where the American team had been disqualified for the roughness of their play. Therefore, at 10.15am on the Sunday morning after the Games closed a lengthy meeting took place in the Examination room with around forty people in attendance. The main resolutions arising from this meeting were as follows:

i.   A tribunal of three members, elected by ballot, be appointed each year to consider and give a decision in any dispute that may arise, should the teams concerned not accept the referee's decision.
ii. In addition, a member of the Stoke Mandeville organising staff act on the tribunal in an advisory capacity.
iii. Stoke Mandeville continue to set up rules for future Games as close as possible to international rules in all games.
iv. In order to encourage archery as a sport for paraplegics there should be a beginner's round in archery and that each team be limited to one beginner.
v.   The distances in the swimming competitions be as follows: Class A – 20 metres, Class B and C – 40 metres.
vi. Club throwing be introduced as a new sport in the 1958 Games
vii. Referees be drawn from any country taking part.

One other major decision came about as a result of the huge growth in the Games and the strain they were placing both upon accommodation and other hospital services. It was decided that a national games would be held in May each year where all of the various British organisations, Spinal Units and individuals would be invited to take part. From these Games a team of the best sportsmen and women would be selected to form a Great Britain national team to participate in the international games. The impact of this change would be two-fold; it would lessen the burden upon the accommodation and other hospital services at the international games by reducing numbers and it would also allow a British team to compete on an equal basis with other nations for the first time. The first national games would take place the following year.

1958 National Games

A number of reports state that the introduction of a national Games, whilst succeeding in making the event more manageable, also helped re-capture a more intimate family feeling for the Games which even Dr Guttmann commented upon in his closing address. The Games took place on Friday 13th & Saturday 14th June. Over two hundred competitors took part representing teams from eighteen organisations and institutions, with each hoping that their athletes would be selected for the first official British team to compete in the International Stoke

Mandeville Games the following month. The Games cost £107 to put on and raised £62 from the sale of programmes.

Programme sellers at the entrance to the Games Grounds

British Organisations and Institutions

Chaseley Home, Eastbourne, Sussex
Spinal Injuries Unit, Lodge Moor, Sheffield
Stoke Mandeville 'Old Boys' living at home
Stoke Mandeville 'Old Girls' living at home
National Spinal Injuries Unit, Stoke Mandeville
Thistle Foundation, Edinburgh, Scotland
Lyme Green Settlement, Macclesfield, Cheshire
Team from Cheltenham
Winford Orthopaedic Hospital, Winford, Somerset
Star and Garter Home, Richmond, Surrey
Coal Industry Social Welfare Organisation, Derbyshire
Duchess of Gloucester House, Isleworth, Middlesex
Spinal Injuries Unit, General Hospital, Hexham, Northumberland
National Spinal Injuries Unit, Stoke Mandeville (Ladies' Team)
Spinal Injuries Unit, Pinderfields Hospital, Wakefield
Spinal Injuries Unit, Promenade Hospital, Southport, Lancashire
Spinal Injuries Unit, Edenhall Hospital, Musselburgh, Midlothian, Scotland
Ministry of Health Spinal Injuries Unit, Rookwood, Cardiff, Wales

Sports: Archery, Dartchery, Javelin, Shot Putt, Snooker, Swimming, Table Tennis, Wheelchair Basketball, Wheelchair Fencing

Guests of Honour

The highlight of the Games for many was the visit late on the Friday afternoon of HRH Prince Philip who arrived by car at 4pm accompanied by the Lord Lieutenant of Buckinghamshire, Sir Henry Aubrey-Fletcher, following a day of visits in Aylesbury. He was only scheduled to stay for thirty minutes, but so interested was he in the events that, much to the consternation of his Aides, he did not depart until 5.15pm. He took time to watch nearly all the different sports and even stopped at Ward 1X, where several acute cases were housed.

HRH Prince Philip watching Junior archery

HRH Prince Philip departing at the controls of a Royal Navy helicopter

On the Saturday following completion of all the events the honour of presenting the medals and prizes was given to Thomas 'Q' Hill who was due to retire the following month following nearly fourteen years of service at Stoke Mandeville as Remedial Gymnast. On completion of his prize giving duties 'Q' was presented with a silver tea service and a cheque by Dr Guttmann in grateful thanks of his long service with both the Spinal Unit and the Games. The Games were completed by a party held in the gym on the Saturday night for all competitors and escorts.

Competitors Qualifying for the First Ever British Team for the 1958 International Stoke Mandeville Games were as follows:

Basketball

Complete Lesions		Incomplete Lesions	
G. Swindlehurst	Lyme Green (Captain)	W. Toman	Duchess of Gloucester House
G. Todd	Duchess of Gloucester House	F. Cole	Lyme Green
D. Platten	Lyme Green	C. Thomas	Lodge Moor
T. Moran	Lyme Green	J. Chadwick	Lyme Green
T. Wann	Thistle Foundation	T. Guthrie	Thistle Foundation

Substitutes

D. Thompson	Duchess of Gloucester House	G. Grundy	Lodge Moor
J. Gibson	Duchess of Gloucester House	R. Scott	Lodge Moor
R. Foster	Lyme Green	Frodshaw	Lodge Moor
J. McBride	Lyme Green	J. Hincliffe	Duchess of Gloucester House
J. Gasgoigne	Lodge Moor	C. Hepple	Pinderfields

Swimming

Junior Girls		Junior Boys	
D. Flint	Cheltenham	P. Waddingham	Stoke Mandeville Old Boy
V. Forder	Stoke Mandeville Old Girl	D. Price	Winford Orthopaedic Hospital
C. Rao	Stoke Mandeville	S. Darrington	Stoke Mandeville Old Boy
D. Randle	High Wycome	M. Goss	Stoke Mandeville Old Boy

Ladies		Men	
J. Laughton	Stoke Mandeville Old Girl	R. Miller	Stoke Mandeville
V. Forder	Stoke Mandeville Old Girl	W. White	Stoke Mandeville Old Boy
B. Anderson	Stoke Mandeville Old Girl	P. Stanton	Stoke Mandeville Old Boy
D. King	Stoke Mandeville Old Girl	S. Miles	Stoke Mandeville Old Boy
S. Telfer	Stoke Mandeville	A. Diamond	Stoke Mandeville
A. Masson	Stoke Mandeville Old Girl	Diver	Winford Orthopaedic Hospital
M. Hatt	High Wycombe	Laughton	Southport

L. Drummond	Stoke Mandeville
A. Brindle	Cheltenham
Brook	Pinderfields
G. Moore	Cheltenham
P. McCranor	Stoke Mandeville Old Boy
Heyes	Southport

Archery

Windsor Round		Columbia Round	
R. Jennings	Stoke Mandeville Old Boy	C. Bradley	CISWO Derbyshire
J. Ross	Duchess of Gloucester House	J. Duggan	Edenhall
M. Sowden	Stoke Mandeville	F. Hall	Pinderfields
J. Laird	Stoke Mandeville Old Boy	D. Gubbins (Mrs)	Duchess of Gloucester House
H. Hill (1st Reserve)	Stoke Mandeville	M. Periscinotti (1st Reserve)	D. of G. House

Dartchery

V. Whitford	CISWO Derbyshire
C. Bradley	CISWO Derbyshire
I. Cathcart	Stoke Mandeville Old Boy
J. Coward	Stoke Mandeville Old Boy
H. Kerr	Stoke Mandeville (1st Reserve)

Throwing the Javelin

Class A		Class B	
D. Thompson	Duchess of Gloucester House	D. Thompson	Duchess of Gloucester House
B. Kamara	Duchess of Gloucester House	R. Scott	Lodge Moor
J. Gasgoigne (1st Reserve)	Lodge Moor	C. Thomas (1st Reserve)	Lodge Moor

Throwing the Club

Class B	
C. Hepple	Pinderfields
R. Scott	Lodge Moor
D. Thompson	Duchess of Gloucester House (1st Reserve)

Table Tennis

	Singles	Doubles
Class A	T. Taylor (Chaseley)	T. Taylor/ A. Wilson (Chaseley)
Reserves	F. Cook (Star & Garter)	F. Cook/ T. Witterick (Star & Garter)
Class B	D. Phillips (Rookwood)	D. Phillips/ J. Hardy (Rookwood)
Reserves	M. Parkin (Lodge Moor)	G. Bolton/ H. Stewart (Stoke Mandeville)
Class C	G. Swindlehurst (Lyme Green)	G. Swindlehurst/ R. Murrell (Lyme Green)
Reserves	P. McCranor (S. M. Old Boy)	J. Gibson/ W. Toman (D. Of G. House)

Fencing

Mens Sabre		Ladies Foil
R. Everson	(Stoke Mandeville)	G. McFarlane (Stoke Mandeville Old Girl)
G. Brookes	(Stoke Mandeville)	J. Brockwell (Stoke Mandeville Old Girl)
D. Winters	(Rookwood)	S. Telfer (Stoke Mandeville)
(Reserve)		(Reserve)

Snooker

C. Keeton (Lodge Moor)
A. Poulter (Stoke Mandeville Old Boy) (Reserve)

Reserves were not required unless notified

1958: 'Great Britain' Finally Makes Its Debut at the Games

The Games of 1958 took place from Thursday 24th to Saturday 26th July and attracted around 250 competitors from twenty nations – a much more manageable number in terms of accommodation. The British team was by far the largest with 83 members. The next largest team was France with 33. Many of the smaller countries such as Malta, Israel and Finland only had about half a dozen athletes each. The withdrawal of the World Veteran's Federation funding may well have played a part in the drop in the number of nations competing as Portugal, Australia and Sweden were all unable to attend for financial reasons. Nations competing for the first time included Lebanon, Northern Rhodesia, Uruguay and India. However, all these nations were actually represented by single patients based at Stoke Mandeville. Bizarrely, Chandra Rao of India is actually listed as a member of the British team qualifying for these Games. It is likely that the organisers chose to re-list her as the sole member of the Indian team (she was from Madras) in order to prevent the number of competing nations dropping too far from the previous year's peak of 24 competing nations. The Games cost £1,126 to put on and the sale of programmes and admission fees raised £210 meaning the Games had a net cost of £916.

Nations Represented

Austria Belgium Finland France Germany Great Britain India Israel Italy
Lebanon Malta Netherlands Northern Rhodesia Norway Pakistan South Africa
Switzerland Uruguay USA Yugoslavia

As well as the addition of Club Throwing to the sports programme archery saw
the addition of two new rounds. For the more advanced archers there was the
Albion round, which increased the maximum distance shot to 80 yards, with 36
arrows being shot at distances of 80, 60 and 50 yards. For the novice archers, as
agreed at the previous year's technical meeting, the Saint Nicholas Round was
added, which involved shooting 48 arrows over 40 and then a further 36 arrows
over 30 yards.

Sports: Archery, Club Throw, Dartchery, Javelin, Shot Putt, Snooker, Swimming,
Table Tennis, Wheelchair Basketball, Wheelchair Fencing
Demonstrations: Club Swinging

Nasir Bissat   Dawn Hare   J. Peroni (URU)

In keeping with Dr Guttmann's continual references to the Olympic Games 1958
saw the introduction of a preliminary activity to the Games similar to that of the
torch relay that was first run at the Berlin Olympic Games of 1936. The relay for
the Stoke Mandeville Games commenced on the Wednesday at 9am when the
Lord Mayor of Manchester read out the message of the Games on the steps of the
town hall from a specially prepared scroll. The Lord Mayor then handed the scroll
to Leo Halford of the Lyme Green Settlement, who was the first of four 'runners'
to carry the scroll on its way to the Games, either by car or by wheelchair. The
scroll was next read out by the Lord Mayor of Sheffield, who then handed it over
to Frank Taylor of the Lodge Moor Spinal Unit for carriage to Birmingham. After
a similar ceremony in Birmingham the scroll was handed to Tony Potter for

carriage to London, where it was read out by the Lord Mayor of London on the steps of the Mansion House. Finally, it was handed to Dick Thompson of the Duchess of Gloucester House for carriage to Stoke Mandeville and the opening ceremony of the Games. The scroll, composed by Dr Guttmann read:

> "The aim of the Stoke Mandeville Games is to unite paralysed men and women from all parts of the world in an international sports movement and your spirit of true sportsmanship today will give hope and inspiration to thousands of paralysed people. No greater contribution can be made to society by the paralysed than to help, through the medium of sport, to further friendship and understanding amongst nations"

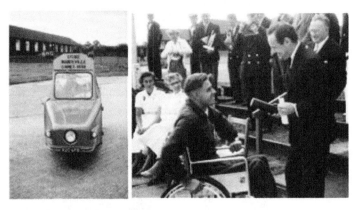

Dick Thompson in his car and handing the scroll to his namesake Richard Thompson, Parliamentary Secretary to the Ministry of Health for the official opening ceremony of the 1958 Games.

Guests of Honour

Guests of Honour for the Games of 1958 included Mr R.M.H. Thompson, Parliamentary Secretary for the Minister of Health, who officially opened the Games; Mr W. Ch. J. M. Van Lanschot, President of the World Veteran's Federation, who took the salute during the wheel-past of nations and the actor Kenneth More, who presented the prizes. During his speech Mr More apparently claimed he had happily accepted the invitation to attend for two reasons. Firstly, he had recently portrayed the World War II flying ace Douglas Bader in the film 'Reach for the Sky'. And, secondly, he had once been standing peacefully on a mountain in Switzerland when someone had skied into him and broken his back, although fortunately without damaging his spinal cord.

Dr Guttmann and Kenneth More

One individual who made a major impact upon everyone competing at the Games was a young German polio victim, Berndt, who hitch-hiked all the way from Berlin to Stoke Mandeville in order to support his team.

The technical meeting of trainers was once again held on the Sunday morning after the Games in order to discuss various proposals and issues pertinent to the following year's Games. In the end there were only two major decisions affecting the next year's Games that were passed:

i.   That the following new classification system, as suggested by the trainers at the meeting, be adopted for the Games of 1959:
      Class A – Cervicals to C7 (inc)
      Class B – C8 – T6 (inc)
      Class C – T7 to T10 (inc) (complete and incomplete lesions)
      Class D – T11 to L2 (inc)
      Class E – Cauda Equina

ii.   That the overall points scoring system for the various competitions to decide the winner of the International Society for the Care of Cripples Challenge Cup for the Best Team competing at 'The Games' be scrapped as it had not proved satisfactory. In its place a Pentathlon event would be introduced made up of five of the sports currently on the Games programme.

1959 National Games

The 1959 National Stoke Mandeville Games took place on Friday 12th and Saturday 13th June. Information regarding these Games is a little sketchy, but it is known that 217 competitors took part from thirteen organisations and institutions from around the UK that can currently be confirmed as having participated and which are listed below. The Games cost £299 to put on and raised £38 from the sale of programmes giving a net cost of £261.

British Organisations and Institutions

Chaseley Home, Eastbourne, Sussex
Spinal Injuries Unit, Lodge Moor, Sheffield
Stoke Mandeville 'Old Boys' living at home
Stoke Mandeville 'Old Girls' living at home
Star and Garter Home, Richmond, Surrey
Thistle Foundation, Edinburgh, Scotland
Lyme Green Settlement, Macclesfield, Cheshire
National Spinal Injuries Unit, Stoke Mandeville
Coal Industry Social Welfare Organisation, Derbyshire
Duchess of Gloucester House, Isleworth, Middlesex
National Spinal Injuries Unit, Stoke Mandeville (Ladies' Team)
Spinal Injuries Unit, Pinderfields Hospital, Wakefield
Ministry of Health Spinal Injuries Unit, Rookwood, Cardiff, Wales

Sports: Archery, Dartchery, Javelin, Shot Putt, Snooker, Swimming, Table Tennis, Wheelchair Basketball, Wheelchair Fencing

The snooker took place in the sports unit, near the swimming pool, with all the other events being hosted on the sports field. Table tennis was housed in a large marquee erected specially for the occasion. It was claimed the holding of a separate British National Games in order to select the British team for the International Games had resulted in an increased keenness and a higher standard of competition amongst the competitors, because they all deemed it such an honour to qualify for the Great Britain Team. In addition, for the first time ever, a ladies section was included in the field events.

Guests of Honour

The guests of honour at this year's Games were Mr J.C.A. Faure, Chairman of the Paraplegic Sports Endowment Fund, who gave an up-date on the Fund's progress and Mr F. Weatherhead, President of the Aylesbury Rotary Club, who presented the prizes. As usual the Games ended with a party with music provided by the R.A.E Westcott Band, who had been entertaining the competitors and spectators throughout the two days of competition.

Aylesbury Rotary Club President Mr F. Weatherhead presenting prizes and giving a speech at the closing ceremony

1959: The Multi-sporters Try the Pentathlon for the First Time

Information on the Games of 1959 is actually quite scarce due to a printer's strike that meant the local papers were not produced when the Games were on and so no reports of the Games are available from those sources. The games that year took place from Thursday 23rd until Saturday 25th July. They attracted only seventeen nations whose participation can be verified from the results, although the names of Australia, Finland and Yugoslavia appear in the programme for the Games. No mention is made anywhere in the available material of the total number of competitors, but the organisers were happy to point out that although the number of nations represented was actually less than the previous year they felt it was a significant feature that those countries that had sent official teams had sent teams that were far larger than in previous years. Cyprus was represented for the very first time by Christos Antoniou, a private patient at Stoke Mandeville. The Games cost £969 to put on and the sale of programmes and admission fees raised £172 meaning the Games had a net cost of £797.

Nations Represented

Austria, Belgium, Cyprus*, Denmark, France, Germany, Great Britain, India, Ireland , Israel, Italy, Malta, Netherlands, Norway, Portugal*, Switzerland, USA
*Supported by WVF

Following on from the decision made at the previous year's meeting of trainers a pentathlon event was added to the sports programme to replace the competition for the team with best overall points score. It consisted of archery, 60m swim, javelin, club and shot put with points being awarded for each event dependent upon time, score or distance in each event.

Sports: Archery, Club Throw, Dartchery, Javelin, Pentathlon, Shot Put, Snooker, Swimming, Table Tennis, Wheelchair, Basketball, Wheelchair Fencing
Demonstrations: Club Swinging

Guests of Honour

The main guest of honour at this year's Games was the Countess Mountbatten of Burma, who was not only a Vice Patron of the Endowment Fund, but also Patron of the National Spinal Injuries Unit itself. Countess Mountbatten took the salute at the wheel-past of nations, supported by Air Chief Marshall Sir Dermot Boyle and Dr Guttmann. She then went on to give a speech and present the trophies and medals. Apparently, due to an organisational error they turned out to be a couple of medals short, but Countess Mountbatten quickly saved the situation by firstly unbuttoning her own then Dr Walsh's button-hole and handing them to the 'delighted' winners in place of their medal.

Once again a Trainer's Meeting was held on the Sunday after the Games. As well as a number of slight rule changes or rule clarifications it was decided that it was necessary to form an International Standing Committee of the Stoke Mandeville Games. In doing so it was decided that Great Britain should be a permanent member of the Committee and that that the Country hosting the Games in future Olympic years should also be a member. It was also decided that the committee should consist of five members and the first five nations voted onto this committee were as follows:

   i.   Great Britain (Dr Ludwig Guttmann)
   ii.   Italy (as the hosts of the 1960 Games) (Dr Antonio Maglio) (Treasurer)
   iii. The Netherlands (as the country that first put the Games on an international basis) (Captain Herman Tjebbes)
   iv.   Belgium (Dr Pierre Houssa)
   v.   France (Mr Michel Boubee)

Dr Guttmann was elected President and Joan Scruton was appointed as Secretary of the committee.

Summing Up the First Twelve Years

It might appear hard to understand how an event that started life with just sixteen wheelchair archers in 1948 as a demonstration to the public that competitive sport is not the prerogative of the non-disabled could, just ten years later, find itself with several dozen international teams and three hundred and sixty competitors in attendance. In fact the Games grew to such an extent that despite several extensions to the accommodation it became necessary to introduce a national Stoke Mandeville Games from 1958 onwards from which a British team would be selected to take part in the international Games a month or so later. There appear to be five possible mechanisms that played key roles in spreading the word regarding the Games to various corners of the globe:

> 1. In the early years much of the driving force for the growth appears to have been down to former patients of Dr Guttmann's who were transferred to other spinal units and took what they had learned, and their enthusiasm for it, with them. Many of them returned year after year to take part in the Games. To a slightly lesser extent this is also true of the doctors and surgeons from all over the world who visited Stoke Mandeville to train under Dr Guttmann and then returned home and incorporated sport into their treatment programmes, such as Dr Ralph Spira from Israel.

> 2. In 1947 the very first edition of 'The Cord' was published. This contained articles and advice of benefit to paraplegics everywhere and often gave space to reports on the sporting goings on at the hospital. Because practical information of assistance to paraplegics was in short supply copies of this journal often got sent abroad to individuals and organisations carrying news of the Games and Dr Guttmann's rehabilitation methods far and wide. The journal continued to be published all the way up until 1983.

3. Dr Guttmann himself was a major player in spreading the word about the Games. He would often travel abroad to conferences, to give lectures and even to give evidence in court cases and would take every opportunity to tell people about the Games and his use of sport as a rehabilitative tool. He would often challenge particular key individuals in other countries to bring a team to the Games the following year as was the case with Sir George Bedbrooke at the Royal Perth Hospital on a visit in 1956. Australia sent their first team to Stoke Mandeville the following year.

4. Dr Guttmann also appears to have been very astute when it comes to politics and what it takes to get an event noticed. Right from the very first Games in 1948 he made sure that high ranking political and social figures and later sports stars and celebrities were present at the Games in order to attract profile and media attention.

5. The final mechanism used by Dr Guttmann to cement the importance of the Games in people's minds, despite the luke-warm response it received when he first suggested it, was his constant comparisons to the Olympic Games. Indeed the welcome notes in the programme for the 1959 International Stoke Mandeville Games clearly state 'it has always been our ambition to model our International Stoke Mandeville Games on the lines of the Olympic Games.' Its affect and design appears to have been two-fold. Firstly to give his patients something tangible to aim for and to give them a feeling of self-worth and, secondly, to catch the attention of the media and people and organisations involved with paraplegics worldwide.

There are also two other key factors that enabled the organisers of the Stoke Mandeville Games to cope with the rapid growth of the Games from a financial perspective:

1. The World Veteran's Federation provided funding to enable veterans to afford the cost of travel to Stoke Mandeville for the Games. Without this funding many of these individuals and teams would have simply been unable to attend as is shown by the absence of Australia, Portugal and Sweden in 1958, when the WVF had withdrawn their financial support to concentrate on other projects.

2. The British Paraplegic Sports Endowment Fund and its much smaller predecessor, the Paraplegic Sports Fund, along with all the generous support and fundraising by numerous individuals and organisations enabled the Games organisers to cope with the increased costs of the growth. It also allowed them to make the necessary additions and upgrades to the facilities in order to cope with not only the increased number of competitors, but also the increase in the numbers of spectators wishing to attend the Games.

Two of the key indicators of the successful growth of the Stoke Mandeville Games are the vastly increased sporting programme over the period and the huge increase in the number of competitors in terms of both individuals and teams. Table one highlights the growth in the sporting programme, which increased from one sport in 1948 to eleven sports just twelve years later. There was also a large growth in the number of events within some sports over the same period, such as archery where the increase was led by improved available space and improved technical ability or a number of other sports where changes in the classification system and increased number of competitors led to events being split into several classification groupings.

Table 1. Growth in the Sporting Programme of the Stoke Mandeville Games (1948 – 1959)

Sport	1948	1949	1950	1951	1952	1953	1954	1955	1956	1957	1958	1959
Archery	X	X	X	X	X	X	X	X	X	X	X	X
Netball		X	X	X	X	X	X					
Javelin			X	X	X	X	X	X	X	X	X	X
Snooker				X	X	X	X	X	X	X	X	X
Club Swinging				D	D	D	D	D	D	D	D	D
Table Tennis				D	X	X	X	X	X	X	X	X
Swimming						X	X	X	X	X	X	X
Dartchery						X	X	X	X	X	X	X
Fencing							D	X	X	X	X	X
Basketball								X	X	X	X	X
Shot Putt										X	X	X
Club											X	X
Pentathlon												X

D: Demonstration

The growth in the number of nations represented at the Games after they first became truly international in 1952 was quite dramatic. Table 2 shows that in just six years the number of nations represented went from two to twenty-four.

Table 2. Growth in the Number of Teams competing at the Stoke Mandeville Games (1948-1960)

Country	1948	1949	1950	1951	1952	1953	1954	1955	1956	1957	1958	1959	Rome 1960
British Organistions	X	X	X	X	X	X	X	X	X	X			
Great Britain											X	X	X
Netherlands					X	X	X	X	X	X	X	X	X
Canada						X	X	X	X	X			
Finland						X	X	X	X	X	X		X
France				P		X	X	X	X	X	X	X	X
Israel						X	X	X	X	X	X	X	X

Austria						X	X	X	X	X	X	X
Belgium						X	X	X	X	X	X	X
Egypt						X						
West Germany						X	X	X	X	X	X	X
Pakistan						X		X	X	P		
Portugal						X			X		X	
Yugoslavia						X	X	X		X		X
Australia				P		P	P	P	X	X		X
South Africa						P	X	X	X			
Malta						P		X	X	X	X	
Malaysia						P	X	X				
United States							X	X	X	X	X	X
Denmark							X	X	X		X	
Norway							X	X	X	X	X	X
Turkey							X					
Italy								X	X	X	X	X
Greece	P	P	P						X			X
Argentina									X			X
Ireland									X		X	X
Sweden									X			X
Switzerland									X	X	X	X
Lebanon											P	X
Northern Rhodesia											P	X
Uruguay											P	
India											X	X
Cyprus											P	
Southern Rhodesia			P									
				2	6	14	18	18	24	20	17	21

P: Individual Patient from Stoke Mandeville or other Unit.

The slight decline in the number of nations in 1958 and 1959 is likely due to the withdrawal of funding by the World Veteran's Federation as mentioned above. However, this funding was re-instated for the first Paralympic Games held in Rome in 1960 and may explain why the number of competing nations rose again, although this may also have been due to the added prestige of competing in the Olympic host city shortly after the Olympic Games had taken place.

References

Anderson, J., 2003, Turned in Tax Payers': Paraplegia, Rehabilitation and Sport at Stoke Mandeville, 1944-56, Journal of Contemporary History, Vol. 38 (3): p. 461-475.

Brandmeyer, G.A. & McBee, G.F., 1986, Social Status and Athletic Competition for the Disabled Athletes: The Case of Wheelchair Road-Racing, in Sherrill, C. (Ed.), 1986, Sport and Disabled Athletes, Human Kinetics; Champaign, Il, p. 181-187.

Brittain, I. & Hutzler, Y., 2009, A social-historical perspective on the development of sports for persons with a physical disability in Israel in Sport in Society, Special Issue: Sport, Culture and Ideology in the State of Israel, Vol. 12(8), 1075-1088.

Cohen, N., 2007, Mind if I Sit? QuadPara Association of South Africa; Pinetown, South Africa.

Craven, Sir P., Paralympic Athletes Inspiring and Exciting the World, presentation at the XIXth British National Olympic Academy, Greenwich, UK on 29th April, 2006.

Goodman, S., 1986, Spirit of Stoke Mandeville: the story of Sir Ludwig Guttmann London: Collins.

Guttmann, L.,1976, Textbook of Sport for the Disabled, Aylesbury, Bucks, UK: HM & M Publishers.

Guttmann, L., Looking Back on a Decade in The Cord, 1954, Vol. 6(4); p9-23.

Guttmann. L., 1952, On the Way to an International Sports Movement for the Paralysed, The Cord, Vol. 5 (3) (October): p. 7 – 23.

LA84 Foundation website, 2009, Norway and Olympism, (http://www.la84foundation.org/OlympicInformationCenter/OlympicReview/197 8/ore123/ore123k.pdf) accessed 24-10-09.

Legg, D., Emes, C, Stewart, D. & Steadward, R, Historical Overview of the Paralympics, Special Olympics and Deaflympics, Palaestra, 20.1 (Winter 2002): 30 – 35, 56.

Letter dated September 3rd, 1956 from Otto Mayer, Chancellor of the International Olympic Committee to Sir Arthur Porritt in response to the nomination of the Stoke Mandeville Games for the Fearnley Cup. (IOC Archives)

Letter dated 27th August, 1956 from Sir Arthur Porritt to Otto Mayer, Chancellor of the International Olympic Committee nominating the Stoke Mandeville Games for the Fearnley Cup. (IOC Archives)

Lockwood, R. & Lockwood, A., 2007, Rolling Back the Years: A history of wheelchair sports in Western Australia, Wheelchair Sports WA Inc; Perth, Australia.

Lomi, C., Geroulanos, E. & Kekatos, E., Sir Ludwig Guttmann – "The de Coubertin of the Paralysed", 2004, Journal of the Hellenic Association of Orthopaedic and Traumatology, Vol 55 (1). (http://www.acta-ortho.gr/v55t1_6.html) accessed 21-04-10.

McCann, C., 1996, Sports for the Disabled: the evolution from rehabilitation to competitive sport, in the British Journal of Sports Medicine, Vol. 30(4), p. 279-280.

Online Olympic Games Museum, 2009, The Sir Thomas Fearnley Cup, (http://olympic-museum.de/awards/fearnley_cup.htm) accessed 24-10-09.

Paraplegia News, 1953-1960.

Paraplegic Sports Endowment Fund Annual Reports and Abstracts of Accounts 1955-1960 (IWAS Archives)

Programme for The 1959 Stoke Mandeville Games (The International Sports Festival of the Paralysed) dated 23rd-25th July. (IWAS Archives)

Programme for the 1957 Stoke Mandeville Games dated 26th-27th July, 1957 (IWAS Archives)

Programme for the Sixth Annual and Second International Inter-Spinal Unit Sports Festival "Stoke Mandeville Games" dated August 8th, 1953. (IWAS Archives)

Scruton, J., 1964, History of Sport for the Paralysed, The Cord, Vol. 17 (1)

Scruton, J., 1959, The National and International 1959 Stoke Mandeville Games, in The Cord, Vol. 11(3/4); p. 7-27.

Scruton, J., 1958, The 1958 National Stoke Mandeville Games, in The Cord, Vol. 10(3); p. 6-16.

Scruton, J., 1957, The 1957 International Stoke Mandeville Games, in The Cord, Vol. 9(4); p. 7-28.

Scruton, J., 1956, International Stoke Mandeville Games, in The Cord, Vol. 8(4); p. 7-21.

Scruton, J., 1955, Reflections on the 1955 International Stoke Mandeville Games, Vol. 8(1); p. 21-28.

Schweikert, H., 1955, Pan Am Jets Take Part in Paralympics, in Paraplegia News, September 1955; p. 12.

The Bucks Advertiser and Aylesbury News Newspaper

The Bucks Free Press Newspaper

The Bucks Herald Newspaper

The Cord, Journal for Paraplegics, Vol. 1(1) – Vol. 12(4)

The Star and Garter Magazine, 1948-1960.

Chapter 2: Rome, Italy 1960

Logo:	Confirmed Participating Nations	21
	Participating Athletes	328 (275 men, 53 women) (Using Official Results)
	Number of Events	117
	Opening Ceremony	Sunday 18th September (5.00pm) Aqua Acetosa
Mascot:	Closing Ceremony	Sunday 25th September (9.00pm) Palazzetto dello Sport
None Known	Officially Opened by	Prof. Camillo Giardina Minister of Health
	Main Stadium	Tre Fontane
	Flame Lit by	No Flame
	Athlete's Oath	None known[2]

Participating Nations (21): Argentina, Australia, Austria, Belgium, Finland, France, Federal Republic of Germany, Great Britain, Greece, Ireland, Israel, Italy, Lebanon, Malta, Netherlands, Norway, Rhodesia, Sweden, Switzerland, United States, Yugoslavia.

---

[2] If you know the name of the aoth taker in Rome please e-mail parahist@hotmail.co.uk

Sports (9): Archery, Athletics, Dartchery, Pentathlon (Archery, Athletics & Swimming Events), Snooker, Swimming, Table Tennis, Wheelchair Basketball, Wheelchair Fencing.

Impairment Groups (1): Spinal Cord Injuries*

*Bill Mather-Brown (2002), one of the Australian competitors in Rome claims the term 'spinal cord injuries' must have been applied to include various forms of paralysis, as distinct from amputees etc. Polio victims such as himself do not necessarily have spinal injuries.

Bids: None

Logo: No special logo was designed for these Games. They simply used the Stoke Mandeville Games logo of a wheelchair wheel wrapped around the world, which had been used at Stoke Mandeville for at least five years previously.

The Selection of Rome as the Host City

Dr Guttmann first discussed the possibly of holding the 1960 International Stoke Mandeville Games away from their spiritual home at the Annual meeting of the World Veteran's Federation held in Rome in May 1959. On 15th June 1955, at the IOC session in Paris, Rome had been selected as the hosts for the 1960 Olympic Games. At the World Veteran's Federation meeting in Rome Dr Guttmann had discussions with the Italian Instituto Nazionale per l'Assicurazione contro gli Infortuni sul Lavoro (INAIL), representatives of the World Veteran's Federation and Dr Antonio Maglio, Director of the Spinal Centre at Ostia in Rome, that had been set up by INAIL in June 1957. Although it was agreed that the task of holding the Games in Rome shortly after the Olympic Games would be an immense undertaking there was great enthusiasm amongst those present along with the promise of financial backing. INAIL agreed to cover the accommodation costs of the visiting teams and the World Veteran's Federation agreed to assist with the travel costs of some of the teams. Given that all former participating countries in the Stoke Mandeville Games gave their willing agreement to the project it was decided to go ahead and make the hosting of the Games in the Olympic host city an experiment 'in the interests of furthering our young sports movement for the paralyzed'. If the experiment worked it was decided that the Games would, where possible, be held in the same city as the Olympic Games in Olympic years, returning to Stoke Mandeville in the intervening years. In order to assist the organizers in Rome Joan Scruton, Secretary of the Spinal Centre at Stoke Mandeville, who had been involved in the organization of the Stoke Mandeville Games from their inception travelled to Rome for a fortnight in October 1959 as a guest of INAIL.

The Games Poster[3]

Although it is assumed by the author that a poster did exist for these Games, neither the author nor anyone he has spoken to have seen it or can remember what it looked like. The search for this poster is on-going.

The Games Opening Ceremony

The opening ceremony for the Games took place on Sunday 18th September at 5.00pm at the Acqua Acetosa sports ground. The ceremony began with the parade of nations led by a large police band. The band were followed by a British ex-serviceman flanked by a male and female Italian competitor carrying the Stoke Mandeville banner. The nations were lead in by the British team as originators of the Games, then each competing nation in alphabetical order, with the Italian team as hosts bringing up the rear. As each team entered the stadium Italian naval cadets raised the appropriate flag. Once all the teams were lined up on the grass facing the saluting base they were inspected by Camillo Giardino, Italian Minister for Health accompanied by Cesare Merzagora, President of the Italian Senate and Dr Guttmann. Renato Morelli, President of INAIL then made a speech of welcome before Prof. Giardina declared the Games officially open. Following a short address by Dr Guttmann the participants then returned to the Village to prepare themselves for the start of competition the following day. No mention has ever been found that an athlete's oath was performed at the opening ceremony in Rome.

The Games Themselves

Dr Guttmann, Joan Scruton and Charlie Atkinson had all visited Rome prior to the Games in order to assist with the organisational preparations at which time they had made definite arrangements to use the Acqua Acetosa Sports Ground for most of the sports. This was in the north-east of Rome on the left bank of the Tiber some 2km from the Foro Italico Olympic Centre, 1 km from the Olympic Village, and Palazzetto dello Sport and some 4 km from the centre of the city. They had also agreed upon the type of accommodation, which had lifts and was suitable for paraplegics, to be used within the Olympic Village which was in the area known as Campo Parioli, in the Flaminio quarter to the north of Rome. INAIL had offered to pay for the accommodation of all team members during their stay in Rome. However, upon arrival in Rome with the British team they found that decisions had been made by people in power that they could only use the Acqua Acetosa for the opening ceremony and that the area of the Village where lifts were installed were no longer available to them. Instead they would have to use the Tre Fontane Sports Ground, some 40 minutes drive by coach from the Village, for most of the sports and worse than that the accommodation they would have to use was built on stilts with a set of 20 steps needing to be negotiated between each floor. Each set of 20 steps doubled back on itself so that

---

[3] If anyone has a copy of this poster or knows the whereabouts of a copy please e-mail parahist@hotmail.co.uk

two sets of 10 steps had to be negotiated between each floor. Ramps had been installed over the steps, but the steps were simply too steep for the ramps to be of any use. These steps can just be seen in the background of the photograph below.

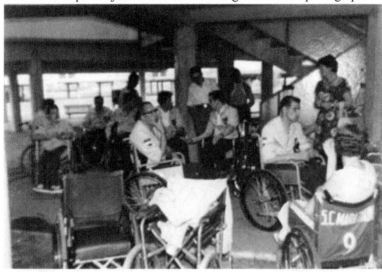

Dutch team relaxing under the stilted section of the accommodation. The steps to the living quarters can be seen in the background.

The implications for this on arrivals day was that the escorts not only had to carry all of the luggage up several flights of stairs, but also many of the athletes and their wheelchairs. This problem was eventually overcome by drafting in Italian lifters to assist the escorts with the lifting throughout the Games. In addition, rather than return to the Village each day for lunch, which would have eaten up valuable time and place great physical strain on all concerned, arrangements were made for picnic lunches to be delivered to the Tre Fontane Sports Ground each day. However, it would have been impossible to hold the table tennis competitions at Tre Fontane, which had no indoor facilities, as the wind would have made play impossible. Permission was, therefore, granted for the use of the Clubroom in the Olympic Village to hold the table tennis competitions. In order to overcome any issues arising during the competitions in Rome it had been decided at the 1950 meeting of trainers and escorts that a special International Tribunal should be elected for the Rome Games to deal with any disputes that might arise. The tribunal in Rome consisted of a member from Switzerland, Norway and the Netherlands with a reserve member from Italy. They were, apparently, only called upon on two occasions in Rome and each time the dispute was settled to the satisfaction of all concerned. Most sources claim there were 400 athletes that participated in Rome. However, this number cannot be borne out by the official results nor a careful analysis of team sizes published in various national reports and in many cases verified by analysis of film footage of the opening ceremony. So far 328 participants have been identified. It is unlikely this number was above 350 even taking into account members of team sports not identified in the official results.

The swimming events were all held on the Saturday, the final day of competition, and were the only sport held that day. The swimming pool used for the Games was the Piscina Foro Italico, which had been used as the warm up pool for the Olympic Games and is connected by an underground passage to the Olympic pool. The pool used by the Paralympians was designed by architect Enrico del Debbio, and was located in a large hall measuring 62m by 36m. One side had windows extending from the floor to the ceiling. On the opposite side there were 6 seating tiers for the public. The pool, which measured 50m × 20m, was lined with marble, whilst the space around the pool was paved with black-and-white marble decorated with aquatic mosaic designs, as were the three walls of the building.

The swimming pool in Rome.

Tre Fontane	Archery, Athletics, Basketball, Dartchery, Fencing, Snooker
Piscina Foro Italico:	Swimming
Olympic Village Club House:	Table Tennis

The Games in Rome saw the addition of four new events that had never been held at Stoke Mandeville. In swimming events were held over 50m for the very first time. In table tennis events just for women took place. Previously the women had competed in the men's events. A full FITA round was added to the archery competition. This consisted of 36 arrows at 90m, 70m, 50m and 30m for men and 36 arrows at 70m, 60m, 50m and 30m for women. Finally precision javelin was added to the athletics field events. The throwing position for this event is the same as for javelin throwing with the aim of trying to score as many points as possible. The javelin used was a junior 600 gram 2.20m one with then throwing from a distance of 10m from the centre of the target and women from 7m. The target consisted of eight concentric rings, one inside the other with the centre ring being 20cm in diameter and each ring after that being 40cm bigger in diameter than the one inside it. The target is marked on the floor and points are scored depending on where the tip of the javelin sticks in. The outer ring would score 2 points. The centre ring scores 16 points. As with archery, cutting a line counts as the higher score. Each competitor had 6 throws with the best five counting towards their final score giving a maximum possible total of 80 points.

Basketball match between the Netherlands and Italy

The snooker was actually played outdoors at Tre Fontane, which had a cinder 400-metre track with 6 lanes and a covered 130m straight for training during bad weather. It was here, in the middle of the covered straight, that the snooker took place. As snooker was not a popular sport in Italy the table had to be shipped from Stoke Mandeville to Ostia in order for the event to take place. After some careful adjustments by Dr Allen, who was in charge of the snooker event, the table was made reasonably level and snooker was one of the few sports that made it through the first day's torrential rain relatively unscathed. The FITA round of the archery had to be cancelled and rescheduled for the next day.

Snooker under the covered athletics straight

The Outstanding Performers in Rome

Without a doubt the outstanding performer in Rome was Maria Scutti of Italy who won 10 gold, 3 silver and 2 bronze medals in athletics, fencing, swimming and table tennis. However, it was in athletics where she really excelled winning 9 gold and 2 bronze medals. Scutti was a class A competitor (most disabled) and yet she was able to win classes A and B in Club Throw, Javelin, Precision Javelin and Shot Put. In addition she won the class C (least disabled) Precision Javelin, took bronze in the class C Club Throw and Javelin and finished fifth in the class C shot Put. Her other gold medal came in the class 4 women's 50m breaststroke. All of the top performers in Rome were women. Zander of Germany won 6 gold and 1 bronze in archery, athletics and swimming. Baroness Berger-Waldenegg of Austria won 5 gold, 1 silver and 2 bronze athletics, swimming and table tennis and Scutti's team mate Anna Maria Toso won 3 gold, 5 silver and 2 bronze in athletics, fencing, swimming and table tennis. Amongst the men Dick Thompson of Great Britain won 4 gold, 1 silver and 2 bronze in athletics and basketball and Ron Stein of the USA who won 4 gold medals in athletics, basketball and pentathlon. In the fencing Italy took a clean sweep of all nine medals from the three fencing events held and the USA won both the complete and incomplete lesion basketball competitions.

The Winners Medal

Great Britain's first ever Paralympic Gold Medal won by Margaret Maughan for the Archery Colombia Round.

The Closing Ceremony

At 9.00pm on Sunday 25th September the closing ceremony for the inaugural Paralympic Games got under way in the Palazzo dello Sport, which had a total seating capacity of 15,000 places and sat on a hill overlooking an artificial lake next to the Viale Cristoforo Colombo. The ceremony took place in the presence of the Patron of the Games, Donna Carla Gronchi, wife of the Italian Prime Minister. Following demonstrations of fencing and table tennis given by teams from Italy and Great Britain Donna Carla presented some of the main trophies for the Games. Dr Guttmann then gave a speech thanking the Italian organizers and awarding INAIL a banner of the Stoke Mandeville Games, which was the highest distinction the International Stoke Mandeville Games Committee could bestow for outstanding service and achievement in the cause of the sports movement for the paralysed. Signor Morelli, President of INAIL, then gave the final speech before Donna Carla Gronchi declared the first Paralympic Games officially closed. Guttmann summed the Games up in Rome by stating that 'It can now be concluded that the first experiment to hold the Stoke Mandeville Games as an entity in another country, as an international sports festival comparable with the Olympic Games and other international sports events for the able-bodied has been highly successful. It justifies the hope that this achievement will be a stimulus to continue in the same pattern'.

An Audience with His Holiness Pope John XXIII

One of the highlights of the Games was the special audience given to all the participants at 11.30am on the morning before the closing ceremony by Pope John XXIII, who addressed the athletes as follows: 'You are the living demonstration of the marvels of the virtue of energy. You have given a great example, which We would like to emphasize, because it can be a lead to all: you have shown what an energetic soul can achieve, in spite of apparently insurmountable obstacles imposed by the body' (Scruton, 1998). The Pope twice appeared on the balcony, the second time with Dr Guttmann and Dr Maglio at his side. The Pope also gave an audience to Father Leo Close from Dublin, a former paraplegic patient of Dr Guttmann's who had been a competitor in the Games. 'He was ordained by special permission of the Pope,' Guttmann wrote, 'and became the first Catholic "priest on wheels".'

Dr Guttmann meets Pope John XXIII

The Final Medal Table

Rank	NPC	Gold	Silver	Bronze	Total
1	Italy	29	29	24	82
2	Great Britain	21	14	19	54
3	Fed. Rep. Germany	15	6	9	30
4	Austria	11	8	11	30
5	United States	11	7	7	25
6	Norway	9	3	4	16
Number of Countries winning a medal					17
% of participating countries winning a medal					81.0

Games Trivia

Both Margaret Harriman and George Mann, competing for Rhodesia, had to produce medical certificates certifying them fit to fly before the airline would issue the tickets.

Jack Whitman won USA's first gold medal in Rome in the archery men's FITA round-on the same day as his 30th birthday.

The American team of twenty four male athletes was sponsored by the Joseph Bulova School of Watch Making in co-operation with the World Veterans Federation, the Paralyzed Veterans of America and the National Paraplegia Foundation.

The team of sixteen athletes and their six helpers from Malta arrived in two aircraft of the Order of St John – the Malta organisers could not have sent such a large team to Rome had it not been for the Order's help.

Mather-Brown (2002) and several members of the Australian team from Rome in a video commemorating the Rome Games made by the Australian Paralympic Committee (2010) claim the some of the officiating by the Italian officials in Rome was rather biased, particularly in fencing and basketball. As an example of this they claim that in basketball if their chair hit an Italian player's chair they were accused of 'charging', but if an Italian player's chair hit theirs they were accused of 'blocking'.

References

Bailey, S., 2008, Athlete First: A History of the Paralympic Movement, John Wiley & Sons Ltd; Chichester, UK.

Harriman, M., 1967, Bring Me My Bow, Victor Gollanz; London, UK.

INAIL, 1960, IX Giochi Internazionali per Paraplegici, Roma 1960: Programma e Resultati delle Gare, INAIL; Rome.

ISMGC, 1959, Report of the Meeeting of Trainers and Escorts held at Stoke Mandeville Stadium on Sunday 26th July 1959 (IWAS Archives)

Japan Olympic Committee Website, 2010,

(http://www.joc.or.jp/english/historyjapan/history_japan_bid02.html) accessed 19-01-10.

Mather-Brown, B., 2002, The Fight in the Dog, Becks Books; Australia.

Scruton, J, 1998, Stoke Mandeville: Road to the Paralympics, Peterhouse Press; Alesbury, UK.

The Cord, 1960, Special Issue: The 1960 International Stoke Mandeville Games for the Paralysed in Rome, Hunt Barnard; Aylesbury, UK.

The Cord, 1959, Stoke Mandeville Calling, Vol. 12(1); p. 22-25.

The Times of Malta, Malta Paralympic Team Back in Triumph, Friday 30th September 1960; p.9.

Chapter 3: Tokyo, Japan 1964

Logo	Confirmed Participating Nations	21
	Participating Athletes	378 (303 men, 75 women)
	Number of Events	144
	Opening Ceremony	Sunday 8th November (10.00am) 'Oda' Track & Field Stadium
Mascot:	Closing Ceremony	Thursday 12th November (5.00pm) Olympic Gymnasium Annexe
	Officially Opened by	H.I.M Crown Prince Akihito
None Known	Main Stadium	'Oda' Track & Field Stadium
	Flame Lit by	No Flame
	Athlete's Oath	Shigeo Aono (Swimmer)

Participating Nations (21): Argentina, Australia, Austria, Belgium, **Ceylon**, **Fiji**, France, Federal Republic of Germany, Great Britain, Ireland, Israel, Italy, **Japan**, Malta, Netherlands, **Philippines**, Rhodesia, **South Africa**, Sweden, Switzerland, United States + three observers from Mexico (Jorge Beltran (Head of Delegation), Dr Leonardo Ruiz + A.N. Other).

(Countries in bold are those appearing at a summer Paralympic Games for the first time)

Sports (10): Archery, Athletics, Dartchery Pentathlon (Archery, Athletics & Swimming events), Snooker, Swimming, Table Tennis, Weightlifting, Wheelchair Basketball, Wheelchair Fencing.

Impairment Groups (1): Spinal Cord Injuries.

Logo: The logo chosen by the Japanese for the Tokyo Games was full of symbolism. An outline of the white dove of peace was used to symbolise love. The logo also incorporated five rings. The word for ring in Japanese is 'wa' which has two meanings. It can mean ring, but it also means 'harmony'. The rings also symbolise wheelchairs. Original the rings were laid out in a 'W' formation like the Olympic rings, but following a complaint from the IOC the design was changed to a 'V' shape to represent the athletes' victory in overcoming the problems in their lives.

Bids: None

The Selection of Tokyo as the Host City

In truth there was no real selection process for the Games of 1964. The Games committee, having successfully taken the Games to Rome in 1960, were keen to continue this association with the Olympic host city. They were fortunate that during the Games in Rome a Japanese government official, named only as Mrs Watanabe, was attending a conference in Rome and took time out to attend the Games. Mrs Watanabe was so enthused by what she saw that she agreed on her return to Tokyo to pave the way for Dr Guttmann to approach the necessary authorities about Tokyo hosting the Games of 1964. This was followed by a visit to Stoke Mandeville by Dr Yutaka Nakamura, an orthopaedic surgeon from Beppu, who spent three months studying under Dr Guttmann at Stoke Mandeville. In 1962 the first Japanese team of two athletes attended the International Games at Stoke. They were accompanied by Dr Nakamura and Mr Yoshisuke Kasai, a high ranking Japanese government official who went on to become Chairman of the organising committee for the Tokyo Games and then, for many years, an Executive Board member of the International Stoke Mandeville Games Committee. The final part of the preparation for the Games was that in June 1964 Dr Guttmann, Joan Scruton and Charlie Atkinson all flew to Tokyo to carry out site visits and to take part in organising committee meetings in order to ensure everything would be ready for the Games in November.

Transportation to Tokyo

Hosting the Games in Asia actually made it possible for The Philippines to participate in the Games for the very first time and also allowed countries such as Australia to send bigger teams than usual. Participants from ten of the countries plus the observers from Mexico made their own arrangements to travel to Tokyo. Arrangements for the British and most of the European teams was made through Stoke Mandeville, who following negotiation through brokers, managed to charter two planes. The KLM plane would pick participants up in Amsterdam and

London and the Air France flight in Paris, London and Hamburg. Air France officials, noting how much easier the narrow chair KLM used made transporting passengers up the aisles of the plane during the boarding process, apparently had one made overnight in order to make their own passengers more comfortable during boarding.

On arrival at Haneda Airport in Tokyo all of the competitors received a warm and friendly welcome. They were unloaded from their planes and carried to awaiting buses by members of the Japanese Defence Force. On arrival at the village they were once more greeted with a friendly welcome and a garland of paper cranes, which in Japanese culture represent peace and long life.

Japanese Defence Force members unloading arriving athletes

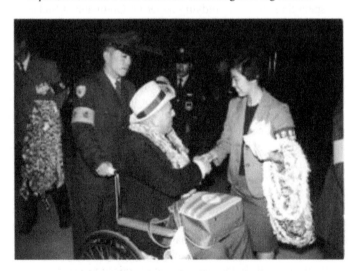

A warm welcome for all new arrivals

The Games Poster

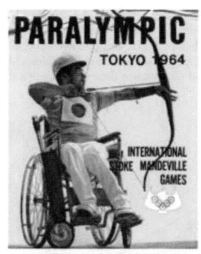

There were actually three versions of the Tokyo Games poster produced for the Games. Two large posters (103 x 72cm) were produced. One, all in English, was for the international market. The poster shown below was for major advertising locations within Japan. A third, smaller poster, was produced for the domestic market for use within shops, offices and other locations to advertise the Games.

The Games Opening Ceremony

The opening ceremony for games occurred at 10.00am on Sunday 8th November in bright sunshine. It was attended by Crown Prince Akihito, who officially opened the Games and his wife Princess Michiko, as well as a host of Japanese government officials. In addition to the usual speeches the parade of nations was lead by a marching band of young Japanese girls, after which the Crown Prince and the Princess inspected the teams on the field. The athlete's oath was taken by Japanese swimmer, Shigeo Aono, and was followed by the release of hundreds of pigeons. The opening ceremony concluded with a demonstration of traditional Japanese fencing by members of the Defence Force.

Teams lined up at Oda Field for the opening ceremony

The Games Themselves

Given that the organising committee of the fourteenth Olympic Games only handed the Olympic village over to Mr Kasai and his organising committee on 5th November, three days before the Games were due to begin, they did a remarkable job of preparing everything for the arrival of the athletes. As the two photographs below show a great deal of work was done to ensure that the whole of the village was wheelchair accessible.

Two pictures showing the kind of conversion work that had to be carried out to make the athlete's village accessible

Although the Games used the same village as Olympic Games, the only sports facilities they had in common were the National Gymnasium (Snooker, Table Tennis and Weightlifting), although not for swimming as the pool was being converted into a skating rink, and the National Gymnasium Annexe, which was used for some of the wheelchair basketball games after dark. For the swimming events competitors had to be taken by bus to the Tokyo Metropolitan Indoor Swimming Pool. The sports were spread over seven venues:

1. Oda Field: Athletics + Opening Ceremony
2. National Gymnasium: Snooker, Table Tennis, Weightlifting
3. National Gymnasium Annexe: Basketball (Indoor) + Closing Ceremony
4. Basketball (Outdoor) Venue
5. Archery + Dartchery Venue
6. Tokyo Metropolitan Indoor Swimming Pool: Swimming
7. Fencing Venue

The Crown Prince and his Princess flanked by Dr Shigeo Aono, inspecting the teams

Nakamura taking the athletes' oath

Weightlifting for men was the only completely new sport to be added to the programme in Tokyo with medals being competed for in four different weight categories. However, a number of sports including archery, athletics, swimming, table tennis and wheelchair fencing added new events or disciplines to their programmes. Athletics in particular added track events for the first time with a wheelchair dash, slalom and relay being competed for. Discus was also added to the field event programme.

Weightlifting – the newest sporton the programme

The Outstanding Performers in Tokyo

The outstanding performers in terms of gold medals in Tokyo were both American. Amongst the men Ron Stein won seven gold medals in track and field and wheelchair basketball and amongst the woman Rosalie Hixson won six gold medals in track and field and swimming. Two other women, Lynnette Gilchrist of Rhodesia in track and field and swimming and Anna Maria Toso of Italy won five gold medals each. In terms of total medals Ms Toso was the top performer winning 5 gold, 5 silver and 1 bronze medal in track and field, swimming and fencing. Amongst the men the top performer was Tim Harris of America who won 2 gold, 5 silver and 3 bronze medals in track and field, swimming and wheelchair basketball. The host nation, Japan's, only gold medal was won by

Watanabe and Ikari playing together in the men's class C table tennis doubles. In terms of total individual medals their best performer was T. Matsumoto who won two silver medals in the archery FITA and Albion team events and a bronze medal in the Dartchery mixed pairs open event. Japan only had three female competitors in their team and so C. Inoue and F. Ogusawara did well to win a bronze medal in the women's class C table tennis doubles, especially given Japan's relative inexperience of international competition in disability sport at that time.

Ron Stein (USA) on the way to one of his seven gold medals

The Winners Medal

A total of 610 medals were made by Mr George Butler, engineering instructor in the Occupational Therapy department attached to the National Spinal Injuries Unit at Stoke Mandeville Hospital, with the help of patients who cut the medals from bars of brass and turned and polished them. Mr Butler then engraved each medal, including the symbol of the relevant sport, and then covered them in a gold, silver or bronze coating.

The Games Closing Ceremony

At 5.00pm on Thursday 12th November the closing ceremony for the second Paralympic Games got under way in the National Gymnasium Annexe. They were once again attended by Crown Prince Akihito and Princess Michiko, who gave out a number of special prizes to outstanding athletes at the Games. The five thousand seat stadium was full with some people having to stand. The twenty-one teams were lined up on the arena floor surrounded on both sides by Defence Force members carrying the flags of each nation. As the flag bearers entered the arena one hundred and fifty girls wearing white blouses sang a song dedicated to the Paralympics and world peace. Following a speech by Dr Guttmann in which he thanked the organising committee and the Japanese people for putting on such a wonderful spectacle, the Stoke Mandeville Games flag was officially lowered and handed over to Dr Leonardo Ruiz as the representative of the Mexican Organising Committee for the 1968 Games. Mr Hirokuni Dazai, Vice-Chairman of the Organising Committee, declared the Games officially closed at around 5.40pm. The athletes left the arena to strains of Auld Lang Syne with young Japanese students and children clamouring for the hats of the athletes and officials as souvenirs.

Teams lined up in the Olympic Stadium Annexe for the closing ceremony

Time Issues

Due to circumstances beyond the control of the ISMG Committee all of the sporting events, as well as the opening and closing ceremonies, had to be squashed into four and a half days, which made organising the schedule an extreme headache given that many of the sportsmen and women regularly entered a number of different sports. In reviewing the Games at the ISMGC on November 13, immediately after the Games, all concerned agreed that four days was far too short a period, especially given the increasing numbers of sports and events and the numbers of competitors taking part in each. It was, therefore, decided that future Stoke Mandeville Games held in Olympic years should last for seven days excluding opening and closing ceremonies.

Impact of Games on Japanese Society

The Games and the media coverage of them within Japan had quite a profound impact upon the way people with disabilities were viewed within Japan. At the ISMG Committee meeting, held in conjunction with the annual Stoke Mandeville Games of 1965, Mr Kasai, Chairman of the Tokyo Organising Committee confirmed that since the Games there had been an increasing interest in the welfare of the disabled within Japan and that the Ministry of Labour were building a factory to provide jobs for paraplegics by the side of Lake Shigain in Nagano. This factory eventually spread into a chain of factories all over Japan under the banner of Sun Industries.

Sport for People with Other Disabilities

Although not part of the official 'Paralympic' Games held in Tokyo the Japanese authorities put on a National Games for the Handicapped on Friday 13th and Saturday 14th November, immediately following the Games. This was for amputees, blind and visually impaired and deaf athletes. As well as representatives from around twenty-five Japanese prefectures a small team of German athletes also took part in these Games, which were once again patronised by Crown Prince Akihito and his wife.

The Final Medal Table

Rank	NPC	Gold	Silver	Bronze	Total
1	United States	52	42	32	126
2	Great Britain	18	23	20	61
3	Italy	14	15	14	43
4	Australia	12	10	9	31
5	Rhodesia	10	5	3	18
6	South Africa	8	8	3	19
Number of Countries winning a medal					17
% of participating countries winning a medal					81.0

Games Trivia

The Games organizers actually had three names for the Games. These were:

- The International Stoke Mandeville Games (Dr Guttmann's preferred choice)
- The Tokyo Games for the Physically Handicapped

- Paralympics (The Organising Committee's preferred choice, because it sounded nice)

The Organising Committee actually produced three different sets of information for the Games, which were identical except for the name of the Games.

The Tokyo Games are the first Games known to have some kind of rudimentary accreditation card for athletes and officials:

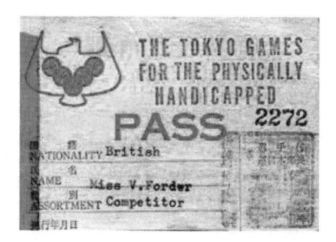

One of the sponsors for the Tokyo Olympic Games was the Peace Tobacco Company, which also produced a Cigarette Packet design to commemorate the Paralympic Games:

Restarts for field events in javelin, shot put and discus were ordered by officials on the first day of competition as bitterly cold headwinds disrupted competition.

Results sheets for the men's and women's precision javelin events went missing on the Monday following throw offs for tied places and were not found until the Wednesday. Although the results appeared in some foreign newspapers they were completely missed out of the official results for the Games.

According to the ISMG Executive Committee minutes Deutschen Versehrtensportverbandes (DVS), the organisation that usually represented Germany at the annual Stoke Mandeville Games, boycotted the Games in Tokyo and instead Germany were represented by an independent team under the leadership of Mr Weiss of the Johannes Strasbinger Haus in Wildbad. It appears that this boycott was due to a dispute between Gerd Brinkmann, the then President of DVS and Dr Guttmann over events at a meeting of the International Working Group for Disabled Sport held on 5th June 1963, which eventually lead to the resignation of Dr Guttmann from the International Working Group.

References

Anon, 1965, Undaunted against great odds, International Review of the Red Cross, Vol. 5(49); 202-210.

Australian Paraplegic, 1964, With the Australian Paraplegic Team in Tokyo, Vol. 3(4); 3 – 25.

Guttmann, L., 1965, The International Stoke Mandeville Games for the Paralysed: Tokyo, 1964, Physiotherapy, (March), Vol. 51; 78-83.

Harriman, M., 1967, Bring Me My Bow, Victor Gollanz; London, UK.

Minutes of the Meeting of the International Stoke Mandeville Games Committee held at Stoke Mandeville Hospital on Wednesday 21st July 1965 (IWAS Archives)

Minutes of the Meeting of the International Stoke Mandeville Games Committee held in Tokyo on Friday 13th November 1964 (IWAS Archives)

Scruton, J., 1998, Stoke Mandeville: Road to the Paralympics, Peterhouse Press; Aylesbury, UK.

The Cord, 1965, Special Issue: The 1964 International Stoke Mandeville Games for the Paralysed in Tokyo, Hunt Barnard; Aylesbury, UK.

The Cord, 1964, Preparations for the Stoke Mandeville Games and Scientific Meeting in Tokyo, Vol. 16 (3); 20 – 22.

The Japan Times, November 1965.

The Mainichi Daily News, November 1965.

Chapter 4: Tel Aviv, Israel 1968

Logo:	Confirmed Participating Nations	28
I.S.M.G.1968	Participating Athletes	730 (554 men, 176 women) (According to Official Results)
	Number of Events	188
	Opening Ceremony	Monday 4th November (3.15pm) University of Jerusalem Stadium
Mascot:	Closing Ceremony	Wednesday 13th November (6.00pm) Tel Aviv Fair Grounds
	Officially Opened by	Yigal Allon Deputy Prime Minister of Israel
None Known	Main Stadium	National Stadium Ramat Gan
	Flame Lit by	No Flame
	Athlete's Oath	Zvi Ben-Zvi (Athlete)

Participating Nations (28): Argentina, Australia, Austria, Belgium, **Canada**, Denmark, **Ethiopia**, Finland, France, Federal Republic of Germany, Great Britain, **India**, Ireland, Israel, Italy, **Jamaica**, Japan, **Korea**, Malta, Netherlands, **New Zealand**, Norway, Rhodesia, South Africa, **Spain**, Sweden, Switzerland, United States. **(Countries in bold are those appearing at a summer Paralympic Games for the first time)**

NB. A number of newspapers reported that a single female competitor from Uruguay participated in Tel Aviv when describing the opening ceremony, but no mention of such a competitor can be found in the official results, which lists team sizes alongside medals won.

Sports (11): Archery, Athletics, Dartchery, Lawn Bowls, Pentathon (Archery, Athletics & Swimming Events), Snooker, Swimming, Table Tennis, Weight Lifting, Wheelchair Basketball, Wheelchair Fencing.

Impairment Groups (1): Spinal Cord Injuries.

Logo: The logo used in Tel Aviv was simply an amalgamation of the three interlocking wheelchair wheels (representing Friendship, Unity and Sportsmanship) used by the Stoke Mandeville Games at the time and the term I.S.M.G. 1968 (International Stoke Mandeville Games 1968)

Bids from prospective host cities: Buenos Aries, Argentina, New York, USA and Tel Aviv, Israel.

The Selection of Tel Aviv as the Host City

Present at the Tokyo Paralympic Games in 1964 was Dr Leonardo Ruiz, from the Instituto Mexicano de Rehabilitacion, as part of an observation team looking at the possibilities for the Games to be held in Mexico City, hosts for the Olympic Games of 1968. A year later at the next Games committee meeting a letter from the head of the rehabilitation centre stating that things were progressing well was read out. Due to the worries about the impact of the altitude on paraplegics it was decided that the Americans should take a team to Mexico City to investigate. However, when their team manager, Ben Lipton, tried to arrange this he received a letter from the President of the rehabilitation centre stating that due to financial constraints and accessibility issues with facilities Mexico City would be unable to host the Games. Following offers from Buenos Aires, Argentina, New York, USA and Tel Aviv, Israel it was decided that the 1968 Games would be held in Israel. At the next meeting of the International Stoke Mandeville Games Committee Mr Arieh Fink, President of the Israeli Stoke Mandeville Committee confirmed that the Israeli Government was 'most enthusiastic' about hosting the Games, especially as it would coincide with both the Twentieth Anniversary of the State of Israel and the Twentieth Anniversary of the Stoke Mandeville Games. The Israeli President, Mr Zalman Shazar, had agreed to be Patron of the Games and a budget had been calculated at nearly £50,000.

The Games Poster

NB. This is not a de fact copy of an original poster as one has not been found. It has been pieced together from photographic and video sources that have included images of an original poster.

The Games Opening Ceremony

Deputy Prime Minister, Mr Yigal Allon (centre) with Sir Ludwig

The opening ceremony for the Games actually occurred at the University of Jerusalem Stadium, where nearly twenty thousand spectators witnessed the 'wheel-past' of athletes and performances by a military band, a girls choir and a group of folk dancers. Speeches and messages of welcome were given by Deputy Prime Minister, Mr Yigal Allon, standing in for President Shazar who was recovering from illness, Mr Arieh Fink and Sir Ludwig Guttmann, Founder and President of the Games. Mr Zvi Ben-Zvi, an Israeli paraplegic from the 1947-48 War of Independence, and one of the first Israeli participants at the 1954 Stoke Mandeville Games, gave the oath on behalf of the athletes to conduct themselves according to the three ideals of the Games: Friendship, Unity and Sportsmanship.

Opening Ceremony at the University of Jerusalem Stadium

The Games Themselves

The Games turned out to be a great success attracting twenty-eight nations, seven more than at either of the previous Games, and a total of 730 athletes (554 Men and 176 Women), nearly double the number at any previous Games. The Games were held from 4th to 13th November 1968 with the athletes, officials and administrators either being housed at the Kfar Maccabiah or Ramat-Aviv hotels. All of the sports events were held in or around the ILAN Sports Centre for the Disabled, which acted as the administrative headquarters for the Games. The sports were spread over five venues:

Hayarkon Scouts Club:	Snooker.
ILAN Sports Centre for the Disabled:	Basketball, Fencing, Swimming.
National Stadium Ramat Gan:	Archery, Track and Field.
Ohel Shem School:	Basketball, Precision Javelin, Slalom, Table Tennis, Weightlifting.
Ramat Gan Bowling Club:	Lawn Bowls.

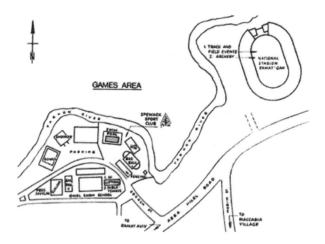

Under the direction of Gershon Huberman, Chairman of the Sports Committee, the sports programme had enlarged considerably compared with the 1964 programme in Tokyo. New events such as Lawn Bowls, women's Basketball and the 100m wheelchair race for men were introduced. This was the first time bowls had appeared on the Games programme outside of Britain as bowls clubs had apparently been afraid of the wheelchairs ruining the greens. However the Ramat Gan Club apparently got around this partially by laying plywood boards across the green to allow the wheelchairs to move around the green. Considerable damage was still done to the green by the wheelchairs, but despite this Max Spitz of the Israel Bowling Association still claimed that it had been a rare privilege to host the tournament, 'which had produced not only bowling and sportsmanship of the highest quality, but was an education to Israeli society as a whole'.

Swimming at the ILAN Sports Centre for the Disabled

From an Israeli sporting perspective the highlight of the Games was probably the men's wheelchair basketball final in which the host nation came up against the

USA, who had won every Paralympic men's basketball final up to that date. At previous Games the wheelchair basketball had been split into two classes – complete and incomplete lesions. However, for the 1968 Games the two groups were combined so that there was only one competition for the men. The final drew huge interest. It was due to start at 9pm, but was delayed due to disorderly crowds trying to get into the venue. The stands, built to accommodate two thousand people, were full by 5pm. Despite mounted police being drafted in to control the crowds it is estimated that by the time the game started some six thousand spectators had entered the grounds. Amongst those watching were the US Ambassador Walworth Barbour and Israeli Defence Minister Moshe Dayan, who helped present the medals after the game was over. In a thrilling match which Israel lead 21-16 at half-time, Israeli Captain Baruch Hagai finally led Israel to a historic and hard-fought 47-37 victory. Israel also went on to take victory in the women's wheelchair basketball event winning all four of their matches in a five team round robin tournament.

Moshe Dayan congratulates a member of the winning Israeli team.

Roberto Marson of Italy was proclaimed the outstanding athlete of the Games having won nine individual gold medals (three in field events, three in swimming and three in fencing) and one team fencing gold medal, making a total of ten gold medals. Another outstanding athlete was Lorraine Dodd, 24, from Australia. She set three Swimming records in her class, all on the same day. Ed Owen, 20, of the USA returned home with seven medals—two golds in Athletics, a gold for the Pentathlon, two golds in Swimming, a silver in Basketball, and a bronze in

Javelin. The top performing Israeli athletes at the Games were Zipora Rubin-Rosenbaum with five gold and one silver medal from wheelchair basketball, field events and the pentathlon and, for the men, Baruch Hagai with three gold medals from the wheelchair basketball and the table tennis singles and doubles events. Israel eventually finished third in the overall final medal table behind USA and Great Britain, their best position in a Paralympic Games to date and one which they have only equaled on one other occasion in Toronto in 1976.

The Winners Medal

Paralympic Gold medal and medal certificate from Tel Aviv, 1968

The Games were not just about the sport however. Participants were given the opportunity to tour the Holy Land with all participants and officials being taken by bus to a number of sites. These included Nazareth where they were greeted by both the Arabic Mayor of Nazareth, Mr Mousa Kteily, and the Jewish Mayor of Upper Nazareth, Mr Mordechai Allon. Archiship Isodoros of the Greek Orthodox Church gave a communal blessing to all present on behalf of all of the religious denominations of Nazareth and songs were sung by two choirs of Arabic and Jewish schoolchildren respectively. After the ceremony the competitors were taken to two kibbutzim (Afikim and Beit Zera) near Lake Tiberias for lunch and on their way back to Tel Aviv the buses stopped by the River Jordan where each competitor was presented with a small bottle of holy water which they witnessed being drawn from the river by volunteers.

At 6pm on Wednesday November 13th the closing ceremony of the third Paralympic Games got under away at the Tel Aviv Fair Grounds. In the presence of the Deputy Prime Minister, Yigal Allon, and the Mayor of Tel Aviv, Mordechai Namir, some of the trophies were presented and a display was given by dancers from three kibbutzim in the Jordan Valley. The Deputy Prime Minister officially declared the Games closed and congratulated all the participants upon the contribution they had made towards world unity.

Final Medal Table

Rank	NPC	Gold	Silver	Bronze	Total
1	United States	33	27	39	99
2	Great Britain	29	20	20	69
3	Israel	18	21	23	62
4	Australia	15	16	7	38
5	France	13	10	9	32
6	Fed. Rep. Germany	12	12	11	35
Number of Countries winning a medal					22
% of participating countries winning a medal					78.6

Games Trivia

Members of the German team, when applying for visas, had to complete a questionnaire about their political past e.g. – whether they had been de-Nazified and in what category, which was a national law in Israel at the time.

In order to try and do away with the political race between nations to prove their superiority, as was occurring in the Olympic Games, the Games in Tel Aviv had no official medal table and dispensed completely with the playing of national anthems and raising of national flags during medal ceremonies.

In order to overcome possible political issues surrounding the participation of Rhodesia in Tel Aviv the Israeli immigration officials sought and gained permission from Britain to allow Rhodesian athletes entry to Israel without looking at their passports. Each athlete filled out a landing card and their visa was stamped directly onto it without the passport being shown. Rhodesia was banned from the Mexico Olympic Games following political pressure spearheaded by Great Britain.

These were the first Games to have a special commemorative stamp to honour the hosting of the Games depicting two wheelchair basketball players in action. The Games youngest competitor was 13 year old Constance Meikle from Jamaica who broke the world record in the 50m breaststroke event for her class

References

Ashbury Park Press, NJ, USA, November 10th 1968; Stamp News.

Guttmann, L., 1968, Report on the 1968 International Stoke Mandeville Games in Israel, (IWAS Archives)

IPC Website
    (http://www.paralympic.org/release/Main_Sections_Menu/Paralympic_ Games/Past_Games/Tel_Aviv_1968/index.html) Accessed 14-01-08.

Jerusalem Post Newspaper, November 1968

Letter from Sir Ludwig Guttman to Dr Pierre Houssa of Belgium dated 21st November 1966, Belgian Paralympic Archives, Brussels.

Letter from Rolulo O'Farrill Sr, President of the Instituto Mexicano De Rehabilitacion, to Mr Ben Lipton, dated 7th June 1966. Belgian Paralympic Committee Archives, Brussels.

Minutes of the Meeting of the International Stoke Mandeville Games Committee Held on Friday 13th November, 1964 in Tokyo. IWAS Archives, Stoke Mandeville.

Minutes of the Meeting of the International Stoke Mandeville Games Committee Held at Stoke Mandeville Hospital on Wednesday 21st July, 1965, pt70. IWAS Archives, Stoke Mandeville.

Minutes of the Meeting of the International Stoke Mandeville Games Committee Held at Stoke Mandeville Hospital on 25th February, 1967. pt 83. IWAS Archives, Stoke Mandeville.

Minutes of the Meeting of the International Stoke Mandeville Games Committee Held at Stoke Mandeville Hospital on 26th July, 1967, pt 90 (1). IWAS Archives, Stoke Mandeville.

Minutes of the Meeting of the International Stoke Mandeville Games Committeeheld at Brugmann Hospital, Brussels on 20th September 1968, p. 5. IWAS Archives, Stoke Mandeville.

Nowak, A., 2008, Politics and the Paralympic Games: Disability Sport in Rhodesia-Zimbabwe in the Journal of Olympic History, Vol. 16(1), p. 52.

Official Results of The 17th International Stoke Mandeville Games in Israel (IWAS Archives)

Scruton, J.,1998, Stoke Mandeville: Road to the Paralympics, Peterhouse Press, Aylesbury, UK.

The 17th International Stoke Mandeville Games for the Paralysed in Israel, Timetable of Sports Events. (Author owned copy).

Chapter 5: Heidelberg, Germany 1972

Logo	Confirmed Participating Nations	43
	Participating Athletes	984 (According to Official Results) (Split approx. 697men, 287women)
	Number of Events	188
	Opening Ceremony	Wednesday 2nd August (5.00pm) University of Heidelberg Sports Ground
Mascot:	Closing Ceremony	Wednesday 9th August (7.30pm) Marquee in Games Village
None Known	Officially Opened by	Gustav W. Heinemann President – F.R. of Germany
	Main Stadium	University of Heidelberg Sports Ground
	Flame Lit by	No Flame
	Athlete's Oath	Marga Flöer (Athlete)

Participating Nations (43): Argentina, Australia, Austria, **Bahamas**, Belgium, **Brasil**, Canada, **Czechoslovakia**, Denmark, **Egypt**, Finland, France, Federal Republic of Germany, **Gibraltar**, Great Britain, **Hong Kong**, **Hungary**, India, Ireland, Israel, Italy, Jamaica, Japan, **Kenya**, Korea, **Malaysia**, Malta, **Mexico**, Netherlands, New Zealand, Norway, **Peru**, **Poland**, **Portugal**, Rhodesia,

Romania, South Africa, Spain, Sweden, Switzerland, **Uganda**, United States, Yugoslavia. **(Countries in bold are those appearing at a summer Paralympic Games for the first time)**

Sports (11): Archery, Athletics, Dartchery, Lawn Bowls, Pentathlon (Archery, Athletics & Swimming Events), Snooker, Swimming, Table Tennis, Weightlifting, Wheelchair Basketball, Wheelchair Fencing.

Impairment Groups (1): Spinal Cord Injuries.

Logo: According to a member of the Heidelberg Organising Committee the logo for the 1972 Games was derived from the outline of a photograph of an un-named local archer.

Bids: None

The Selection of Heidelberg as the Host City

As the Olympic Games of 1972 were to be held in Munich Sir Ludwig and the other ISMG Committee members made every effort to persuade the Munich Organising Committee to put on the Stoke Mandeville Games as well. However, despite Sir Ludwig and Mr Walther Weiss, a German member of the ISMGC, visiting Willi Daume, the President of the German National Olympic Committee it proved impossible to make this happen. The official reason given was that the plan for the City of Munich to convert the Olympic Village into private housing could not be altered or delayed. Efforts to find suitable alternative accommodation by the German Disabled Sports Federation (DSV) also proved fruitless. As an alternative Mr Weiss suggested Heidelberg in the state of Baden-Württemburg, where the Games would coincide with the 15th anniversary of the introduction of modern rehabilitation practices within the state. The Games Organising Committee was chaired by Professor Volkmar Paeslack, Director of the Spinal Injuries Centre in the Orthopaedic University Clinic in Heidelberg and the Games were supported by financial contributions from the government of Baden-Württemburg, the German Bundestag and the Federal Government with additional support provided by German and American Forces as well as numerous local organisations, businesses and individuals.

The Games Poster

The Games Opening Ceremony

The opening ceremony for the Games took place on Wednesday 2nd August on the University of Heidelberg sports ground beginning at 5.00pm. The 9th Army Music Corps of the Airborne Division led the procession followed by three athletes from Great Britain, Israel and the Federal Republic of Germany carrying the Games flag. They were followed by the teams, lead by Great Britain as the originators of the Games, in alphabetical order, with the Federal Republic of Germany, as hosts, bringing up the rear. Following speeches of welcome by Eberhard Rosslenbroich, President of DSV, and Sir Ludwig Guttmann, President of the ISMGC, the Games were officially opened by Gustav Heinemann, President of the Federal Republic of Germany, who would go on to officially open the Olympic Games in Munich just over three weeks later. President Heinemann took this opportunity to present Sir Ludwig with the Gold Star of the Great Cross of Merit of the Federal Republic of Germany.

Gustav Heinemann and Sir Ludwig Guttmann at the opening ceremony

This was followed by the taking of the oath on behalf of the participants by Marga Flöer from Germany who had won two gold medals in Swimming in Tel Aviv four years earlier and went on to win another gold medal for pentathlon in Heidelberg, having won the silver in that event in Tel Aviv. The oath went as follows:

> In the name of all competitors I promise that we will take part in these games, respecting and abiding by the rules which govern them, in the true spirit of friendship, unity and sportsmanship for the glory of sport and the honour of our teams.

The Games Themselves

Once again the Games increased in size with fifteen countries appearing at a summer Paralympic Games for the first time and over two hundred more competitors taking part compared to Tel Aviv four years earlier. The Athletes and escorts were accommodated in the Rehabilitation Centre, which had twelve hundred accessible beds, and a nearby trade school, which housed the remaining escorts. This was thanks to the assistance of Werner Boll, Director of the Foundation Rehabilitation. The sports themselves took place within the sports grounds of the Institute for Sport and Sports Science of the University of Heidelberg and the neighbouring National Institute for Sport. Snooker and Lawn Bowls caused some problems for the organisers as neither sport was really played in Germany at that time. However the organisers managed to get hold of a snooker table and laid an artificial carpet on which lawn bowls could be played. Events for tetraplegic athletes were added to the programme in a number of sports for the first time, but given the rise in overall athlete numbers individual athletes were limited to taking part in six individual events plus team events. In addition each country was limited to a maximum of three competitors in each individual event class e.g. Men's Javelin 2.

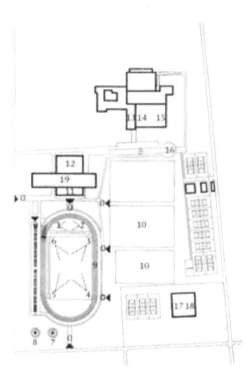

0   Entrance
1 – 6   Shot Put, Discus and Javelin
7 – 8   Precision Javelin
9   Wheelchair Dash
10   Archery
11   Fencing
12   Table Tennis
13   Weightlifting
14   Basketball
15   Swimming
16   Wheelchair Slalom
17   Bowls
18   Snooker
19   Press Centre

As with four years earlier one of the highlights of the Games in Heidelberg was the men's wheelchair basketball final. It was contested once again by Israel and the USA. With less than a minute to play Israel were leading 58 – 53 and looking on course to retain their title. However, a disqualified basket for Israel and one in the dying seconds for the USA meant the Americans snatched the title by the narrowest of margins: 59 – 58.

Track race in Heidelberg depicting different propulsion methods for wheelchairs.

The Outstanding Performers in Heidelberg

Perhaps due to the limitation on the number of events any individual could enter and perhaps also due to an increased level of competition in Heidelberg the number of athletes winning large numbers of medals dropped dramatically. The outstanding athlete of these Games was van der Schyff from South Africa who won four gold medals in Swimming and two silver and a bronze medal in athletics field events. The next most successful athlete was Carol Bryant of Great Britain who won four gold and one bronze medal in athletics, fencing and table tennis. She was closely matched by Ingrid van Benden and Marijke Ruiter, both from the Netherlands, who each won four gold medals in swimming. The best male competitors in Heidelberg appear to have been Roberto Marson of Italy with three gold and a silver medal in fencing and Patrick Reid, a tetraplegic from Jamaica, who won three gold and a bronze medal in athletics and swimming.

The Winners Medal

Full Set of Paralympic Medals from Heidelberg, 1972

The Games Closing Ceremony

The closing ceremony for the Games in Heidelberg took place on the evening of Wednesday 9th August, beginning at 7.30pm in the Marquee in the Games Village that had been used for entertainment throughout the Games. Following a musical introduction cups and trophies were presented to the individual winners and the team captains of the winning teams. This was then followed by closing speeches from Vice-Chancellor and Minister for Foreign Affairs Walter Scheel, Mayor of Heidelberg Reinhold Zundel and Sir Ludwig Guttmann, who officially declared the Games closed. The closing ceremony was followed by an International Gala Evening in the same venue with performances from Dunja Rajter and the Les Humphries Singers.

Media Coverage of the Games

According to the minutes of an ISMGC Technical Sub-Committee meeting held in December 1971 the Games in Heidelberg were due to be covered by German television on four occasions – twice as special items and twice amongst the sport and news items. The organising committee also undertook to produce a commemorative film in English and German that was presented to each competing nation upon completion. The minutes also note a letter from Ealing Films of Boston, USA requesting exclusive United States and Canadian film rights for the Games, which was agreed to by the meeting. The two local newspapers Heidelberg Tageblatt and the Rhein-Neckar-Zeitung gave daily coverage of the events at the Games.

The Fencing venue with participants being interviewed for television

Other Disability Groups in Heidelberg

Bailey (2008) claims that demonstration events were held in Heidelberg for blind athletes in goalball and 100m on the track, but does not cite a source for this information. According to discussions with several individuals involved in the organising committee for the Heidelberg Games no such events took place. They are certainly not recorded or mentioned in the official results anywhere. The programme for the Games does, however, mention a sports exhibition by 300 members of the German Sports Association for the Disabled (DSV) at 9.00am on Saturday 5th August as a 'special event'. The DSV was a multi-sports association and it is possibly this event that Bailey is referring to, although no further details of where it was to be held or what events would be exhibited were given in the programme.

The Final Medal Table

Rank	Country	Gold	Silver	Bronze	Total
1	Fed. Rep. Germany	28	17	22	67
2	United States	17	27	30	74
3	Great Britain	16	15	21	52
4	South Africa	16	12	13	41
5	Netherlands	14	13	11	38
6	Poland	14	12	7	33
Number of Countries winning a medal					31
% of participating countries winning a medal					72.1

Games Trivia

Two times Olympic marathon champion Abebe Bikila of Ethiopia, who was spinally injured in a car accident near his home in Addis Ababa in 1969, was entered to compete in the archery St Nicholas Round for tetraplegics in Heidelberg, having competed at Stoke Mandeville in 1971. However, for reasons unexplained the whole of the Ethiopian team failed to arrive in Germany for the Games.

Kenya's only medal in Heidelberg was a gold medal in the men's 25 m freestyle class 2 swimming event. It was won by John Britton, who had also won the gold medal for the same event in Tel Aviv four years earlier. However, on that occasion he was swimming for Great Britain and had moved to live in Kenya in the intervening years.

References

Bailey, S., 2008, Athlete First: A History of the Paralympic Movement, John Wiley & Sons Ltd; Chichester, UK.

Committee of the XXI Stoke Mandeville Games, 1973, 1000 Competitors 1000 Winners, Committee of the XXI Stoke Mandeville Games; Heidelberg, Germany.

ISMGC, 1972, Minutes of the Meeting of the International Stoke Mandeville Games Committee held at the Berufsförderungswerk, Heidelberg on 29th July 1972. (IWAS Archives)

ISMGC, 1971, Minutes of the Preliminary Meeting of the International Stoke Mandeville Games Technical Sub-Committee held at Stoke Mandeville on Saturday 4th December 1971. (IWAS Archives)

ISMGC, 1971, Minutes of the Meeting of the International Stoke Mandeville Games Committee held at Stoke Mandeville on 30th July 1971. (IWAS Archives)

ISMGC, 1971, Minutes of the Meeting of the International Stoke Mandeville Games Committee held at Stoke Mandeville on 26th July 1971. (IWAS Archives)

ISMGC, 1969, Minutes of the Meeting of the International Stoke Mandeville Executive Committee held at Stoke Mandeville on 27th July 1969. (IWAS Archives)

Programm - XXI. Weltspiele der Gelähmten, Committee of the XXI Stoke Mandeville Games; Heidelberg, Germany.

Scruton, J, 1998, Stoke Mandeville: Road to the Paralympics, Peterhouse Press; Alesbury, UK.

Chapter 6: Örnsköldsvik, Sweden 1976

Logo	Confirmed Participating Nations	16
WINTER OLYMPIC GAMES for the disabled	Confirmed Participating Athletes	198 (161 Men, 37 Women)
	Number of Events	53
	Opening Ceremony	Saturday 21st February
	Closing Ceremony	Saturday 28th February
Mascot:	Officially Opened by	Bertil Löfberg (Regional Governor – County of West Norrland)
None Known	Stadium	Kempehallen (for Opening and Closing Ceremonies)
	Flame Lit by	No Flame
	Athlete's Oath	Bertil Lundmark (Nordic Skier)

Participating Nations (16): Austria, Belgium, Canada, Czechoslovakia, Finland, France, Great Britain, Japan, Norway, Poland, Sweden, Switzerland, United States, Uganda, West Germany, Yugoslavia.

NB. Australia was unofficially represented at these Games by Ron Finneran, who competed but is not officially recognised as he did not fall into either the amputee or visual impairment categories.

Sports (2): Alpine, Cross Country.

Impairment Groups (2): Amputees, Blind and Visually Impaired.

Logo: The word Örnsköldsvik literally translates as 'Eagle shield's bay'. The logo for the Örnsköldsvik winter Olympic Games for the Disabled, therefore, consisted off an eagle carrying a shield over water flanked below on either side by an alpine and a cross country skier – the two sports contained within the Games.

The selection of Örnsköldsvik as the Host City: According to the IPC winter Paralympic Games history book the idea of organising the first winter Paralympic Games first arose in 1974 during a break of the annual general meeting of the International Sports Organisation for the Disabled (ISOD). The Swedish delegation, at the suggestion of ISOD Vice President Bengt Nirje, put forward the suggestion that they, through the Swedish Sports Organisation for the Disabled (SHIF), would take responsibility for organising the event, which those present at the general assembly gratefully accepted. The winter Paralympic Games had been born.

The Games Poster

The Games Opening Ceremony

Relatively little is known about the opening and closing ceremonies of the first winter Paralympic Games in Örnsköldsvik other than that they were relatively simple affairs. The opening ceremony took place in the Kempehallen on the evening of Saturday 21st February when around 1500 spectators witnessed the historic moment when the Regional Governor of the County of West Norrland, Bertil Löfberg, declared the world's first winter Olympic Games for the Disabled open. Although 17 nations are often reported as taking part in the opening ceremony Australia's Ron Finneran, who travelled to Sweden at his own expense, was deemed ineligible to compete as his impairment, Polio, did not fit into either the amputee and visually impaired groups taking part in the Games.

The Games Themselves

A total of 198 athletes from 16 nations competed in 53 medal events over 2 sports. There was also a demonstration in Ice Sledge Racing. It is perhaps not surprising that the medal table at the first winter Paralympic Games was completely dominated by the European nations who had a long history of success in non-disabled skiing, with the Scandinavian countries dominating the Nordic events and countries such as Germany, Switzerland and Austria dominating the Alpine events.

According to Ted Fay many of the racing classes in Örnsköldsvik had very few athletes and, thus, a number of athletes were declared the winner by virtue of just finishing their race. Canadian Lorna Manzer became the first athlete to win medals in both alpine and cross country events at the same Paralympic Games. However, her gold medal in the 5km cross country event had no other competitor in her particular class. As Fay points out this makes it very difficult to assess the athletic ability and performance level of many of the medallists in Örnsköldsvik due to a lack of a reasonable critical mass of athletes in their respective racing class.

The Outstanding Performers in Örnsköldsvik

A total of nine athletes left Sweden with three gold medals apiece. In the alpine events they were Eva Lemezova of Czechoslovakia, Irene Moillen and Heinz Moser from Switzerland and Petra Merkott and Annemie Schneider of West Germany. In the cross country events they were Birgitta Sund of Sweden, Morten Langeroed of Norway and Teuvo Sahi and Pertti Sankilampi of Finland.

The Winners Medal

Winners medal and participants diploma from Örnsköldsvik

The Closing Ceremony

Even less is currently known about the closing ceremony in Örnsköldsvik than the opening ceremony. It is known that it was attended by the young King of Sweden, Carl Gustaf XVI. He was accompanied by Regional Governor Bertil Löfberg who had opened the Games. The King was greeted by over 4000 of his subjects, and toured several sites in Örnsköldsvik before officially presiding over the official closing of the first Winter Olympics for the Disabled.

The Final Medal Table

Rank	NPC	Gold	Silver	Bronze	Total
1	Fed. Rep. of Germany	10	12	6	28
2	Switzerland	10	1	1	12
3	Finland	8	7	7	22
4	Norway	7	3	2	12
5	Sweden	6	7	7	20
6	Austria	5	16	14	35
Number of Countries winning a medal					9
% of participating countries winning a medal					56.3

Games Trivia

As the winter Paralympic Games in Örnsköldsvik did not contain athletes with a spinal cord injury they could not really be called 'Paralympic Games' in the Paraplegic Olympic sense that it was then used. ISOD, therefore, chose to call the Winter Games in Örnsköldsvik the 'Winter Olympics for the Disabled'. 1976 was also the first year in which the summer Paralympic Games contained other impairment groups and so they decided to call the summer Games in Toronto the 'Olympiad for the Disabled'. The Paralympic use of the terms Olympic and Olympiad were first drawn to the attention of the IOC by the International Ski Federation in September 1975. This led to a protracted period of discussion and dispute between the IOC and the disability sport movement that lasted up to the early 1990s.

Two Swedish teams played an exhibition match in Ice Sledge Hockey at 1976 Paralympic Winter Games in Örnsköldsvik. However, Ice sledge hockey did not become an official event until the Paralympic Games at Lillehammer in 1994.

Postage mark commemorating the opening day of the first Winter Olympics for the Disabled

References

Brittain, I., 2008, The Evolution of the Paralympic Games in Cashman, R. et al, Benchmark Games: The Sydney 2000 Paralympic Games; Walla Walla Press, Petersham, NSW, p. 19-34.

Fay, T., 2011, Winter Paralympic Games: Founding Legacies 1976 – 1980 in Legg, D. & Gilbert, K., Paralympic Legacies, Commonground Publishing; Champaign, Il., p. 165-172.

Janhnke, B. & Schüle, K, 2006, Paralympic Winter Games 1976 – 2006: Örnsköldsvik – Torino, RLC; Paris, France.

Chapter 7: Toronto, Canada 1976

"A time to be together"

Logo:	Confirmed Participating Nations	40
	Participating Athletes	1369 (1105 men, 264 women) (Amended from Games programme)
	Number of Events	447
	Opening Ceremony	Tuesday 3rd August (7.30pm) Woodbine Race Track
Mascot: None Known	Closing Ceremony	Wednesday 11th August (6.30pm) Centennial Park Stadium
	Officially Opened by	Mrs Pauline McGibbon Lieutenant Governor
	Main Stadium	Centennial Park Stadium
	Flame Lit by	Joanne McDonald (Wheelchair Athlete + Table Tennis), Dave Wall (Blind Swimmer + Athlete), Hans Noe (Amputee Swimmer)
	Athlete's Oath	Eugene Reimer (Wheelchair Athlete)

Participating Nations (40): Argentina, Australia, Austria, Bahamas, Belgium, Brasil, **Burma**, Canada, **Colombia**, Denmark, **Ecuador**, Egypt, Ethiopia, Fiji,

Finland, France, Federal Republic of Germany, Great Britain, Greece, **Guatemala**, Hong Kong, **Indonesia**, Ireland, Israel, Italy, Japan, Korea, **Luxembourg**, Mexico, Netherlands, New Zealand, Norway, Peru, Poland*, South Africa, Spain, Sweden, Switzerland, Uganda, United States.
(Countries in bold are those appearing at a summer Paralympic Games for the first time)

* Poland withdrew during competition due to the participation of South Africa.

NB: Cuba, Hungary, India and Jamaica arrived in Toronto, but withdrew prior to competition due to the participation of South Africa.

Sports (14): Archery, Athletics, Dartchery, Goalball, Lawn Bowls, Pentathon Shooting, Snooker, Swimming, Table Tennis, Volleyball (Standing), Weightlifting, Wheelchair Basketball, Wheelchair Fencing.

Impairment Groups (3): Amputees, Blind & Visually Impaired, Spinal Cord Injuries

Logo: Designed by Peter G. Robinson, a Toronto graphics designer and Chairman of the Games Graphics Committee, the logo consisted of three elements i. an equilateral triangle with rounded corners representing the pyramid of the international sports movement for the disabled. This was made up of three colours with each colour representing a participating impairment group – blue (paraplegics), magenta (amputees) and orange/red (blind). ii. A pictogram of a human figure with arms raised in a gesture of achievement and representing the handicapped (sic) rising above disability through participation in sport and iii. three interlocking rings derived from the traditional symbol of the Stoke Mandeville Games (three wheelchair wheels representing friendship, unity and sportsmanship). Apparently the three rings may also be interpreted as deriving from the traditional five-ring symbol of the Olympic movement, with the loss of two rings symbolically representing some disability.

Bids: Toronto only

The Selection of Toronto as the Host City

There appears to be some confusion over exactly when Canada offered to host the Games of 1976. Guttmann (1976) claims that it was decided in 1971 by the Praesidium of the International Stoke Mandeville Games Federation (ISMGF) and the International Sports Organisation for the Disabled (ISOD) that the 1976 Games should be held in Canada. No record of this decision can be found in the ISMGF minutes, but as Guttmann was President of both organisations it is possible the original decision is contained within the ISOD minutes. However, the minutes of the International Stoke Mandeville Games Committee held at Stoke Mandeville and dated 26th July 1971 do note that Dr Robert Jackson from Canada had been invited to attend as an observer due to the fact that the 1976

Olympics Games would take place in Canada. The minutes of the ISMG Council meeting four days later note that Dr Guttmann hoped that in 1976 the Canadians would be able to organise Games for amputees and blind, in addition to the International Stoke Mandeville Games. By the time of the next meeting of the International Stoke Mandeville Games Committee in Heidelberg on 29th July 1972 Dr Jackson had formed a Games Committee under the aegis of the Canadian Wheelchair Sports Association. Canada had also sent seven observer groups to Heidelberg in preparation for the 1976 Games. According to Greig (2005) Jackson approached Montreal, the 1976 Olympic host city, as his first choice venue, but they showed little interest and the idea was quickly turned down. The minutes of the ISMGF meeting held at Stoke Mandeville on 16th July 1973 show that Jackson and his Committee then approach specific cities, where they showed a film of the 1968 Tel Aviv Games. One of the cities, Jackson's home town of Toronto, was the only one to show any real interest in the project. A letter received from the Municipality of Metropolitan Toronto Parks Department was received detailing their interest and according to the minutes a final decision to host the Games was taken in September of that year. On 18th September 1973 the Council of the Municipality of Metropolitan Toronto voted to support the Games and to contribute an amount not exceeding half a million Canadian dollars to the running costs (Greig, 2005).

The Games Poster

The Games Opening Ceremony

The opening ceremony for the Games in Toronto took place on Tuesday 3rd August at Woodbine Racetrack. Accounts of the number of spectators attending the event vary from 19,000 to 24,000. Prior to the Parade of Nations entertainment was provided in the form of the Kalev Estienne Rhythmic Gymnasts, The Jim Skye Six-Nations Dancers and Trick Riding Show and a musical ride by the Metropolitan Toronto Police to the accompaniment of the Royal Regiment of Canada. Guest of Honour for the opening ceremony was the Lieutenant Governor Mrs Pauline McGibbon and her husband who arrived in a carriage escorted by Metropolitan Police on horseback. Other guests included Mr William G. Davis, The Prime Minister of the Ontario Government; Minister Welsh of the Ontario Government; Mr Godfrey, Chairman of the Metropolitan Government of Toronto; Mayor of Etobicoke, Dennis Flynn and ambassadors and other representatives of the particip ating nations. The Lt- Governor, Dr Robert Jackson and Dr Guttmann took the 'Salute of the Parade of Nations'. Despite pulling out of the Games after their arrival in Toronto the Jamaican team did apparently take part in the parade of nations, although they did not wear team uniform. The Lt-Governor officially declared the Games open and then the flame was lit by three Canadian participants representing each of the three different impairment groups taking part in the Games. Eugene Reimer, a Canadian athlete who had competed in Canada's first team at the Games in Tel Aviv in 1968 then took the oath on behalf of the athletes before a spectacular firework display brought proceedings to an end. The Oath went as follows:

> In the name of all the competitors I pledge we will abide by the rules that govern the Games, that we will be modest in victory, gracious in defeat and at all times participate in a manner that will bring honour to our teams

The Games Themselves

For the first time ever in Toronto the Games were widened to include events for disability groups other than spinal cord injuries. Amputees and blind and visually impaired athletes competed for the first time, which lead to the addition of two new impairment specific sports to the programme. These were goalball for the blind and visually impaired and standing volleyball for the amputees.

Despite the problems caused by the participation of the team from South Africa outlined below there were still nearly fourteen hundred athletes from forty nations present in Toronto. Six nations were participating in the Games for the very first time. The Paraplegic athletes and their escorts were housed at York University and the amputee and blind athletes and their escorts were housed at Toronto University. Both sites were about 25 minutes from the Games site, which was at the Centennial Park of the Borough of Etobicoke. The individual sports were held at the following venues:

Centennial Park Fields: Archery, Dartchery, Equestrian

Centennial Park Olympium:	Goalball, Swimming, Volleyball (Standing), Wheelchair Basketball
Centennial Park Stadium:	Athletics
Centennial Park West Arena:	Table Tennis, Weightlifting, Wheelchair Fencing
Etobicoke Lawn Bowling Club:	Lawn Bowls
No. 2 Division Police Facilities:	Shooting
Seneca School:	Snooker

The South African Problem

The issue of the impact of the South African team's participation in the Torontolympiad upon the organisation of the Toronto Games is a complicated one. Given the space available for this only a broad overview will appear here. Readers wanting more details on this issue should see Grieg (2005) and Brittain (2011). South African teams had competed at the Paralympic Games since Tokyo, 1964 and at all of the Games held at Stoke Mandeville in the intervening years with the exception of 1969. According Guttmann (1976) up until 1975 South Africa sent alternate teams of black participants and white participants to the Stoke Mandeville Games, although it appears to have been the all white teams that competed in the 'Paralympic' Games. Menzo Barrish, the Chairman of the South African organisation later pointed out that 'whilst the practice of the Association was one of non-discrimination, the environment within which it had to operate continued to be a discriminatory one. For this reason, the activities of the Association over a long period were, Barrish claimed, a microcosm of the social battle that was going on in South Africa.

With the next Paralympic Games due to be held in Toronto the first hint for the organisers that the participation of a South African team might cause problems came in May 1974 when the Canadian Minister for Health and Welfare released a statement informing all sports federations that it would not fund athletes travelling to South Africa because of its apartheid practices. As the Federal Government had promised funding of C\$500K for the Games the organising committee sought clarification from the Minister who in November 1974 wrote urging that South Africa not be invited as their presence would have embarrassing repercussions. South Africa was duly notified that it would not be invited. However, both the ISMGF and ISOD of whom the South African organisation was now a full member in good standing were against the expulsion and as such following a meeting in May 1975 the organising committee informed the South African organisation that a team would be welcome provided they had integrated trials and sent an integrated team, which may well have had some impact upon their decision to send their first ever integrated team to Stoke Mandeville in 1975. In the end South Africa sent a team of around thirty including nine black athletes. The political ramifications of South Africa's participation impacted upon both the financial situation for the Games and also the number of countries participating. Eight countries withdrew either before or during the Games on the order of their governments. These were Kenya, Sudan and Yugoslavia who withdrew before the Games and Cuba, Jamaica, Hungary, India and Poland who turned up in Toronto, but either withdrew prior to the start of the Games or like Poland competed for several days (winning enough medals to place seventh in the medal table). Poland finally withdrew after a failed appeal to the organising committee to have the South African team thrown out.

Reports of athlete reactions to the intrusion of politics into their Games appear to show that, in general, the intrusion was resented and unwelcome. Indeed on Thursday 5th August, having won the class 3 discus event, Eric Russell, a university student from Brisbane, Australia, refused his gold medal in protest at the intrusion of politics into the Games. Russell claimed he was upset by governments, stressing he meant all governments, attempting to mix sport with politics. However, following a press conference where Russell explained his actions to the media, and statements were made by Dr Jackson and Dr Guttmann, Russell finally accepted his medal from Dr Guttmann.

Despite the fact that the Federal Government withdrew its funding from the Toronto Games and despite the withdrawal of several countries from the Games due to the participation of the South African team, there appears to have been no attempt by the Government to prevent the entry of the South African team into Canada. Whether this was as a result of the mounting media and public support for the Games and the integrated South African team's participation or whether it was merely a reflection of the low importance the Government associated with the Games themselves and their potential impact is hard to assess.

Outstanding Competitors in Toronto

The outstanding athlete of the Toronto Games was Marijke Ruiter, a class 5 paraplegic, from the Netherlands who won seven gold medals in swimming. Five of these came in individual events and two from relays. The outstanding male athlete was Uri Bergman, a class 6 paraplegic, from Israel who won six gold medals in swimming – four in individual events and two in relays. Other athletes worthy of a mention include the two youngest competitors at the Games, 14 year olds Jose Evertsen and Martin Kers from the Netherlands, both single-arm amputee swimmers. Jose won five individual gold medals and Martin won two gold and two silver medals in individual events. Not to be outdone 15 year old Elena-Marie Bey, better known as Nina, from the USA won four gold medals, one silver and one bronze in swimming. Amongst the smaller nations Metwali Ahmed Khadr from Egypt won four gold medals in the athletics field events. However, perhaps the most remarkable story of a medallist at these Games is that of Stephen Kempf from the USA, who had only been disabled in January whilst working as a fireman when a ceiling fell in on him. Shortly before he was due to leave for Toronto to take part in the Games he fell from his wheelchair resulting in a single fracture of a bone in his throwing arm. Following consultation with his doctor he arrived in Toronto with his arm in a brace from thumb to elbow, which he then removed for competition to comply with the rules. Despite this he still managed to win a gold medal in the class 1B discus in a new world record. He wasn't finished there however. He went on to win a silver medal in the shot put and a further gold medal in the 25m freestyle swimming event.

The Winners Medal

Paralympic Silver Medal and bronze medal certificate from Toronto, 1976

The Closing Ceremony

The closing ceremony for the Toronyolympiad occurred on Wednesday 11th August in the Centennial Park Stadium at 6.30pm following completion of several finals at the Olympium. The simple ceremony began with the entrance procession of all the teams with Canada bringing up the rear as the host nation. This was followed by the awarding of the Carling O'Keefe Brewery award for the outstanding individual performance of the Games, which went to Canada's Arnie Boldt, a single leg above the knee amputee, who leapt over a magnificent 1.86m in the high jump.

Arnie Boldt – winner of the award for the outstanding individual performance of the Games

Following speeches by Dr Jackson, Chairman of the organising committee and Dr Guttmann, Dennis Flynn, Mayor of Etobicoke, officially declared the Games closed. As the closing song was sung by 15 year old Kevin Page, who had also composed it, the Games flag was lowered, folded and presented to Dr Guttmann for safe keeping until the next Games four years later. Finally, to the strains of Auld Lang Syne the Olympiad flame slowly grew smaller until it flickered and died and the assembled crowds made their way out of the stadium. The athletes and officials then made their way to the University of York where an evenings entertainment was laid on in the beer tent.

Final Medal Table

Rank	NPC	Gold	Silver	Bronze	Total
1	United States	66	44	45	155
2	Netherlands	45	25	14	84
3	Israel	40	13	16	69
4	Fed. Rep. Germany	37	34	26	97
5	Great Britain	29	29	36	94
6	Canada	25	26	26	77
Number of Countries winning a medal					32
% of participating countries winning a medal					80.0

Games Trivia

Toronto was the first Games to have its own daily newsletter running from Wednesday 4th to Thursday 12th August and included stories, photographs, event schedules etc for the Games.

Wilma Rudolph, triple Olympic Gold medallist in Rome, who had polio as a child and wore leg braces until the age of eight, attended the Games as a representative of Pony Sporting Goods who outfitted teams at the Torontolympiad.

Hungarian paraplegic athlete Imre Szelenyi claimed political asylum after disappearing late at night from the team accommodation at York University. Apparently he hopped in a taxi and tried to explain in broken English that he wanted asylum, but needn't have bothered as the taxi driver turned out to be a Hungarian immigrant.

On the evening of Friday 6th August Sharon Myers (29), an American paraplegic athlete and swimmer, was injured when a blind runner veered off the track and ran into her. Sharon suffered a seven stitch cut on her cheek, a black eye and a knee injury when she was thrown from her chair.

Israeli athlete and ultra-orthodox Jew Shmuel Chaimovitch slept at the weightlifting venue overnight so he wouldn't have to travel on the Sabbath. His decision proved to be a good one as he won the gold medal in a new Game's record.

Peter Hans van der Vis of the Netherlands won a bronze medal in the 200m for wheelchairs only to be outdone by his wife Cis van der Vis who won a silver medal in the Precision Javelin.

References

Barrish (1992) *Letter from Menzo Barrish to Paul Luedtke dated 29th April 1992.* Stoke Mandeville, UK: (IWAS Archives).

Brittain, I. (2011: in press) South Africa, Apartheid and the Paralympic Games. *Sport in Society* (Special Edition on Issues in Disability Sport)

Canadian Paralympic Committee Website, 2009, Organization History, (http://www.paralympic.ca/page?a=229&lang=en-CA) accessed 21-10-09.

Coetzee, G.J. & Van Der Merwe, F.J.G. (1990) South Africa's Participation in the International Stoke Mandeville Games. In *South African Journal for Research in Sport, Physical Education and Recreation,* 13(1), 79-85

Greig, D. (2005) *South African Apartheid and the 1976 Torontolympiad: A Historical Analysis of Influential Actions and Events Affecting the 5th Paralympic Games.* Unpublished Masters Thesis, Ontario, Canada: University of Windsor.

Greig, D. (2003) *Conflict, Perseverance, and Legacy: A Historical Analysis of the 1976 Torontolympiad.* Paper presented at the North American Society of Sports History, 23-26 May, Ohio State University, Colombus, Ohio.

Guttmann, L. (1976) Reflection on the 1976 Toronto Olympiad for the Physically Disabled. In *Paraplegia,* 14, 225-240.

Guttmann, L. (1976) *Report on the Olympiad for the Physically Disabled held in Toronto, Canada, from 3rd – 11th August, 1976.* Unpublished Report. Stoke Mandeville, UK: IWAS Archives.

Jackson, R.W. (1977) What Did We Learn From The Torontolympiad? In *The Canadian Family Physician,* 23: 586-589.

Minutes of the meeting of the International Stoke Mandeville Games Committee held in Heidelberg and dated 29th July 1972 (IWAS Archives)

Minutes of the meeting of the International Stoke Mandeville Games Federation Executive Committee held at Stoke Mandeville Stadium and dated 16th July 1973 (IWAS Archives)

Minutes of the meeting of the International Stoke Mandeville Games Council held at Stoke Mandeville Stadium and dated 30th July 1971 (IWAS Archives)

Minutes of the meeting of the International Stoke Mandeville Games Committee held at Stoke Mandeville Stadium and dated 26th July 1971 (IWAS Archives)

Olympiad for the Physically Disabled, 1977, Torontolympiad 1976, Olympiad for the Physically Disabled; Toronto, Canada.

The Globe and Mail Newspaper, 1976, Cheers, fanfare open Olympiad for disabled, Wednesday 4th August, Section 4, p.1.

Torontolympiad Daily News, 1976, Vol. 1(1) (4th August) – Vol. 1(9) (12th August).

Chapter 8: Geilo, Norway 1980

Logo:	Confirmed Participating Nations	18
	Confirmed Participating Athletes	299 (229 Men, 70 Women)
	Number of Events	63
	Opening Ceremony	Friday 1st February (6.00pm)
Mascot:	Closing Ceremony	Thursday 7th February (7.00pm)
	Officially Opened by	HRH Crown Prince Harald
None Known	Stadium	Geilo Idrettshallen (for Opening and Closing Ceremonies)
	Flame Lit by	HRH Crown Prince Harald
	Athlete's Oath	Morten Langerød (Nordic Skiing)

Participating Nations (18): **Australia**, Austria, Canada, Czechoslovakia, **Denmark**, Finland, France, Great Britain, **Italy**, Japan, **New Zealand**, Norway, Sweden, Switzerland, United States, Uganda, West Germany, Yugoslavia **(Countries in bold are those appearing at a winter Paralympic Games for the first time)**

Sports (3): Alpine, Cross Country, Ice Sledge Speed Racing.

Impairment Groups (3): Amputees, Blind and Visually Impaired, Spinal Cord Injuries.

Logo: The logo for the Games consisted of the Geilo city emblem at the time of a stylised snowflake held between the antlers of two reindeer facing each other along with the logo of the International Stoke Mandeville Games Federation (ISMGF) which was combined with a flaming torch. The inclusion of the ISMGF logo hints at the power of ISMGF, or possibly Dr Guttmann who was President of ISMGF and ISOD, given that it was ISOD who founded the winter Games.

The selection of Geilo as the Host City: The decision to select Geilo, Norway as the hosy city for the 1980 winter Paralympic Games was taken at a joint meeting of the International Stoke Mandeville Games Federation (ISMGF) and the International Sports Organisation for the Disabled (ISOD) held at Stoke Mandeville on Saturday 23rd July 1977 at 5pm.

The Games Poster

DE 2. OLYMPISKE
VINTERLEKER
FOR HANDICAPPEDE

FOR HANDICAPPEDE

GEILO   1.–7.
         FEBRUAR
         1980

NORGES HANDICAPIDRETTSFORBUND

The Games Opening Ceremony

The official programme for the second Olympic winter Games for the Handicapped outlines the programme for the opening ceremony that was held on Friday 1st February starting at 6.00pm in the Sports Hall in Geilo as follows:

1. Introduction of the flags of the participating nations.
2. The Olympic Games Fanfare.
3. Prime Minister Odvar Nordli welcomes the visitors to Norway.
4. The Norwegian National Anthem.
5. Address by the Chairman of the Norwegian Sports Organisation for the Disabled, Jan Molberg.
6. Greetings from ISOD Vice-President Marcel Avronsart and ISMGF and ISOD Secretary General Joan Scruton.
7. Address by the Mayor of the Municipality of Hol, Per M. Bakkegård
8. HRH Crown Prince Harald announces the opening of the Games and lights the Olympic Flame.

HRH Crown Prince Harald lights the Olympic fame

9. Morten Langerød pronounces the Olympic Oath.
10. The organizers receive the Olympic flag.
11. Erling Stordahl recites 'Ridderspranget' (The Knight's Leap) accompanied on the violin by Aage Wallin.
12. The Olympic Hymn
13. Per Asplin entertains for fifteen minutes.
14. Musical Conclusion.

The Games Themselves

Games Postcard showing some of the venues

A total of 299 athletes from 18 nations competed in 63 medal events over 3 sports. Ice Sledge Racing was added to the programme alongside alpine and Nordic skiing events. In the Ice Sledge Racing women had to complete the distance of 100m, 500m and 800m and men competed over 100m, 500, and 1500m. The Ice Sledge Racing track was, according to Ted Fay, an outdoor, natural track laid over a high school cinder running track, which was apparently common in Norway and other countries near the Arctic Circle at that time. There was also a demonstration in Sledge Downhill Racing, which apparently acted as a precursor to alpine sit-skiing. The athletes were housed in six hotels; the Bardøla Mountain Hotel, the Geilo Hotel, the Geilo Sportell, the Highland Hotel, the Holms Hotel and the Ustedalan Mountain Hotel. The competition schedule in Geilo was as follows:

Saturday 2nd February	10.00am	Cross Country (5km Men & Women)
		Cross Country (10km Men)
	10.30am	Giant Slalom (Men & Women)
Sunday 3rd February	10.30am	Giant Slalom (Men & Women)
	3.00pm	Ice Sledge Racing (100m & 500m Men & Women)
Monday 4th February	10.00am	Cross Country (10km Men & Women)
		Cross Country (20km Men)
	2.30pm	Ice Sledge Racing (1500m Men & 800m Women)
Tuesday 5th February	10.00pm	Training – Slalom

Wednesday 6th February	11.00am Training – Sledge Downhill

Wednesday 6th February

11.00am Training – Sledge Downhill
10.30am Slalom (Men & Women)
12.30pm Sledge Downhill (Demonstration)

Thursday 7th February

10.00am Cross Country Relay Race (Men & Women)
10.30am Slalom (Men & Women)

Ted Fay (R) guides one of the visually impaired American skiers in the cross country events

The Outstanding Performers in Geilo

The outstanding performers in Geilo were Britt Mjaasund Oejen of Norway for the women who won 5 gold medals in cross country and Ice Sledge Racing and for the men Eric Sandbraaten, also of Norway, who won 3 gold and 1 bronze medal in the same disciplines.

The Winners Medal

The Closing Ceremony

Very little is currently known about the closing ceremony for the Geilo winter Paralympic Games other than that it was quite a low key affair.

The Final Medal Table

Rank	NPC	Gold	Silver	Bronze	Total
1	Norway	23	21	10	54
2	Finland	15	7	12	34
3	Austria	6	10	6	22
4	Sweden	5	3	8	16
5	Switzerland	4	2	3	9
6	USA	4	1	1	6
Number of Countries winning a medal					10
% of participating countries winning a medal					55.6

Games Trivia

According to Ted Fay, a guide with the USA cross country team in Geilo, the United States actually sent two separate teams to Geilo organised by disability and sport type. The Alpine team was comprised of locomotor disabilities, whilst the cross country team was comprised of blind and visually impaired athletes. Fay claims that this was typical at the time and demonstrated the nasty and often discriminatory behaviour of disability politics and hegemony based on the pecking order of disability type that was prevalent in that period.

The American team in Geilo

In connection with the Games in Geilo the Norwegian Sport Organisation for the Disabled and the State Office for Youth and Sport in Norway arranged the First International Medical Congress on Sports for the Disabled at the Ustaoset Mountain Hotel about 10km from Geilo. The congress was aimed at physicians, scientists, teachers and all persons concerned with scientific advances, educational activities, practical work and current research in the field of sports for the disabled.

Sir Ludwig Guttmann had been advised by his doctors not to attend the Games in Geilo because of the extreme cold and altitude. ISMGF were, therefore, officially represented by Vice-President Ben Lipton and Secretary General Joan Scruton.

References

Fay, T., 2011, Winter Paralympic Games: Founding Legacies 1976 – 1980 in Legg, D. & Gilbert, K., Paralympic Legacies, Commonground Publishing; Champaign, Il., p. 173-180.

International Stoke Mandeville Games Federation, Minutes of Executive Committee Meeting held at Stoke Mandeville Stadium, Aylesbury, Bucks, England on Tuesday 26th July, 1977.

International Stoke Mandeville Games Federation, Minutes of Council Meeting held at Het Dorp, Arnhem, The Netherlands, Tuesday 1st July 1980.

Program for de 2. Olympiske Vinterleker for Handicappede (Norwegian & English) (Author copy)

Chapter 9: Arnhem, The Netherlands 1980

Logo:	Confirmed Participating Nations	42
	Confirmed Participating Athletes	1973 (1503 men, 470 women) (From Games programme)
	Number of Events	587
	Opening Ceremony	Saturday 21st June (2.00pm)
	Closing Ceremony	Saturday 5th July (10.30am)
Mascot:	Officially Opened by	Princess Margriet
	Main Stadium	The 'Olympic' Stadium, Papendal National Sports Centre
	Flame Lit by	Harry Venema (Basketball), Vera Rotgans-Schipper (Swimmer), Joke Van Rijswijk (Athlete), Chris De Groen (Swimmer)
	Athlete's Oath	Irene Schmidt (Table Tennis)
	Official's Oath	Henk Boersbroek (Athletics Official)

Participating Nations (42): Argentina, Australia, Austria, Bahamas, Belgium, Brasil, Canada, Colombia, Czechoslavakia, Denmark, Egypt, Ethiopia, Finland,

France, Federal Republic of Germany, Great Britain, Greece, Hong Kong, **Iceland**, Indonesia, Ireland, Israel, Italy, Jamaica, Japan, Kenya, Korea, **Kuwait**, Luxembourg, Malta, Mexico, Netherlands, New Zealand, Norway, Poland, Spain, **Sudan**, Sweden, Switzerland, United States, Yugoslavia, **Zimbabwe. (Countries in bold are those appearing at a summer Paralympic Games for the first time)**

Sports (14): Archery, Athletics, Dartchery, Goalball, Lawn Bowls, Pentathon (Archery, Athletics & Swimming Events), Shooting, Swimming, Table Tennis, Volleyball (Sitting & Standing), Weightlifting, Wheelchair Basketball, Wheelchair Fencing, Wrestling.

Impairment Groups (4): Amputees, Blind & Visually Impaired, Cerebral Palsied, Spinal Cord Injuries

Logo: The logo used by the organising committee was designed by Joop Smits of the PRAD advertising agency. It represents an unfurled Dutch flag adorned with the number '80' to represent the year of the Games. The '80' is also made up of three interlocking rings, which, as with previous Games were meant to represent Friendship, Unity and Sportsmanship.

Mascot: The organisers of the Games decided upon the a pair of squirrels to be the mascots for the Games, apparently because a squirrel, in its lifetime, gets many hard nuts to crack, not unlike people with disabilities who, on a different level, face many problems as well. They chose to have a pair of squirrels because men and women take part in the Games. They then invited members of the public to submit designs for the squirrels and this contest was won by Mrs Opheusden of St Michielsgestel.

Bids: Denmark, Mexico, Netherlands, Poland, South Africa, USA.

The Selection of Arnhem as the Host City

At a meeting of the International Stoke Mandeville Games Federation in October 1976 Guttmann, in his role as President, reported that his attempts to gain a response from various quarters in Moscow as to the possibility of them hosting the 1980 Games had gone unanswered. At that time they had received alternative bids from USA, Mexico, Poland and South Africa. At the same meeting a year later Guttmann reported that he had tried numerous different avenues to get a response from Moscow, but that not a single reply had been forthcoming. A joint meeting was then held between the ISMGF and ISOD Executive Boards on 23rd July 1977. At that point six bids had been received with the Netherlands and Denmark having added their names to the candidate list. However, Poland had withdrawn their application due to technical difficulties and Mexico had not followed up on their original application leaving USA, South Africa, Denmark and the Netherlands to be considered. AS the 1984 Olympic Games were to be held in the USA it was not felt appropriate to hold the 1980 Games there. There was also a feeling the the Games should be held in Europe and so following a presentation by Mr Westerneng as Chairman of the Dutch Sports Organisation for the Disabled it was decided that the Dutch should be awarded the summer Games for 1980.

The Games Poster

Olympische Spelen voor Gehandicapten
Arnhem   21 Juni – 5 Juli   Veenendaal

The Opening Ceremony

The opening ceremony for the Arnhem Games took place on Saturday 21st June at 2.00pm in the 'Olympic' Stadium. Although the weather conditions made it necessary to cancel a proposed parachute landing in the stadium the rain did at least hold off. The entertainment portion of the ceremony began with barrel organ music by 'De Korsikaan' from Nijmegan and was followed by folk music by 'De Cannenburgher Boerendansers' from Vaassen, the 'Meuelenvelders' from Doesburg and ''t Olde Getrouw' from Varsseveld. Further music was supplied by the Royal Dutch Infantry and the Royal Airforce Band. The end of this section was timed to coincide with the arrival of Princess Margriet and her husband by helicopter. Mr van Emden, Chairman of the organising committee then welcomed the athletes and led a minutes silence in honour of Sir Ludwig Guttmann who had dies earlier in the year. Princess Margriet then declared the Games officially open, which was the cue for a huge display of jazz, free exercise and streamer displays by girls from the Royal Dutch Gymnastics Union. Following the raising of the flags of the 42 nations competing in the Games Princess Margriet lit the Olympic flame and handed it over to four Dutch competitors representing each of the four disability groups in the Games - Harry Venema (Basketball - Paraplegic), Vera

Rotgans-Schipper (Swimmer - Amputee), Joke Van Rijswijk (Athlete - Blind), Chris De Groen (Swimmer – CP) – to actually light the cauldron. Irene Schmidt, a Dutch paraplegic table tennis player then took the oath on behalf of the athletes and for the first recorded time in the history of the Games Henk Boersbroek, an athletics official, took the oath on behalf of the officials. The ceremony then came to a conclusion with a parade of the 42 competing teams led by Canada with the Netherlands as host nation bringing up the rear.

Princess Margriet declares the Games officially open

The Games Themselves

These were the first Games to occur following the death of Sir Ludwig Guttmann in March 1980 and as a result many tributes to his name and his legacy took place. The Games in Arnhem also saw the participation for the very first time of approximately 122 cerebral palsied athletes, who competed in four classes (A – D, with A being the most disabled). The number of classes in the amputee group grew from the four for single amputees in Toronto to nine classes in Arnhem that included both double and multiple amputations. The teams were all housed in The Oranjekazerne in Schaarsbergen – a military camp appropriately named after the Dutch Royal Family, given that HRH Princess Margriet was Patroness of the Games in Arnhem. The Village also had its very own Mayor for the duration of the Games – Sabine de Jong van Ellemeet. Snooker was dropped from the programme in Arnhem, possibly because it was not a well known sport in the Netherlands and so no facilities were available. Sitting Volleyball was added allowing amputees, cerebral palsied and paraplegics to all compete together and wrestling for the blind was also added to the programme. The venues for the different sports were as follows:

De Vallei Swimming Pool, Veenendal:	Swimming + Pentathlon Swimming Events
Rijnhal, Arnhem:	Wheelchair Basketball
Papendal Sports Centre:	All other Sports

Games postcard showing Papendal from the air

The South African Issue

Once again the issue of the participation of the multi-racial team from South Africa was raised in the build up to the Games in Arnhem. South Africa had continued to compete at the Stoke Mandeville Games in the period 1977 to 1979 with a racially integrated team. However, a small number of nations boycotted these Games as a result, including Jamaica, Finland and Yugoslavia. In July 1977 the decision was taken to award the 1980 Paralympic Games to Arnhem in the Netherlands, following a lack of any response from the Olympic organizers in Moscow. However, the Dutch Parliament, following much debate, decided that if the organizers of the 1980 Games allowed South Africa to compete they would be forced to withdraw their offer of financial support for the Games. Unlike, the Toronto organisers the organisers in Arnhem took the decision to cancel the South African entry.

Outstanding Competitors in Arnhem

The outstanding performer in Arnhem was Swanepoel, a female class 5 paraplegic from the Federal Republic of Germany who won 6 gold and 2 silver medals. She won 5 individual gold medals in the pool as well as a gold medal in the lawn bowls singles for ladies classes 2-5. She also won silver in shot put and discus at the track. There were six other competitors in Arnhem who won five individual gold medals. Five of them were swimmers – three paraplegics from

Poland, G. Ignaczuk, Agnieszka Ogorzelska and Andrzej Surala; an amputee from Sweden, Annelie Ahrenstrand and partially sighted Trischa Zorn from the USA. Although it cannot be confirmed from the current available results it would appear probable that both Ignaczuk of Poland and Zorn of the USA also won two further relay gold medals taking each of their totals for the games in Arnhem to seven. At the track Anne Farrell, a single below the knee amputee from Canada demonstrated her all around athletic ability by winning 5 gold medals in shot put, long jump, javelin, discus and the 100m.

The Winners Medal

Paralympic Gold Medal from Arnhem, 1980

The Closing Ceremony

The closing ceremony took place on the morning of Saturday 5th July in the same stadium where it had opened some two weeks earlier. As with the opening ceremony the weather meant that the planned parachute jump once again had to be cancelled. The ceremony was attended by the Dutch Health Minister Mr Ginjaar and Secretary of State for Culture, Recreation and Social Work Mr Wallis de Vries. Alfred van Emden, Chairman of the organising committee declared the Games officially closed and as the Royal Dutch Army band played the Olympic hymn the flags of ISMGF and ISOD were lowered, folded and delivered to Joan Scruton, Secretary General of ISMGF and Marcel Avronsart, the newly elected President of ISOD for safe keeping. Finally, the Olympic flame was slowly extinguished and the traditional parade of the competing nations brought the ceremony to a close.

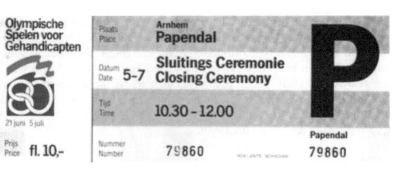

Closing ceremony ticket

The Use of Olympic Terminology

The bringing together of athletes from both ISMGF and ISOD into one Games in Toronto in 1976 had raised two problems with regards to a name for the Games. As they now included blind and amputee athletes they could no longer be called the International Stoke Mandeville Games, nor could the term 'Paralympic', as it was then understood (Paraplegic Olympics), be applied. The use of Olympic terminology both in Toronto and Örnsköldsvik in 1976 led to a great deal of communication between Sir Ludwig and the IOC over this use of Olympic terminology. This led to a tentative agreement by Guttmann that the Games would stop using Olympic terminology in return for IOC Patronage and support. However, having not had this confirmed at the time in was decided that the summer Games in Arnhem were to be entitled the Olympics for the Disabled 1980. This came to the attention of the IOC and in February 1978 Madame Berlioux wrote to Sir Ludwig regarding the use of Olympic terminology. Sir Ludwig responded by stating that he was still awaiting official written confirmation of the IOC decision to recognise ISMGF. Throughout the remainder of 1978 correspondence flowed backwards and forwards between Madame Berlioux and Sir Ludwig in order that a solution could be found and patronage officially bestowed upon ISMGF by the IOC. However, throughout this period several issues arose, both politically and practically, that prevented a solution being reached. These included the use of the term 'Olympic' by the Special Olympics organisation in the USA who had been granted use of the term by the United States Olympic Committee. This came to light when the Special Olympics Organisation made an application to join ISOD in 1978. In addition, the IOC wished to officially recognise only one organisation representing the whole of the disabled sports movement and despite ISOD and ISMGF having the same President in Sir Ludwig they were constitutionally two separate entities. Finally, South Africa were full members of both ISOD and ISMGF and competed with a totally racially integrated team. However, the IOC stance at the time was that South Africa was banned from Olympic competition and they, therefore, felt unable to recognise an organisation that allowed South Africa to participate.

In the autumn of 1979, less than three months after his eightieth birthday, Sir Ludwig suffered a coronary thrombosis and despite a brief recovery died in March 1980 (Goodman, 1986). News of Sir Ludwig's death was obviously slow in reaching the IOC as in an internal memo in late March 1980 Lord Killanin wrote to Madame Berlioux that he thought they hadn't heard from Sir Ludwig for a while because he had become very old. He ends the memo by stating that nevertheless 'the correct thing would be that (a) these Games should not take place in the Olympic country (b) they should not be called the Olympic Games but whatever games they like, under the patronage of the I.O.C.'. With the death of Sir Ludwig the attitude of the IOC seemed to harden somewhat as the possibility of litigation was raised for the first time. Firstly, Madame Berlioux wrote to Mr Idenburg, President of the Netherlands Olympic Committee in May 1980 asking him if anything could be done under Dutch law to stop the use of the title 'Olympics for the Disabled'. Then, rather bizarrely, considering the Games finished on July 5th she wrote to Mr Henrik Meijers, Managing Director of the Sports Division for the Games on October 17th , asking if it was not too late for him to drop the word 'Olympics'. She concluded by indicating the possibility of litigation.

Buses in Arnhem using Olympic terminology

The Final Medal Table

Rank	NPC	Gold	Silver	Bronze	Total
1	Poland	76	50	52	178
2	United States	75	66	54	195
3	Fed. Rep. Germany	68	48	46	162
4	Canada	64	35	31	130
5	Great Britain	47	33	21	101
6	Netherlands	33	31	37	101
Number of Countries winning a medal					40
% of participating countries winning a medal					95.2

Games Trivia

The youngest competitor at the Games was 11 year old David Foppolo, a double above the elbow arm amputee, who not only won an individual bronze medal in the 2 x 50m individual medley and a silver medal in the 3 x 50m freestyle relay for class E1-F1, but also gained himself a 14 year old Dutch girlfriend who was also a swimmer at the Games.

Despite Stoke Mandeville being the spiritual home of the Paralympic Games the Games in Arnhem were the very first to have a programme made about them by the BBC. The 60 minute documentary was narrated by former rugby union player Cliff Morgan who had himself spent a year in a rehabilitation centre following a stroke ten years earlier and was broadcast on BBC1 at 7.00pm on the 17th July.

Cato Zahl Pedersen, a 21 year old student from Norway and an arm amputee won four gold medals in athletics in Arnhem to add to the three gold medals he had won in the second winter Paralympics in Geilo six months earlier.

On Monday 30th June a blind Judo demonstration was held in the sports hall at Papendal organised by Great Britain, Israel and the Netherlands. Eleven judokas, three with black belts, took part from the three organising countries plus Japan. Blind judo went on to replace blind wrestling at the Paralympics in Seoul eight years later and remains on the programme to this day.

In order to assist blind and visually impaired athletes get around the venue at Papendal the Games organisers had braille maps produced so participants could get around the various event sites.

References

Olympic Village Daily, Issues 1 – 13 (21st June – 5th July 1980) (Author Copies)

Papps, H.A., Report on the Olympics for the Disabled, Holland 1980 (Unpublished – Author Copy)

Rückert, H., 1980, Olympics for the Disabled Holland 1980 Commemorative Book, Stichting Olympische Spelen voor Gehandicaten; Arnhem.

Sainsbury, A.J. Great Britain Team Manager's Report – Paraplegic Section, Olympic Games for the Disabled, Holland 1980 (Unpublished – Author Copy)

Chapter 10: Innsbruck, Austria 1984

Logo:	Confirmed Participating Nations	21
UNTER DEM PATRONAT DES INTERNATIONALEN OLYMPISCHEN COMITÉS III. WELTWINTERSPIELE FÜR KÖRPERBEHINDERTE INNSBRUCK 1984 AUSTRIA	Confirmed Participating Athletes	419 (325 Men, 94 Women)
	Number of Events	107
	Opening Ceremony	Saturday 14th January (6.00pm)
Mascot: None Known	Closing Ceremony	Friday 20th January (4.00pm)
	Officially Opened by	Dr Rudolph Kirchschläger (President of Austria)
	Stadium	Innsbruck Olympic Ice Stadium (Opening and Closing Ceremonies)
	Flame Lit by	Peter Perner (Alpine Skier)
	Athlete's Oath	Unknown[4]

Participating Nations (21): Australia, Austria, Belgium, Canada, Czechoslovakia, Denmark, Finland, France, Great Britain, Italy, Japan, **Netherlands**, New Zealand, Norway, Poland, **Spain**, Sweden, Switzerland, United States, West Germany, Yugoslavia. **(Countries in bold are those appearing at a winter Paralympic Games for the first time)**

---

[4] If you know the name of the individual who took the oath please e-mail parahist@hotmail.co.uk

Sports (3): Alpine, Cross Country, Ice Sledge Speed Racing.

Impairment Groups (5): Amputees, Blind and Visually Impaired, Cerebral Palsied, Les Autres and Spinal Cord Injuries.

Logo: The logo for Innsbruck was a combination of three parts. The centre of the logo shows a stylised depiction of the Goldenes Dachl (Golden Roof) – one of Innsbruck's most famous landmarks. Above this was the Olympic rings, which the IOC had agreed to the use of based upon certain conditions (see below). Below the Golden Dachl was five broken rings aimed at depicting the disability of the participants taking part. It also contained the words 'Under the patronage of the International Olympic Committee' beneath the Olympic rings.

The Selection of Innsbruck as the Host City

The earliest reference to the selection of Innsbruck found so far is in the minutes of the founding meeting of the International Co-ordinating Committee held in Leysin, Switzerland in March 1982, where it is clear the decision had been taken by ISOD at an earlier unspecified date.

The Games Poster

The Games Opening Ceremony

As with several of the other opening and closing ceremonies for the early winter Games relatively little is known about the content of the ceremonies that occurred in Innsbruck in 1984. It is known that IOC President Juan Antonio Samaranch was in attendance and gave a speech whilst the Olympic flag was hoisted in the Olympic Ice Stadium where the opening ceremony was held on Saturday 14th January from 6.00pm. The Games were officially opened by the President of Austria, Dr Rudolph Kirchschläger, and the flame was lit by Peter Perner, an Austrian alpine skier. The name of the individual who took the athlete's oath is currently unknown.

The Games Themselves

In 1981, both the International Blind Sport Association (IBSA) and the Cerebral Palsied-International Sports and Recreation Association (CP-ISRA) broke away from ISOD to become independent bodies. However, at a meeting in Leysin, Switzerland, in March 1982, the four international bodies (ISMGF, ISOD, IBSA, CPISRA) joined together to form the International Co-ordinating Committee (ICC). While remaining independent in terms of the development of their own disability groups, the four organisations used ICC to better co-ordinate the major games for athletes with a disability. This also provided the opportunity for one single body to relate to the IOC as a representative of the disabled groups that participated in the contentiously named Olympics for the Disabled.

A meeting took place between ICC and the IOC in February 1983, at which President Samaranch made it clear that the IOC wished the disabled sports movement to become part of the Olympic movement. In return for the removal of Olympic terminology from their events, he added that he was willing to offer the disabled sports movement both IOC patronage and financial assistance. A major result of this meeting was an agreement by the IOC that a demonstration disabled skiing event could take place at the Sarajevo Winter Olympic Games in 1984 and, if successful, a demonstration event might also be added to the Los Angeles Summer Games. This was confirmed at a meeting of the IOC Executive Board in early summer of 1983.

Earlier, in late 1982, the IOC had shown a willingness to work closely with the disabled sports movement when its Executive Board meeting in October 1982 agreed to allow the use of the Olympic rings in the logo for what were called the 1984 World Winter Games for the Disabled. This had been granted on the understanding that the term 'Olympic' would be dropped from ISODs preferred title of '3rd Winter Olympic Games for the Disabled'. Samaranch also agreed to attend the Games in person. This was to be the start of a much closer working relationship between the IOC and the disability sports movement.

A total of 419 athletes from 21 nations competed in 107 medal events over 3 sports. The large increase in the number of participants and medal events is largely due to the fact that cerebral palsied and Les Autres athletes took part in the winter Games for the first time. The Innsbruck Paralympic Winter Games were the first Paralympic Games, winter or summer, organised by the newly formed International Co-ordinating Committee (ICC). The venues for the three sports were as follows:

Mutters:	Alpine Skiing
Natters:	Nordic Skiing
Olympic Ice Stadium:	Ice Sledge Speed Racing

The American Nordic team in Innsbruck

A competitors racing bib

The Outstanding Performers in Innsbruck

There were four athletes in Innsbruck that won 4 gold medals each. In the alpine events they were Helmut Falch of Austria, Paul Dibello from the United States and Gunilla Ahren of Sweden and in the Ice Sledge Speed Racing Lahja Haemaelaeinen of Norway.

The Winners Medal

The Closing Ceremony

Very little is currently known about the closing ceremony for the Innsbruck 1984 winter Paralympic Games other than that it commenced at 4.00pm on Friday 20th January in the Olympic Ice Stadium and was attended by Queen Silvia of Sweden.

The Final Medal Table

Rank	NPC	Gold	Silver	Bronze	Total
1	Austria	34	19	17	70
2	Finland	19	9	6	34
3	Norway	15	13	13	41
4	Fed. Rep. of Germany	10	14	10	34
5	USA	7	14	14	35
6	Sweden	7	2	5	14
Number of Countries winning a medal					14
% of participating countries winning a medal					66.7

Games Trivia

Thirty male alpine giant slalom skiers from four different racing classes including both leg and arm amputees were selected from Innsbruck to compete in an exhibition event at the Sarajevo winter Olympic Games held on Saturday 11th February. However, as with all the Olympic exhibition events, both summer and winter, that followed the athletes were not considered part of their respective national Olympic teams, where not allowed to stay in the Olympic village, could not march in the opening or closing ceremonies and were not allowed to wear the uniforms of their respective national teams.

There was a severe lack of snow in Innsbruck at the time of the Games and so the organisers were forced to call upon the Austrian army to help bring snow down from the nearby high glaciers and prepare the race tracks by hand.

The rules for the Nordic skiing at Innsbruck 1984 were unusual in that they actually allowed more than one relay team from the same nation to compete. This meant that Austria were able to take gold and silver in the Men's 3x2.5 km Relay Gr I-II and Finland to take gold and silver in the Men's 4x5 km Relay LW2-9. This rule was changed for subsequent Games.

References

Brittain, I., 2008, The Evolution of the Paralympic Games in Cashman, R. et al, Benchmark Games: The Sydney 2000 Paralympic Games; Walla Walla Press, Petersham, NSW, p. 19-34.

Fay, T., 2011, Winter Paralympic Games: Founding Legacies 1984 – 1988 in Legg, D. & Gilbert, K., Paralympic Legacies, Commonground Publishing; Champaign, Il., p. 173-180.

Minutes of the Meeting of the Co-operative Committee of CP-ISRA, IBSA, ISMGF and ISOD held on March 11th 1982 at Hotel Central Residence, Leysin, Switzerland.

Speech of the IOC President for the World Championships of Winter Sports for the Disabled – Innsbruck, 14th January 1984 (Author copy)

Tiroler Tageszeitung, 16-1-1984, Eröffnungsfeier der Welt winter speile – Ausdruck der Lebensfreude (Opening ceremony of the World Winter Games - an expression of joy)

Chapter 11: New York, USA 1984

Logo:	Confirmed Participating Nations	45
	Confirmed Participating Athletes	1750 (From Official Report) (Gender split ~ 1278 men, 472 women based upon ratio of known participants)
	Number of Events	973*
	Opening Ceremony	Sunday 17th June (2.00pm)
	Closing Ceremony	Friday 29th June (6.00pm)
Mascot: Dan D. Lion	Officially Opened by	President Ronald Reagan
	Main Stadium	Mitchel Park Track
	Flame Lit by	Jan Wilson (Amputee) Kevin Stark (Blind) Margo Maddox (Cerebral Palsy) William Lehr (Les Autres)
	Athlete's Oath	Ólavur Kongsbak (Faroe Islands - Swimmer)
	Official's Oath	Jack Abramson (Swimming Coordinator)

*A number of events such as table tennis team results and some athletics events were missed out of the official results altogether and so are not accounted for in this figure

Participating Nations (45): Argentina, Australia, Austria, Belgium, Brasil, Burma, Canada, **China**, Denmark, **Democratic Republic of Germany**, Egypt, **Faroe Islands**, Federal Republic of Germany, Finland, France, Great Britain, Greece, Hong Kong, Hungary, Iceland, India, Indonesia, Ireland, Israel, Italy, Japan, Kenya, Korea, Kuwait, **Liechtenstein**, Luxembourg, Mexico, Netherlands, New Zealand, Norway, Poland, Portugal, Spain, Sweden, Switzerland, **Thailand**, **Trinidad & Tobago**, United States, Yugoslavia, Zimbabwe.
(Countries in bold are those appearing at a summer Paralympic Games for the first time)

Sports (15): Archery, Athletics, Boccia, Cycling, Equestrian, Football (7-a-side), Football (Wheelchair), Goalball, Lawn Bowls, Powerlifting, Shooting, Swimming, Table Tennis, Volleyball (Sitting & Standing), Wrestling

Impairment Groups (4): Amputees, Blind & Visually Impaired, Cerebral Palsied, Les Autres.

Logo: On Saturday 16th June Keven Lewis, Director of Wheelchair Sports for the Los Angeles Olympic Organising Committee (LAOOC) presented the Games Director Michael Mushett with a Torch used in the Los Angeles Olympic Games for use in the opening ceremony the following day. This was the first time this had ever happened and signified the growing links between the Olympic movement and the fledgling Paralympic movement. It is appropriate then that the logo for the Games in New York was a flaming torch.

Mascot: Designed by Maryanne McGrath Higens, a Long Beach Resident who taught art at the Lawrence, L.I. Junior High School. He is a friendly Lion in a jogging suit and running shoes and he wears the logo of the Games on his jacket. The children of the Human Resources School in Albertson, L.I. took on the project of providing a name for the mascot and held a full-scale election complete with posters, banners, electioneering and speeches. The race, with nominations from every class was very close. The winning name was the suggestion of the ninth graders in the class of Mary Anne Cicchillo.

Bids: USA only (See previous chapter).

The Selection of Long Island, New York as the Host Venue

In 1980 the National Wheelchair Athletics Association (NWAA), following a recommendation from their then Chairman Ben Lipton, approved the submission of a bid to the International Stoke Mandeville Games Federation (ISMGF) to host a competition that would involve only athletes who were eligible under ISMGF rules. This came about after Mr Lipton persuaded them that a Games involving other disability groups would be unwieldy and almost impossible to organise within the USA. Mr Lipton presented this proposal to the ISMGF Executive Committee, of which he was Vice President, at a meeting in the Olympic Village in Arnhem on 24th June 1980 and again at the ISMGF Council meeting at Het Dorp, Arnhem on Tuesday 1st July 1980 with a promise that if the proposal was accepted every effort would be made to ensure that a Games for other disability groups would be organised around the same time at a different venue. Although there were many present at the Council meeting that were responsible for sport for all disability groups within their own countries and whose preference was for a single Games their Chairman reminded them that the responsibility of ISMGF was for the paraplegic Games. They also raised many questions regarding potential extra costs for the nations of having to attend separate Games. Despite this Mr Lipton was given a mandate to pursue his negotiations to find a site for the 1984 Games for ISMGF athletes only. In response to the questions and criticisms made at the ISMGF Council meeting Mr Lipton went away and wrote an NWAA position paper for holding separate Games, which was circulated to the nations in October of 1980.

NWAA Position Paper for Holding Separate Games

On 24th October 1980 Benjamin Lipton, Chairman of the National Wheelchair Athletic Association (NWAA) in the USA, sent out a letter stating the case for the decision made by National Wheelchair Athletic Committee to conduct wheelchair competitions only, with wheelchair competitions being those recognised by the International Stoke Mandeville Games Federation (ISMGF). Despite this the letter states that they were intent on preserving and advancing the integrity of sports for all disabled and although they had decided to advocate separate Games they viewed their decision as contributing to this objective. The paper attached to the letter begins by outlining the various rationales advanced at that time as to why multi-disabled Games were considered the way forward and then it takes each of these rationales and gives reasons why the NWAC consider them to be incorrect. The NWAC advanced five rationales as to why they considered the putting on of separate Games for each disability group to be the way forward. Their over-arching reason for the decision was a belief that the Games should be about the athletes and athletic competition not as a means of advancing the cause of disabled people in general.

> *The question of economy*: The general feeling at the time was that by having all of the disability groups competing in one place at one time was that a consolidated event served to concentrate the limited resources of the host nation thereby reducing the need for duplication of manpower and funding. However, NWAA disagreed with this principle stating that too many dissimilarities amongst the disability groups calling upon diverse resources meant that it would be very difficult to achieve any real worthwhile economies.

> *Rehabilitation objectives*: It was also argued that there were positive rehabilitation objectives obtained when the various disability groups

were brought together in the same physical and social environments. NWAA felt that this argument was predicated upon the false assumption that if you force people together for athletics purposes that would automatically use the occasion for the desired psycho-social and rehabilitation purposes. They argued that human relationships do not predictably improve nor does understanding advance when contrived circumstances compel people to interact.

Performance identity: A slightly less prominent argument that had been used to justify the 1976 and 1980 Games was a belief that newer, emerging competitive organisations needed the direct and immediate association with the older organisations such as ISMGF in order to develop and sustain their own programmes.

NWAA argued that by having separate Games for each disability group it would be far easier for either the general public or the media to understand and appreciate the performances of that particular disability group, rather than the information overload that would come from a multi-disabled Games.

Number affected: By holding separate Games the NWAA suggested that more athletes from each disability group would be able to participate, whereas in the previous two Games team sizes had had to be capped due to a limit on available space. This appears to be somewhat at odds with their arguments relating to economy, but they felt that the caps on nations capable of entering more athletes in any or all of the disability groups would help raise standards by increasing the depth of competition.

Administrative freedoms: NWAA felt that by hosting separate competitions for each of the disability groups this would enable the different disability organisations a great deal more freedom in the services they could provide their athletes and they way in which they ran their own Games.

The paper from the NWAA concludes by clearly stating that they had no interest in undoing all of the hard work and all of the achievements that had occurred up to that point in the development of sport for the disabled. To that end they suggested that a co-ordinating council made up of two representatives of each organisation be established in order to overcome the potential dangers that can occur when several groups pursue similar objectives at the same time.

Ben Lipton was Chairman of the US National Wheelchair Athletics Association from 1957 to 1980, when he was replaced by Dale Wiley, Chairman of the Steering Committee trying to organise the wheelchair Games at the University of Illinois – the very Games that Ben Lipton had initiated. Following his replacement on the NWAA board Ben Lipton appears to have had nothing more to do with the wheelchair games being planned for Illinois. However it appears not to have been the end of his involvement in the International Games planned for other disabilities in 1984. According to Mike Mushett, one morning in May of 1982 Ben Lipton walked into the office of Nassau County Executive Francis Purcell looking for a home for what promised to be the second largest sports event in the world for the year of 1984 (Mushett, 1984). Lipton, a neighbour of Purcell, promptly asked him to host the third International Games for the Disabled in Nassau County in 1984. Despite having all the potential problems of hosting the Games explained to him Purcell decided it was worth the effort and in the early autumn of 1982 Mike Mushett was employed as Games Director and preparations for the Games to include amputees, blind & visually impaired, cerebral palsied, Les Autres athletes began in earnest

The Games Poster

The Games Opening Ceremony

Occasional showers greeted the 14000 spectators packed into the Mitchel Park stadium on Sunday 19th June for the 2pm start of the Games Opening Ceremony. Events began with Master of Ceremonies William B. Williams, a New York radio personality, giving a short welcome speech and introducing the first group of entertainers that included Bill Buzzeo and the Dixie Ramblers, Richie Havens, The New Image Drum and Bugle Corps, the ARC Gospel Chorus and the Square Dance Extravaganza. This was followed by speeches from the Nassau County Executive Francis Purcell, a spiritual message from Bishop Bailyand words of welcome from the United National Under-Secretary Shuaib Utham Yolan.

Four helicopters then landed on the baseball field behind the stadium marking the arrival of President Reagan who entered the stadium to the strains of All Hail the Chief plyed by the All American Concert Band. Once President Reagan was settled in place Jiggs MacDonald, a famous Sports Announcer, began the roll call of countries for the march in of the 1750 athletes from 45 countries.

The parade was led by the Netherlands as the hosts of the 1980 Games and each country was preceded by Boy and Girl Scouts from Nassau and Suffolk counties bearing placards with the country's name. One athlete from Austria apparently broke ranks during the parade to present President Reagan with a bouquet of flowers.

President Reagan at the Opening Ceremony

On completion of the parade Cathy Lee Crosby, the Official Hostess for the Games, greeted the athletes and this was followed by short speeches from Commander Archie Cameron, President of the recently formed International Co-ordinating Committee of Sports for the Disabled (ICC), US Senator Alphonse D'Amato and New York State Governor Mario Cuomo. For the first time ever at a summer Paralympic Games the flags of the Olympic and United States Olympic Committees were raised followed by the Games flag and the flags of ISOD and ISMGF. Opera star Elaine Malbin then sang 'Dedicated Athletes' by Robert Bloom and Placido Impollona.

Master Timmy Towers, who had carried the Los Angeles Olympic Torch on its journey through New York City then entered the stadium carry a Los Angeles Olympic Torch given to the Games by the Los Angeles Organising Committee and handed it over to President Reagan. He then handed the torch to Jan Wilson, representing the amputee athletes who ran with it to the base of the stand that would hold the flame for the duration of the Games. She was joined their by Kevin Stark representing blind and visually impaired athletes, Margo Maddox representing athletes with cerebral palsy and William Lehr representing Les Autres athletes and together they lit the flame. Bob Beamon, Olympic Champion from Mexico City and world record holder for long jump at the time acted as Oath Officer for the Games. Ólavur Kongsbak, aswimmer from the Faroe Islands took the oath on behalf of the athletes and Jack Abramson, the swimming co-ordinator for the Games took the oath on behalf of the officials.

President Reagan was then introduced by Francis Purcell and he gave the official welcome on behalf of the USA and declared the Games officially open. The ceremony then concluded with more entertainment from 'The Spinners', Bill Buzzeo and The All Americans.

The lighting of the Olympic flame with a torch from the Los Angeles Olympic Games

The Games Themselves

Perhaps unsurprisingly the official commemorative book for the Games in New York, *The Road to Glory*, paints a picture of a highly successful, well run event. However, a number of sources, and one in particular, paint a somewhat different story. Odeda Rosenthal was a Professor of Humanities at a local Community College on Long Island who spoke five languages and acted as Liaison-Translator for the Austrian Team at the Games. In a series of articles she highlights many issues that occurred at the Games ranging from poor communication to volunteer bus driver who didn't know the route to event scheduling problems that caused some teams and individuals to miss their events completely. By way of explanation of these problems Rosenthal claims Programme Director, Robert Koch and Games Director, Michael Mushett, although having Masters degrees in Recreation, had no experience or understanding of international events or how to run large programmes and yet still made no effort to get any help even when it was clear they were unable to cope. This appears to concur with the comments of Bailey (2008) who claims that the official report on the Games written by the International Co-ordinating Committee by Hans Lindström states that 'there were too few responsible for too much'. Rosenthal also claims that the Director of Media, Hank McCann was able to achieve hardly any press or TV coverage. Nor was there apparently very much advertising and no attempt at a build up of interest in the lead up to the Games. Attendance was apparently dismally low, which is often borne out by the empty stands shown in many of the photographs. Rosenthal claims tickets started at $20, but by the end of the first week were down to $3 with children and seniors being bussed in at special rates in an attempt to fill the empty stands.

However, Rosenthal appears to save her greatest criticism for the police and in particular the Police Chief, George Maher who she claims was on a 'macho ego trip' and who apparently forever took the opposite tack of anything that was suggested to sort out the mess. Before the Games started $3.5million was apparently set aside for police overtime – the same amount as was set aside for the total running costs of the Games. Rosenthal then paints the possibility that the huge Police overtime budget was less to do with the claimed fear of terrorism and more to do with attempts by the then County Executive, Francis Purcell to get himself re-elected. He and Republican Senator D'Amato were apparently responsible for getting President Reagan to attend the opening ceremony at a time when the President had cut funding for the disabled to the point when nearly all programmes had been killed.

Certainly some of the claims made by Rosenthal appear to be borne out by other sources. Baum, writing for Newsday, a local newspaper, reports that the first day of competition was marked by organisational confusion. Goldstein, also writing for Newsday, reports the poor attendance at the Games. Apparently a quarter of million spectators were anticipated, but by the end of the second week it was expected that the figure was unlikely to reach seventy-five thousand. By way of explanation Goldstein cites the Director of Media, Hank McCann, as stating 'It's quite basic…the general public believes it cannot handle watching disabled people do anything'. The poor turn out of spectators actually led to the number of Police on duty being cut from 900 in the first week to 325 in the second week. There are many reports of organisation hiccups and administrative errors. Indeed, the authors own research has shown that many medals were awarded for events that don't appear in the official results and so some athletes will never take their rightful place in Paralympic history.

All of this said the overall impression of the Games reported by many is of a friendly atmosphere where volunteers and workers tried their hardest under difficult circumstances to make the Games memorable for all concerned. It shouldn't be forgotten that the Games were organised in just under two years, on a tight budget and had to cater for over two thousand competitors and officials. The events themselves were held on five separate sites:

Caumsett State Park:	Equestrian
Eisenhower Park:	Cross Country, Cycling, Lawn Bowls
Hofstra University:	Swimming, Table Tennis

Mitchell Park:	Archery, Athletics, Football (7-a-side), Shooting
Nassua Community College:	Boccia, Football (Wheelchair), Goalball, Powerlifting, Volleyball (Sitting & Standing)

The Games in New York saw the addition of a further impairment group to the Games. Les Autres, literally meaning 'the others' includes all motor disabilities except amputees, medullar lesions and cerebral palsy, for example muscular dystrophy, multiple sclerosis, arthrogryposis, Friedrich's ataxia and arthritis. This grouping also includes athletes with restricted height. Boccia, Football (7-a-side) and Road Cycling were added to the sporting programme in New York. The largest team in New York was, unsurprisingly, the Americans with 198 competitors. The smallest was from Liechtenstein with just 2 competitors.

Outstanding Competitors in New York

There were four participants, all swimmers, in New York who won five individual gold medals each. They were Jolanda Romero, a CP class 5 from the Netherlands; Erling Trondsen, a class 3 amputee from Norway and two partially sighted swimmers from the USA, John Morgan and Trischa Zorn. Numerous internet based articles regarding Zorn actually claim that she won ten gold medals in New York, but this cannot be confirmed from the official results and the articles do not list the events for the missing medals. Newspaper articles of the time would appear to indicate that in Zorn's case the lower estimate is an accurate tally and that ten is very unlikely. The USA Ladies team did win the 4 x 100m Medley relay for classes B1 to B3 and so a sixth gold medal for Zorn can probably be fairly safely assumed. This is one of the key problems with the results from New York, which appear to have missed out a growing number of medal events that took place.

The Winners Medal

Paralympic Bronze Medal from New York, 1984

The Closing Ceremony

The Closing Ceremony began at 6pm on Friday 29th June with the final qualifying heats for the men's 1500m and women's 800m wheelchair races for the demonstration events to take place at the Olympic Games beginning a month later in Los Angeles. Amongst the women 14 year old Sacajeweja Hunter of Washington qualified fourth to take part in Los Angeles. The Closing Ceremony itself began when an honour guard of 75 Nassau County police officers took up position at the entrance to the track. The County's Police Bag Pipers then marched in followed by placard bearers with the name of each participating country and a representative from that country carrying their flag. Following this the athletes of all nations mixed together entered the stadium to the strains of 'March of the Nobles' played by the Symphony for United Nations and gathered on the infield. Games Director Mike Mushett then gave a short speech acknowledging the presence of the hosts of the next summer Games in Seoul four years later. Mr Gee Woo Lee from the Seoul delegation read out an invitation to all the athletes to take part in the 1988 Games.

The Games in New York were officially closed by Commander Archie Cameron, President of ICC, with the words:

> 'I declare the Third International Games for the Disabled closed and I call upon all disabled athletes of all countries to assemble four years from now in Seoul, South Korea to celebrate with us the Fourth International Games for the Disabled'

The flags of the Games were then lowered and carried back to the reviewing stand by American athletes Dick Lallier, Shaun Graham, Karen Farmer, Todd Hodgin, Bill Denby and Cathy Brown where they were handed over to Dr William T. Callahan, President of the Games Executive Board, who in turn handed them over to Mr Gee Woo Lee. Farewell addresses on behalf of the athletes by Cynthia Good and on behalf of the officials by Fred Koch were then read out followed by a spiritual message by the Reverend Dr Harold Wilke. The ceremony then concluded with the extinguishing of the flame. The stadium lights were turned off and each person in the stadium unsheathed a light stick they had been provided with, whilst a huge firework display commenced overhead.

The Cost of the Games

As with the Games in Illinois the fundraising for the Games in New York were not without problems. Initially Avis Corp. Chairman Howard Miller volunteered to be chairman of the board of directors and head up the fundraising campaign. He was president of United Cerebral Palsy and a finance official of the United States Olympic Committee. However, early in 1983 he left Avis Corp. and Long Island and it was not until November of that year the board appointed Bill Callahan to replace Miller as well as appointing a professional fundraiser, Michael Manzer who put together a marketing strategy to attract funding. The cost of the Games was estimated at $8.238million of which $4.5million was to cover the costs of the overtime bill for the 900 police officers providing security for the Games. Of the remaining a large proportion of it was covered by a federal government grant of $850,000 and the state of New York provided $550,000 plus $263,000 for National Guard support.

Spectator Attendance At the Games

The organisers of the Games had hoped to at least match, if not surpass, the 100,000 spectators from Arnhem in 1980 and the 108,000 spectators in Toronto in 1976. As a result they had budgeted for $200,000 of income from ticket sales. However, after four days officials were forced to reappraise the situation when the estimates for the first three days attendances were given as 1400 for Monday, 2200 for Tuesday and 2500 for Wednesday. Extrapolating this would give a total spectator attendance for the Games of just under 25,000 people – way below the hoped for attendances. Mike Mushett stated at the time that 'unfortunately, one of the biggest problems with people not coming out is that they have not come to terms with dealing with disabled people'.

The Final Medal Table

Rank	NPC	Gold	Silver	Bronze	Total
1	United States	106	99	82	287
2	Great Britain	80	84	86	250
3	Canada	52	60	54	166
4	Sweden	49	30	26	105
5	Netherlands	47	41	19	107
6	Fed. Rep. Germany	45	44	34	123
Number of Countries winning a medal					39
% of participating countries winning a medal					86.7

Games Trivia

New York was the very first time that China had competed in the Paralympic Games and it was all down the hard work of a British ex-patriot, David Griffiths, who was working at the time as General Manager of the Jubilee Sports Centre in Hong Kong. David, a former manager of Wembley Stadium, ran almost fifty miles a day for over fifty days from Beijing to Hong Kong and raised nearly two and a half million dollars in the process. This money was then used to send a team from Hong Kong and a team from China to the Games in New York, as well as to kit them out.

David Griffiths in Union Jack shorts with members of the Chinese team

Ronan Tynan, an outgoing Irishman and double leg amputee, was elected the most sportsmanlike male individual at the Games. He also won three gold and one silver medal in throwing events at the track. The award for female athletes went to Janet Rowley, a blind field event athlete from the USA.

Ronan Tynan – voted most sportsmanlike male individual at the Games

When one of the Irish delegation lost their wallet containing $400 the police officers took up a collection at $5 per man and returned the money to the Irish athlete.

Reference

British Sports Association for the Disabled, 1985, Handbook 1985, BSAD; London

British Les Autres Sports Association, 1984, Sports Association Handbook 1984, BLASA; Edinburgh, UK

British Sports Association for the Disabled, 1984, Stoke and New York to Seoul Commemorative Publication, BSAD; London

Daily Torch: The Official Newspaper for the Athletes, Issue 1-14, 16-29 June 1984 (Author Copies – Issues 12 & 14 missing)

International Games for the Disabled, 1984, Official Results (Author Electronic Copies)

Mushett, M., 1984, The 1984 International Games for the Disabled, in Sherrill, C. (Ed.), The 1984 Olympic Congress Proceedings (Volume 9): Sport and Disabled Athletes, Human Kinetics; Champaign, Illinois, p. 251-266.

Newsday, The Long Island Newspaper, Saturday 16th June – Saturday 30th June 1984.

Rosenthal, O., 1984, Blunders at the Games (Unpublished – Author copy)

Rosenthal, O., 1984, Farewell to the International Games (Unpublished – Author copy)

Rosenthal, O., 1984, Untitled piece on Rosenthal's experiences at the 1984 Games (Unpublished – Author copy)

Stampleman, B.(Ed), 1984, The Road to Glory, Steve/James & Associates; New York

VIIth World Wheelchair Games or VIIth Paralympic Games, 1984, Final Report Part 1, Nashville, Tennessee (Author Copy)

VIIth World Wheelchair Games or VIIth Paralympic Games, 1984, Final Report Part 2, Nashville, Tennessee (Author Copy)

VIIth World Wheelchair Games or VIIth Paralympic Games, 1984, Final Report Part 3, Nashville, Tennessee (Author Facsimile Copy)

Chapter 12: Stoke Mandeville, UK 1984

Logo:	Confirmed Participating Nations	41
	Confirmed Participating Athletes	1097 (From Official Report) (Gender split ~ 829 men, 268 women based upon ratio of known participants)
	Number of Events	343
	Opening Ceremony	Sunday 22nd July (11.15am)
	Closing Ceremony	Wednesday 1st August (5.00pm)
Mascot:	Officially Opened by	HRH Prince Charles
	Main Stadium	Stoke Mandeville Stadium Track
None Known	Flame Lit by	Terry Willett (Fencer)
	Athlete's Oath	John Harris (Athlete)
	Official's Oath	Ronald Nicholls (Shooting Official)

Participating Nations (40*): Australia, Austria, Bahamas, **Bahrain**, Belgium, Brasil, Canada, Denmark, Ecuador, Egypt, Federal Republic of Germany, Finland, France, Great Britain, Guatemala, Hong Kong, Iceland, Ireland, Israel, Italy,

Jamaica, Japan, **Jordan**, Kenya, Korea, Kuwait, Malta, Mexico, Netherlands, New Zealand, Norway, **Papua New Guinea**, Poland, Spain, Sweden, Switzerland, Trinidad & Tobago, United States, Yugoslavia, Zimbabwe. **(Countries in bold are those appearing at a summer Paralympic Games for the first time)**
* Colombia appear in the list of competing countries in the Official Results book for these Games, but no Colombian athlete's name appears in the actual results of the sports and all newspapers refer to 40 countries.

The Papua New Guinea team competing in their very first Paralympic Games

Sports (10): Archery, Athletics, Lawn Bowls, Shooting, Snooker, Swimming, Table Tennis, Weightlifting, Wheelchair Basketball, Wheelchair Fencing

Impairment Groups (1): Spinal Cord Injuries.

Bids: Originally South Carolina, USA. Then split to University of Illinois (Wheelchairs) and Long Island, New York (Other Disabilities). University of Illinois Games finally moved to Stoke Mandeville, UK following financial difficulties.

Logo: The organisers reverted to using the same logo as the one used in the very early days of the Stoke Mandeville Games in the mid- to late 1950s and the very first Paralympic Games in Rome 1960. The fact that the Games were once again of spinal cord injuries only also enabled the organisers to officially attach the term Paralympic to the Games in its original meaning of 'paraplegic Olympics'.

The Selection of Stoke Mandeville as the Host Venue

An NWAA memo dated 5th June 1980 states the Ben Lipton appointed an Ad Hoc Steering Committee for the 1984 Paralympics of five people: Dale Wiley, Stan Labanowich, Pat Karman, Bob Syzman and Sy Bloom. At a meeting of the Steering Committee in Arnhem on 6th July 1980 Dale Wiley was elected Chairman of the Committee. One of the first jobs this steering committee set itself was to scout for potential venues for the Games. After initially contacting some two hundred potential sites for the Games by June 18th 1981 the Steering Committee had identified eight possible venues to host the wheelchair games. These were:

- Daniel Freeman Hospital, Los Angeles
- University of California, Santa Barbara
- University of Washington, Washington State
- University of Illinois, Champaign, IL.
- Michigan State University, East Lansing
- Long Island, New York (Hofstra University, Adelphi University, Nassau Community College)
- University of Massachusetts, Amherst
- Arlington, Texas

Sometime in the second half of 1980 Dale Wiley replaced Ben Lipton as Chairman of the NWAA and so at the ISMGF Executive Committee meeting on 30th July 1981 it was Wiley who reported that at that time they were looking seriously at three sites. One was in the Los Angeles area of California, but the Los Angeles Organising Committee for the Olympic Games were apparently not very receptive to the idea. The second possible venue was Arlington, Texas who had been given a target date of 15th August to decide if they were capable of hosting the Games there. The third potential venue is not listed. In August 1981 the site selection committee met in Pomona, California during a training camp for the US men's and women's national teams. At that meeting the committee ranked their top two selections as Arlington, near to Dallas in Texas and the University of Illinois. Upon further investigation by Pat Karman, however, it was discovered that none of the potential venues in that area (Southern Methodist University, University of Texas at Arlington, Texas Christian University) had sufficient accessible accommodation to house all the Games personnel. It was, therefore, decided to move forward with the bid from the University of Illinois, which had a long tradition in wheelchair sports. However, it should be made clear that in a letter dated 23rd October 1980 when the University of Illinois offered to host the Games they also made it very clear that they would not be involved in fund raising, nor would they assume any debts incurred as a result of putting on the Games. The Chancellor of the University of Illinois, John Cribbet, officially wrote to Dale Wiley to accept the invitation to host the Games on 8th December 1981.

The reasons why the Games at University of Illinois never actually went ahead are long, messy and complicated, but in short they involve a spectacular failure to raise funds despite going through more than five professional fundraising organizations in less than three years, poorly defined management structures that led to the Chairman of the Board Dale Wiley and Executive Games Director Tim Nugent at loggerheads and several issues with the United States Olympic Committee around the naming of the Games. The University of Illinois finally pulled out of their contract in January of 1984 after failing to receive sufficient proof that funding would be in place in time to put on the Games. Despite last ditch appeals to President Reagan and the Los Angeles Organising

Committee to name but a few the decision to move the Games to Stoke Mandeville from the originally proposed site of Champaign, Illinois was finally taken in March of that year. However, this left relatively little time to put on a Games for over 1000 competitors and 700 officials and escorts. In attempting to raise the money to build new facilities at Stoke Mandeville many years previously Guttmann had stated 'we'll build a sports stadium and an Olympic Village, so that the disabled athletes of the world will always have their own Olympic facilities here at Stoke Mandeville when other doors are closed to them'. How wise those words must have appeared to those who had known him as the events of 1984 had unfolded.

In order to put on the Games the British Paraplegic Sports Society set a fundraising target of £420,000. They were greatly assisted this by the media. Joan Scruton was invited by the BBC to give a television interview where she emphasised that Britain had to succeed where the USA had failed. This interview was apparently seen by a director from the American corporation United Technologies, who happened to be in England at the time and led to a OTIS Elivator PLC, subsidiary of United Technologies, donating £53,000, which resulted in the building, in a record number of weeks, of a specialist amenities building at the Ludwig Guttmann Sports Centre. £66,000 was raised through a German television campaign. The Sports Council made a grant of £20,000 to improve the sports field. Invacare/ Carters were also another major sponsor, but it was the response of the British public at large, through organisations such as Round Table, Rotary and numerous other organisations, companies and individuals that really saved the day. By the time the Games started they had raised all but £50,000 of the target and this was achieved within a couple of months of the completion of the Games.

The Games Poster

VII World Wheelchair Games

The Games Opening Ceremony

On Sunday 22nd July, after landing his helicopter on the nearby Buckinghamshire County Council sports field, HRH Prince Charles made his way to the Stoke Mandeville stadium where he was escorted to the dais for the opening ceremony by Horace Poole, Chairman of the British Paraplegic Sports Society and Dr Robert Jackson, President of the International Stoke Mandeville Games Federation. Mr Poole then invited Dr Jackson to make a welcoming speech to the athletes on behalf of ISMGF.

Team Manager Tony Sainsbury leads out the British team at the opening ceremony

After getting Mr Poole to present Prince Charles with a presentation set of winners medals as a gift Dr Jackson then invited Prince Charles to officially open the Games. Following the playing of the National and ISMGFD Anthems and the raising of the Games flag British athlete Terry Willett wheeled onto the track carrying the Olympic flame in a specially adapted wheelchair, that had been designed and constructed by three apprentices from the Aylesbury Vale Industrial Training Centre. Athlete, John Harris, and shooting official, Ronald Nicholls then took the oaths on behalf the competitors and official respectively. At 11.45am pigeons were released and Prince Charles went on a walkabout to meet and talk to the athletes accompanied by Mr Poole, Dr Jackson, Lord Westbury and Joan Scruton. Commentary upon the events at the Opening Ceremony was provided by television personality Esther Rantzen, with whom Prince Charles stopped to chat briefly before leaving the stadium.

Terry Willett with Prince Charles

John Harris takes the athletes oath

The Games Themselves

Given the short period of time available to organise these Games it is hardly surprising that the only major addition to the sporting programme was a wheelchair marathon for 78 competitors starting in Chalfont St Peter at 7.15am on Sunday 29th July, making its way through Amersham and Wendover, and finishing at Stoke Mandeville stadium. Bailey (2008) claims that the venues used for the Games were more impressive than in the past, using the best amenities available in the vicinity of Aylesbury. Although, this appears on the whole to be true Sainsbury (1984) describes the venue for the fencing as a 'disaster' and was even more scathing of the organisation of the fencing competition itself. He doesn't, however, go into much detail as to why. The venues for the sports were as follows:

Aylesbury Civic Centre:	Table Tennis, Weightlifting
Aylesbury Grammar School:	Wheelchair Fencing
Grange School, Aylesbury:	Archery
High Wycombe Sports Centre:	Swimming
Stoke Mandeville Sports Stadium:	Athletics, Lawn Bowls, Shooting, Snooker, Wheelchair Basketball

Accommodation used for the Games at Stoke Mandeville included William Harding School, Hampden Hall Agricultural College on the Wendover Road, some beds in Stoke Mandeville Hospital and Kermode Hall at the Royal Air Force Halton Camp in nearby Wendover.

Outstanding Competitors at Stoke Mandeville

The outstanding performer in Stoke Mandeville was Marc de Vos, a class 3 paraplegic from Belgium, who won seven gold and one silver medal on the track and if it hadn't been for his own team mate, Paul van Winkel, pipping him into second in the 400m he would have had eight gold medals. Marc and Paul helped Belgium to a clean sweep of the three track relays over 100m, 200m and 400m for classes 2-5 contributing three gold medals to each of their totals in the process. Three other participants won six individual gold medals each. On the track Monica Saker a class 4 paraplegic from Sweden and Ingrid Lauridsen, a class two paraplegic from Denmark, were both unbeatable over all distances for their class on the track. Only Saker's victory over Lauridesen in the 'Queen of the Straight' 100m ladies class 1A-6 prevented Lauridesen from winning a seventh gold medal. Instead she had to be content with a bronze in that event. In the pool Marcia Bevard, a class 4 paraplegic from the USA also proved unbeatable in all four of the swimming strokes winning six individual gold medals in the process. At least eight other athletes won five gold medals each.

Monica Saker (SWE) winner of six gold medals on the track and 'Queen of the Straight'
over 100m for Ladies classes 1A-6.

Slalom Event at Stoke Mandeville, 1984

The Winners Medal

Paralympic Bronze Medal from Stoke Mandeville, 1984

The Closing Ceremony

The Closing Ceremony commenced on Wednesday 1st August at 5pm with a parade of up to six athletes and their team manager entering the stadium behind a placard bearing their country's name. Once these representatives were lined up on the infield their remaining team members and escorts took up position behind them. Mr Horace Poole then introduced Mr Nick Jones of IBM who made the presentation of the medals to the successful basketball teams. This was followed by the presentation of the first ever Sir Ludwig Guttmann Awards, named in his honour, and presented to an athlete and an administrator for outstanding contribution to sport for the spinally paralysed. The winner of the athletes' award was Dr Rosa Schweizer of Austria and the winner of the administrators' award was Joan Scruton, Secretary General of ISMGF. Mr Poole then introduced the retiring President of ISMGF, Dr Robert Jackson, who in turn introduced his successor, Dr John Grant from Australia to the audience. Dr Jackson then declared the Games officially closed after which the Olympic flame was extinguished, the Olympic hymn sung and the flags of the Games and the competing nations were lowered. The Games flag was then taken to the podium whereupon Dr Jackson handed it over to Kim Hyong Shik, a representative from Korea as hosts of the next Games in 1988. The ceremony concluded with the national anthem and the singing of Auld Lang Syne.

Kim Hyong Shik receives the Games flag from Bob Jackson

The Final Medal Table

Rank	NPC	Gold	Silver	Bronze	Total
1	Fed. Rep. Germany	37	32	40	109
2	Canada	35	22	15	72
3	France	33	30	22	85
4	Sweden	31	13	8	52
5	United States	30	33	47	110
6	Great Britain	28	29	26	83
Number of Countries winning a medal					33
% of participating countries winning a medal					82.5

Games Trivia

The Olympic flag as well as the flags of all of the competing nations were hung out in Aylesbury Market Square from Monday 16th August. Within 48 hours the

Olympic flag had been stolen and the flags of Jamaica and Italy had been taken down, ripped up and posted through the letter box of a nearby public house. However, it was possible to repair these two flags and re-hang them, only for them to go missing again, along with the flags of Iceland and Ireland, within 24 hours. It cost £135 of tax payers money to replace to re-place the missing flags.

One of the Swiss team, Walter Boiller, had competed in the FITA round archery event every year that the Games had been held at Stoke Mandeville since 1957.

References

Bailey, S., 2008, Athlete First: A History of the Paralympic Movement, John Wiley & Sons Ltd; Chichester, UK.

Paraplegiker: magazin der Querschnittgelähmten, September 1984.

Pursuit, Newsletter of the VII World Wheelchair Games, Issues 1 – 12 (Sunday 22nd July – Thursday 2nd August 1984)

Sainsbury, A.J., 1984, Report of the British Team Manager – VIITH World Wheelchair Games (Author Copy)

Scruton, J., 1998, Stoke Mandeville: Road to the Paralympics, Peterhouse Press; Aylesbury, UK.

The Bucks Herald Newspaper, Thursday 26th July, Thursday 2nd August, Thursday 9th August.

VIIth World Wheelchair Games or VIIth Paralympic Games, 1984, Final Report Part 1, Nashville, Tennessee (Author Copy)

VIIth World Wheelchair Games or VIIth Paralympic Games, 1984, Final Report Part 2, Nashville, Tennessee (Author Copy)

VIIth World Wheelchair Games or VIIth Paralympic Games, 1984, Final Report Part 3, Nashville, Tennessee (Author Facsimile Copy)

Chapter 13: Innsbruck, Austria 1988

'The Easy Games - The Games with a Heart'

Logo:	Confirmed Participating Nations	22
UNTER DEM PATRONAT DES INTERNATIONALEN OLYMPISCHEN COMITÉS	Confirmed Participating Athletes	377 (300 Men, 77 Women)
	Number of Events	96
IV. WELTWINTERSPIELE FÜR KÖRPERBEHINDERTE INNSBRUCK 1988 AUSTRIA	Opening Ceremony	Monday 18th January (6.00pm)
Mascot:	Closing Ceremony	Sunday 24th January (4.00pm)
	Officially Opened by	Dr Kurt Waldheim (President of Austria)
None Known	Stadium	Innsbruck Olympic Ice Stadium (Opening and Closing Ceremonies)
	Flame Lit by	Josef Meusberger + Brigitte Rajchl (Alpine Skiers)
	Athlete's Oath	Josef Griel (Athletics + Table Tennis (Summer Games) + Ice Sledge Hockey)

Participating Nations (22): Australia, Austria, Belgium, Canada, Czechoslovakia, Denmark, Finland, France, Great Britain, Italy, Japan,

Netherlands, New Zealand, Norway, Poland, Spain, Sweden, Switzerland, United States, **USSR**, West Germany, Yugoslavia. **(Countries in bold are those appearing at a winter Paralympic Games for the first time)**

Sports (4): Alpine, Biathlon, Cross Country, Ice Sledge Speed Racing.

Impairment Groups (5): Amputees, Blind and Visually Impaired, Cerebral Palsied, Les Autres and Spinal Cord Injuries.

Logo: The logo used in 1988 was exactly the same as used in 1984. It was a combination of three parts. The centre of the logo shows a stylised depiction of the Goldenes Dachl (Golden Roof) – one of Innsbruck's most famous landmarks. Above this was the Olympic rings, which the IOC had agreed to the use of based upon certain conditions (see chapter 10). Below the Golden Dachl was five broken rings aimed at depicting the disability of the participants taking part. It also contained the words 'Under the patronage of the International Olympic Committee' beneath the Olympic rings.

Bids: None. Innsbruck requested to host the Games after the refusal of the Calgary Olympic Organisers to host and lack of any other bids.

The Selection of Innsbruck as the Host City

Due to organisational problems with the Calgary 1988 Organising Committee, bought about by an apparent lack of manpower, it was not possible to hold the Paralympic winter Games at the same venue as the 1988 Olympic Winter Games as was to be the case with the summer Games in Seoul. Innsbruck was finally persuaded to step in and organise the Games for a second consequetive time. The contract for the Games was finally signed between members of the ICC governing body and the Organising Committee of the IVth World Winter Games for the Disabled, represented by Secretary General Bertl Neumann and Treasurer Helmut Heiseler, in Arnhem on June 19th 1987.

The Games Poster

The Games Opening Ceremony

As with the opening and closing ceremonies at earlier winter Paralympic Games little is known about the ceremonies for the 1988 Innsbruck winter Paralympic Games. The opening ceremony took place on Monday 18th January, starting at 6.00pm. The Games were officially opened by Dr Kurt Waldheim, President of Austria at the time, and the ceremonies took place in the Innsbruck Olympic Ice Stadium, as they had four years earlier. The Paralympic flame was lit by Josef Meusberger and Brigitte Rajchl, two Austrian Alpine Skiers and the athletes' oath was taken by Josef Griel, who was an Ice Sledge Hockey player in Innsbruck and had previously competed for Austria in the summer Games in both Athletics and Table Tennis.

The Games Themselves

A total of 377 athletes from 22 nations competed in 96 medal events over 4 sports with Biathlon being added to the programme for the first time. Competitors shot twice from the prone position using air rifles on a 10 metre range whilst completing the 7.5km course. Sit-skiing was also introduced as another event in both the Alpine and Nordic competitions. As happened in 1984 there was a major shortage of snow in the valleys and mountains of medium altitude surrounding Innsbruck. The organisers were, therefore, forced to put in a great deal of work to move the alpine and Nordic events to venues at a higher altitude. The Nordic events were moved from Natters to Seefeld and the alpine events were moved from Mutter to Pfriemesköpfl. Even then snow had to be transported in order to complete the Nordic track in Seefeld.

An American cross country skier in action in Seefeld

The venues used for the four sports on the programme in 1988 were, therefore, as follows:

Innsbruck Olympic Ice Stadium: Ice Sledge Speed Racing
Pfriemesköpfl (moved from Mutter):   Alpine Skiing
Seefeld (moved from Natters):   Biathlon, Cross Country Skiing

Once again the Games were attended by Queen Silvia of Sweden who attended both the Nordic events in Seefeld and the alpine events in Pfriemesköpfl, continuing a keen interest in sport for the disabled that had begun with the hosting of the very first winter Paralympic Games in Örnsköldsvik, Sweden in 1976, when HRH King Carl Gustaf of Sweden was the patron.

The Outstanding Performers in Innsbruck

The most successful athlete in Innsbruck was Norway's Knut Lundstroem who won 3 gold medals in cross country events and 4 gold medals in Ice Sledge Speed Racing over 100m, 500m, 1000m and 1500m, making 7 gold medals in total. For the women Norway's Ragnild Myklebust won 2 gold medals in cross country events and 3 gold medals in Ice Sledge Speed Racing making 5 gold medals in total.

The Winners Medal

Miguel Angel Perez Tello (ESP) with one of his two silver medals for cross country skiing

The Closing Ceremony

Currently nothing is known about the closing ceremony other than that it took place in the Innsbruck Olympic Ice Stadium on Sunday 24th January commencing at 4.00pm.

The Final Medal Table

Rank	NPC	Gold	Silver	Bronze	Total
1	Norway	25	21	14	60
2	Austria	20	10	14	44
3	Fed. Rep. of Germany	9	11	10	30
4	Finland	9	8	8	25
5	Switzerland	8	7	8	23
6	USA	7	17	6	30
Number of Countries winning a medal					15
% of participating countries winning a medal					68.2

Games Trivia

Despite being unable to host the 4th winter Paralympic Games themselves the organizing committee of the winter Olympic Games in Calgary, Canada did agree to the second alpine and first ever cross country skiing exhibition events for athletes with a disability one month later. (For results please see appendix 2)

Despite the fact that Biathlon and sit-skiing events were added to the programme the number of participants (419 to 377) and the number of medal events (107 to 96) actually decreased from four years previously. Ted Fay attributes this to nations instigating high qualifying standards to their national teams combined with an overall increase in the skill and competitiveness within the various racing groups.

References

Brittain, I., 2008, The Evolution of the Paralympic Games in Cashman, R. et al, Benchmark Games: The Sydney 2000 Paralympic Games; Walla Walla Press, Petersham, NSW, p. 19-34.

Fay, T., 2011, Winter Paralympic Games: Founding Legacies 1984 – 1988 in Legg, D. & Gilbert, K., Paralympic Legacies, Commonground Publishing; Champaign, Il., p. 173-180.

International Sports Organisation for the Disabled Newsletter, 1988, No.1. (Author Copy)

Chapter 14: Seoul, South Korea 1988

'United For The Challenge'

Logo:	Confirmed Participating Nations	60
	Confirmed Participating Athletes	3059 (2380 men, 679 women)
	Number of Events	732
	Opening Ceremony	Saturday 15th October (2.40pm)
	Closing Ceremony	Monday 24th October (5.20pm)
Mascot: Gomdoori	Officially Opened by	President Roh Tae-Woo
	Main Stadium	Olympic Stadium
	Flame Lit by	Lee Jae-Woon (Blind Athlete) (assisted by Kim Hyun Mee – Olympic Handball Gold Medallist)
	Athlete's Oath	Kim So-Boo (Table Tennis)
	Official's Oath	Chung Bong-Soo (Athletics official)

Participating Nations (60): Argentina, Australia, Austria, Bahamas, Bahrain, Belgium, Brasil, **Bulgaria**, Canada, China, Colombia, **Cyprus**, Czechoslovakia, Denmark, Egypt, Faroe Islands, Federal Republic of Germany, Finland, France, Great Britain, Greece, Guatemala, Hong Kong, Hungary, Iceland, India, Indonesia, **Iran**, Ireland, Israel, Italy, Jamaica, Japan, Jordan, Kenya, Kuwait, Liechtenstein, **Macao**, Malaysia, Mexico, **Morocco**, Netherlands, New Zealand, Norway, **Oman**, Philippines, Poland, Portugal, **Puerto Rico**, **Singapore**, South Korea, Spain, Sweden, Switzerland, Thailand, Trinidad & Tobago, **Tunisia**, United States, **United Soviet Socialist Republic**, Yugoslavia. **(Countries in bold are those appearing at a summer Paralympic Games for the first time)**

NB. A Libyan team, who had not gone through the proper entry procedures arrived in Seoul after the Games commenced and were allowed to take part as observers and participate in the Marathon without entitlement to medals and the closing ceremony without acknowledgement of their presence.

Sports (17 + 1 Demonstration Sport): Archery, Athletics, Boccia, Cycling, Football (7-a-side), Goalball, Judo, Lawn Bowls, Powerlifting, Shooting, Snooker, Swimming, Table Tennis, Volleyball (Sitting & Standing), Weightlifting, Wheelchair Basketball, Wheelchair Fencing, Wheelchair Tennis (Demonstration). **Impairment Groups (5)**: Amputees, Blind & Visually Impaired, Cerebral Palsied, Les Autres, Spinal Cord Injuries

Logo: The logo was designed by Sung Nak-hoon and consisted of five traditional Korean decorative motifs known as tae-geuks, which were meant to represent the five oceans and the five continents. They were arranged in a 'W' configuration meant to represent the first letter of the word 'World' in order to represent the harmony and unity of the disabled worldwide through sport. Their horizontal configuration represented equality and humanity, and the wave shape expressed the willingness and determination of the disabled to become fully active.

Mascot: According to the organisers of the Seoul Paralympic Games bears are well known for their courage and their wisdom and are depicted in the star constellations known as the Great Bear and the Little Bear. The two 'moon-bears' as the organisers describe them, are depicted with the legs tied together in order to show that all mankind can live together peacefully and vigorously whilst still co-operating with each other fully. The Gomdoori, as they were named, were meant to depict the grand celebration of human achievement and accomplishment that the organisers envisaged the Seoul Paralympic Games would be.

The Gomdoori mascots posing with some of the competitors.

The Selection of Seoul as the Host City

There were initially two expressions of interest in hosting the 1988 Paralympic Games. Both Mr Whang from South Korea and Dr Grant from Australia gave outlines of possible bids from their respective organisations at the fourth meeting of the International Co-ordinating Committee (ICC) held at the Civic Centre in Aylesbury, UK on 28th July 1983. However, by the time the sixth meeting of ICC was held in New York on 14th June 1984 only South Korea had followed up its expression of interest with a firm bid and so it was that subject to satisfactory completion of a specially designed ICC questionnaire Seoul was officially awarded the right to host the 1988 summer Paralympic Games.

The Games Poster

The Games Opening Ceremony

The opening ceremony took place on Saturday 15th October and commenced in the Olympic stadium at 2.40pm with twenty minutes of events including 'The blessing of the Heaven' and 'The Festival of Drums'. At 3.00pm the official part of the ceremony began with a Paralympic fanfare and the entry of the President of the Republic of Korea, Roh Tae-Woo. Following the parade of athletes the new ICC flag, which would cause much controversy in the coming years, was handed over to Jens Bromann, Acting President of the International Co-ordinating Committee. Following the customary speeches Roh Tae-Woo declared the Games officially open. The honour of lighting the Paralympic flame went to blind athlete Lee Jae-Woon, who was guided in his task by Kim Hyun Mee – an Olympic handball gold medallist.

Lee Jae-Woon lighting the flame (assisted by Kim Hyun Mee)

The Paralympic oath on behalf of the athletes was then taken by table tennis player Kim So-Boo. Following the Korean National Anthem the athletes exited the stadium to designated seats and at 4.20pm the opening ceremony concluded with a series of cultural and musical displays aimed at beginning the Games through peace and friendship and filling everyone's hearts with joy and excitement.

Kim So-Boo taking the Athlete's Oath Chung Bong-Soo (right), an athletics official, waits to take the official's oath

The Games Themselves

Bailey (2008) describes the games in Seoul as 'the first Paralympic Games of the modern era'. For the first time since 1964 in Tokyo they were returning to the same host city and venues as the Olympic Games - a tradition that has continued ever since. Unfortunately they were not able to use the Olympic village. Instead the athletes were accommodated in ten specially designed accessible apartment blocks, each of fourteen stories. Architects from the city of Seoul visited Stoke Mandeville to discuss their plans, which included three buildings for the exclusive use of wheelchair users. This initially caused some concern to ICC having had previous experience of the time taken to evacuate wheelchair users from a building of many stories, but the architects got round this by fitting outside ramps from the fourteenth floor of each of the three buildings that where easily negotiable. The Paralympic village also included provision for catering, recreation, banking, post office, medical and religious centres and a shopping mall. Wheelchair Tennis was added as a demonstration sport. The sports events were held at four venues:

Chamsil Gymnasium:	Goalball, Swimming, Wheelchair Basketball
Chung-Nip Polio Centre:	Boccia, Snooker
Olympic Park:	Athletics, Cycling, Powerlifting, Swimming, Table Tennis, Weightlifting, Wheelchair Tennis
Sangmu Sports Complex:	Archery, Football, Judo, Lawn Bowls, Shooting, Volleyball, Wheelchair Fencing

The Seoul Olympic Park

On the whole the Games in Seoul ran smoothly, although communication difficulties sometimes arose and the queues for food in the Paralympic village were a daily problem that was never really solved. However, the biggest problem to plague the Games was the cancellation of events after teams had arrived in Seoul, mainly because not enough participants had entered or classification issues led to withdrawals. This led to a meeting of team managers after which a letter of protest signed by 17 of the national team managers was sent to the ICC Paralympic Committee Chairman Colin Rains protesting at the fact that such a large number of events had been cancelled after the teams had arrived in Seoul. The letter demanded that the events be reinstated regardless of the number of competitors. ICC issued a statement in support of the athletes and stated that everything possible would be done to minimise event cancellations.

Letting a visually impaired swimmer know they are nearing the turn

Also included in the Paralympic programme for Seoul was a grand festival of art and cultural activities ranging from exhibitions of Korean sculpture, paintings, handicrafts and culinary art to performances of dance, music, singing and theatre.

The Outstanding Performers in Seoul

Without a doubt the outstanding performer at the Seoul Paralympic Games was Trischa Zorn, a partially sighted swimmer from the USA, who won an incredible ten individual and two relay gold medals in the pool. This feat of twelve gold medals at a Paralympic Games had never been achieved previously nor has it been repeated since. Michael Edgson, a partially sighted swimmer from Canada also had an outstanding Games winning seven individual and two relay gold medals. Away from the pool the most outstanding performer in Seoul was Candace Cable-Brooks, a paraplegic track athlete, who won three individual and two relay gold medals.

Canada bronze medallists in the men's goalball team competition

The Winners Medal

The Games Closing Ceremony

The closing ceremony for the Seoul Paralympic Games took place on Monday 24th October commencing at 5.20pm with a ten minute presentation of a Korean Fantasy, which was followed by the entry of the athletes into the stadium led by 150 flag bearers. The Prime Minister of the Republic of Korea, Lee Hyun-Jae, then made a farewell speech followed by the hoisting of the national flags of Korea and the next Paralympic hosts, Spain. Following spectacular presentations of the 'Ojak Bridge' and 'Parting Ships' Koh Kwi-Nam, President of the Seoul Paralympic Organising Committee and Jens Bromann of ICC gave farewell speeches before handing over the Paralympic flag to Manuel Fonseca from the Spanish National Sports Association for the Disabled representing the hosts of the next Games in Barcelona. Finally the Paralympic flame was slowly extinguished before the final ten minute performance of the night ended with the words 'See you in Barcelona 1992' flashing on the giant electronic scoreboard.

Problems with the Paralympic Logo

It is interesting to note that in the description of the new logo described at the beginning of this chapter neither the Seoul Organising Committee nor the International Paralympic Committee (IPC), who adopted this logo as the logo for the Paralympic movement shortly after the Games, make any mention of the colours used for the tae-geuks, nor the similarity of the logo to the IOC five rings logo and it was this that was to led them into conflict with the IOC. The British Paralympic team for Seoul and the British Paralympic Association, formed in 1989, where amongst the first to incorporate the logo into their own. However, sometime in 1990 the British Olympic Association contacted the IOC pointing out the similarity between the IPC logo and the IOC logo. This lead to the IOC contacting the IPC in January 1991 to express their concerns that the five tae-geuk logo was confusingly similar to the Olympic symbol and requesting that IPC change their logo. The IOC Director of Legal Affairs, Howard M. Strupp made it clear that unless the matter was cleared up to the total satisfaction of the IOC a recommendation would be made to the IOC Executive Board with regard to sanctions to be taken by the IOC against IPC.

This left the IPC Executive Board in a very tricky situation as they were partly reliant on the funding that the IOC were now providing them with and in addition they did not want to jeopardise the working relationship they had recently forged. They, therefore, recommended a change in the logo 'in the spirit of co-operation' with the IOC. However, at the IPC General Assembly in Budapest in 1991 the member nations rejected a change of logo and decided to retain the current logo. The mood amongst the nations appears to have been that they felt they were being dictated to by the IOC rather than there being any kind of true co-operation on both sides. The decision of the general assembly did not go down well with the IOC or other National Olympic Committees worldwide, many of whom wrote to the IOC expressing their concerns over the impact this might have on marketing and sponsorship programmes. Following several meetings and negotiations with the IOC, the last of which occurred on May 4th 1992 the management committee of IPC concluded that they had no option other than to design a new logo, which they forwarded to the member nations for support and which was apparently, on the whole, favourably received. However, it appears that some individuals were still not happy with the actions of the IOC and members of one national Paralympic team produced tee shirts that they intended to wear in protest at the Closing Ceremony of the Barcelona Games in 1992. In the end their protest plans were discovered prior to the closing ceremony and they were prevented from carrying them out for fears of possible bad publicity that might ensue and the potential damage that might be caused to the relationship with the IOC. Given that the IOC had only really discovered the true value of their brand at the Los Angeles 1984 Games and had been extremely short of money prior to this their reaction is possibly understandable. However, it should be noted that these events occurred at a time when the social model of disability was beginning to have a major impact on the disabled population, particularly in the West, and political activism in order to gain fair and equal access to society amongst the disabled community was becoming far more widespread.

Front of Barcelona protest tee-shirt

Reverse of Barcelona protest tee-shirt

The Final Medal Table

Rank	NPC	Gold	Silver	Bronze	Total
1	United States	92	90	91	273
2	Fed. Rep. Germany	76	66	51	193
3	Great Britain	65	65	54	184
4	Canada	54	42	55	151
5	France	47	44	49	140
6	Sweden	42	38	23	103
Number of Countries winning a medal					49
% of participating countries winning a medal					81.7

Games Trivia

Seoul was the first Paralympic Games the Soviet Union had ever taken part in. Team manager, Olga Bogdanova, put their participation down to the broad social changes and re-structuring going on in the Soviet Union at the time under the leadership of Mikhail Gorbachev. However, the team consisted only of 22 blind athletes as sport for other disabilities was not yet properly developed within the Soviet Union.

The Games cost a total of $28,637,142 and made a profit of $1,324,286, which was used to found a Sports Association for the Disabled within South Korea.

The Iranian goalball team was disqualified and sent home from the Games for refusing to play against Israel in a group round game.

The largest team in Seoul was the one from the USA with 376 athletes and 119 staff members.

References

British Paralympic Association, 1989, Celebratory Handbook of the Seoul Paralympics (Author Copy)

Letter dated 16th October 1988 addressed to Mr Colin Rains, Chairman of the ICC Paralympics Committee signed by Mary Margaret Newsom, USA team manager on behalf of seventeen national Paralympic team managers (Author facsimile copy)

Seoul Paralympic Newsletters Nos. 1-12 (Friday 14th – Tuesday 25th October 1988)

Seoul Paralympic Organising Committee, 1989, The 8th Seoul Paralympics: Share in Love to the World, SPOC, South Korea.

Seoul Paralympic Organising Committee, 1989, The Final Report of the Seoul Paralympics Organizing Committee Submitted to the ICC (Author Copy)

Chapter 15: Tignes—Albertville, France 1992

Logo:	Confirmed Participating Nations	24
	Confirmed Participating Athletes	365 (288 Men, 77 Women)
	Number of Events	79
	Opening Ceremony	Wednesday 25th March (4.00pm)
	Closing Ceremony	Wednesday 1st April (5.00pm)
Mascot: Alpy	Officially Opened by	President Francois Mitterand
	Stadium	Lognan Stadium
	Flame Lit by	Luc Sabatier (Nordic Skiing) (assisted by Fabrice Guy)
	Athlete's Oath	Ludovic Rey-Robert (Alpine Skiing)
	Official's Oath	Unknown female[5]

Participating Nations (24): Australia, Austria, Belgium, Canada, Czechoslovakia, Denmark, **Estonia**, Finland, France, **Germany**, Great Britain,

---

[5] If anyone knows the name of the lady that took the official's oath please e-mail parahist@hotmail.co.uk

Italy, Japan, **Liechtenstein**, Netherlands, New Zealand, Norway, Poland, **South Korea**, Spain, Sweden, Switzerland, United States, **Unified Team. (Countries in bold are those appearing at a winter Paralympic Games for the first time)**

Sports (3): Alpine, Biathlon and Cross Country.

Impairment Groups (6): Amputees, Blind and Visually Impaired, Cerebral Palsied, Intellectually Disabled*, Les Autres and Spinal Cord Injuries.

*Demonstration events where held for athletes with an intellectual disability in men's and women's giant slalom, 2.5km cross country for women and 5km cross country for men.

Logo: A bird with broken wings, soaring high across the peak of a mountain was the image, designed by Jean-Michel Folon, used to reflect the sporting abilities of the athletes at the Tignes-Albertville 1992 Paralympic Winter Games.

Mascot: The official mascot, Alpy, designed by Vincent Thiebaut, represented the summit of the Grande Motte mountain in Tignes. Alpy was shown on a mono-ski to demonstrate its athleticism and the colours of white, green and blue were used to represent purity/snow, hope/nature and discipline/the lake.

The selection of Tignes as the Host City

On 16th October 1986 at the IOC session in Lausanne, Switzerland Albertville in France was awarded the right to host the 1992 winter Olympic Games. Almost a year earlier in November 1985 André Auberger, President of the French Sport Federation for the Disabled, had written to Michel Barnier, President of the French Olympic bid committee, to request that they also consider hosting the Paralympic Games should their Olympic bid be successful. On November 3rd 1986 Barnier confirmed his support to the request and on 31st January 1987 at the meeting of the International Co-ordinating Committee in Copenhagen, Denmark the right to host the 1992 winter Paralympic Games was awarded to France. The contract was finally signed on 22nd April 1989.

Signing of the contract for the Tignes winter Paralympic Games

The Games Poster

The Games Opening Ceremony

The opening ceremony for the Tignes winter Paralympic Games commenced at 4.00pm on Wednesday 25th March at the foot of the main competition pistes for the Games. Guest of Honour for the ceremony was President of the French Republic Francois Mitterand who arrived at 5.00pm. The delegations entered the arena in French alphabetical order and every 45 seconds a para-glider in the colours of each country descended into the arena and spread out in front of the delegations. Short speeches by the President of the ICC Jens Broman and the French President were followed by the official opening of the Games by President Mitterand. This was followed by the entrance of the Paralympic flame and the lighting of the Olympic cauldron by French Nordic skier Luc Sabatier assisted by Fabrice Guy. The athletes and officials oaths were then taken by Ludovic Rey-Robert on behalf of the athletes and a currently unknown female official. This was followed by an aerobatic display by six hang-gliders over the stadium to music by French composer Michel Colombier, choreographed by American dancer Dany Ezralow with the harmonica solo being performed by Belgian musician Toots Thielemans. The ceremony ended with the release of balloons to the strains of 'The Ode to Joy' followed by the exit of the team delegations.

The entry of the ICC flag at the Opening Ceremony

The Paralympic Cauldron in Tignes

The Games Themselves

Despite being badged as Tignes-Albertville in all publicity material the fifth winter Paralympic Games actually only took place in Tignes. The fact that the Games only took place in Tignes where there were no ice sport venues, combined with an apparent lack of entries from the nations in ice sport events, meant that only Alpine and Nordic events were held. A total of 365 athletes from 24 nations competed in 79 medal events. For the first time, demonstration events in Alpine and Nordic Skiing for athletes with an intellectual disability and Biathlon for the visually impaired were added to the programme. In addition, this was the first time at a Winter Paralympics that the athletes were all accommodated in an Athlete's Village as opposed to hotels, which had been the case at previous winter Games.

The Games were officially opened by French President Francois Mitterand with the Opening Ceremony and all other ceremonial events being held in front of the finish area for the Alpine Skiing events. This area was named the Lognan Stadium. The Games were covered by 300 journalists and 15 reporters from various television channels. According to the Official Report the Games cost 41,638,810.98 French Francs and actually made a small profit of 392,471.73 French Francs.

Cross country skiing in Tignes

Demonstration Events for Intellectually Disabled Athletes

Women's Giant Slalom
1. Isabelle Redler (FRA) 0.56.46s
2. Barbara Procesi (ITA)   1.47.69

Mens Giant Slalom
1. Norbert Cornero (FRA) 0.44.94
2. Christian Deschaeck (FRA) 0.46.10
3. Michel Jolliet (SUI) 0.46.63

Women's 2.5km Cross Country
1. Ginette Sassignol (FRA) 13.53.1
2. Brigitte Affolter (SUI) 15.45.4
3. Katharina Pliger (ITA) 17.42.3
4. Manuela Arnoldi (AUT) 18.25.4

Men's 5km Cross Country
1. Georges Baralon (FRA) 19.50.0
2. Denis Pichon (FRA) 24.19.5
3. Urs Braun (SUI) 26.56.1
4. Helmutt Thaler (ITA) 26.58.2
5. Thoni Leitner (ITA)29.50.3
6. Rainer Gsthohl (AUT) 34.59.9
7. Christian Bourquin (SUI) 36.46.0
8. Michael Berkmann (AUT) 41.39.
9. Diethar Schreiber (AUT) 49.31.7

The Outstanding Performers in Tignes

The outstanding performer in Tignes was Reinhild Moeller of Germany in the women's Alpine Skiing events who skied to four gold medals. Frank Hoefle, also of Germany, won three gold and 1 silver medal in the Cross Country and Biathlon events. Four other skiers left Tignes with three gold medals each. Nancy Gustafson (USA) and Gerd Schoenfelder (GER) both won three gold in the Alpine Skiing events. Nikolai Ilioutchenko (EUN) and Valeri Kouptchinski (EUN) won three gold medals in the Cross Country Skiing events.

The Winners Medal

Medal ceremony for the Men's slalom LW 3/1/5/7/9 Medals presented by ICC Secretary-General Joan Scruton

The Closing Ceremony

The closing ceremony for the Tignes winter Paralympic Games commenced at 5.00pm on Wednesday 1st April at the foot of the main competition pistes for the Games. The ceremony was attended by Michel Gillibert, State Secretary to the Handicapped and Life Injured, paralysed French sailor Florence Arthaud, who acted as Godmother to the French Paralympic team in Tignes, the Mayor of Lillehammer, hosts to the next winter Paralympic Games in 1994 and representatives from COPTA, ICC and Tignes. The closing ceremony was a simple affair. There was a parade of nations and a descent of all the medal winners together. The ceremony concluded with the extinguishing of the flame and the take-off of a deltaplane bearing the broken-winged bird 'Folon' symbol, which flew away into the distance.

The Final Medal Table

Rank	NPC	Gold	Silver	Bronze	Total
1	USA	20	16	9	45
2	Germany	12	17	9	38
3	Unified Team	10	8	3	21
4	Austria	8	3	9	20
5	Finland	7	3	4	14
6	France	6	4	9	19
Number of Countries winning a medal					19
% of participating countries winning a medal					79.2

Games Trivia

Tignes was the first winter Paralympic Games to carry out doping tests. A total of 36 tests were carried out by a doctor accredited by the French Youth and Sports State Ministry and analysed at the National Doping Detection Laboratory (LAFARGE), which was the only IOC accredited laboratory in France at that time.

Michael Milton won Australia's first ever gold medal at an Olympic or Paralympic winter Games when he won the LW2 Slalom event. The press centre in Tignes was inundated with faxes of congratulations from Australia including one from Australian Prime Minister Paul Keating.

Soviet athlete, Alexei Moshkin was disqualified at the beginning of the week when he missed the start because he couldn't find his guide. The plight of the heartbroken and tearful Moshkin touched the volunteer drivers to the extent that they presented him with a selection of local products including Savoie wine, sausage, ham, champagne and a bottle of brandy.

The IOC and ICC flags were stolen from the arena the day before the downhill events started.

A (clearly French speaking) joker changed the TIGNES sign on the wall at the entrance to the Lognan Stadium to SINGE, which means monkey!

References

Gouby, A. & Fleutiaux, J-P., 1993, 1992 – Tignes – Albertville Vth Paralympic Games Final Report, COPTA; France.

La Gazette des V[es] Jeux Paralympiques de Tignes-Albertville, Vols 1-10 (Author copies)

Chapter 16: Barcelona, Spain 1992

'Sport Without Limits'

Logo:	Confirmed Participating Nations	82 + 13 'Independent Paralympic Participants'
	Confirmed Participating Athletes	3001 (2301 Men, 700 Women)
	Number of Events	489
	Opening Ceremony	Thursday 3rd September (6.00pm)
	Closing Ceremony	Monday 14th September (8.00pm)
Mascot: Petra 	Officially Opened by	HM Queen Sophia of Spain
	Stadium	Estadi Olympic di Montjuic
	Flame Lit by	Antonio Rebollo (Archer) (via Bow and Arrow)
	Athlete's Oath	José Manuel Rodríguez Ibáñez (Athlete)
	Official's Oath	Unknown female official[6]

---

[6] If anyone knows the name and sport of this female official please e-mail parahist@hotmail.co.uk

Participating Nations (82) + Independent Paralympic Athletes (13): Algeria, Argentina, Australia, Austria, Bahrain, Belgium, Brasil, Bulgaria, Burkino Faso, Canada, Chile, China, Chinese Taipei, Colombia, Commonwealth of Independent States (Unified Team), Costa Rica, Croatia, Cuba, Cyprus, Czech and Slovak Federal Republic, Denmark, Dominican Republic, Ecuador, Egypt, Estonia, Faroe Islands, Finland, France, Germany, Great Britain, Greece, Hong Kong, Hungary, Iceland, India, Iran, Iraq, Ireland, Israel, Italy, Jamaica, Japan, Kenya, Kuwait, Latvia, Liechtenstein, Lithuania, Luxembourg,   Macao, Malaysia, Mexico, Morocco, Myanmar, Namibia, Netherlands, New Zealand, Nigeria, Norway, Oman, Pakistan, Panama, Poland, Portugal, Puerto Rico, Seychelles, Singapore, Slovenia, South Africa,   South Korea,   Spain, Sweden, Switzerland, Syria, Tanzania, Thailand, Tunisia, Turkey, United Arab Emirates, United States, Uruguay, Venezuela, Yemen   + Independent Paralympic Athletes (Adzic, Slobodan; Aleksov, Ruzica; Dereta, Zeljko; Dimitrijevic, Svetislav; Djurasinovic, Ilija; Jokovic, Spasoje; Jovanovski, Branimir; Kecman, Simo; Kesler, Zlatko; Krisanovic, Nenad; Rakonjac, Radomir; Velimirovic, Gorica; Vuksanovic, Nada). **(Countries in bold are those appearing at a summer Paralympic Games for the first time)**

Independent Paralympic Participants Tihomir Bogdanovic (Men's Long Jump B2), Miroslav Jancic (Men's Discus B1) and Ljubomir Timotijevic (Men's Shot B2) did not start the events they were entered in and, therefore, cannot be considered to have participated in Barcelona.

Sports (16): Archery, Athletics, Boccia, Cycling, Football (7-a-side), Goalball, Judo, Powerlifting, Shooting, Swimming, Table Tennis, Volleyball (Sitting & Standing),   Weightlifting,   Wheelchair   Basketball,   Wheelchair   Fencing, Wheelchair Tennis.

Impairment Groups (5): Amputees, Blind & Visually Impaired, Cerebral Palsied, Les Autres, Spinal Cord Injuries

Logo: Designed by Josep Maria Trias, the logo was, according to the organising committee, 'a symbolic and figurative design, dynamic in form and strongly Mediterranean in character'. It was based upon a symbolic depiction of a human figure using a wheelchair and the colours are meant to represent the blue of the Mediterranean, the yellow of the sun and the red of life itself.

Mascot: Petra, as the mascot was called, was designed by Javier Mariscal. Petra was designed to appear as a friendly-looking, cheerful character who apparently 'is clever, extroverted, thinks for herself and has many friends. She is a little stubborn, has an impressive store of inner energy and never cries'.

The Selection of Barcelona as the Host City

Following the choice of Barcelona by the International Olympic Committee as the hosts of the XXV Olympiad Barcelona's candidature to host the IX Paralympic Games was unanimously approved by the ICC on 2nd August 1987 at their twelfth meeting in Aylesbury. In April 1989 the Barcelona Olympic Organising Committee created its own Paralympic division and on 20th July 1989 signed an agreement with ICC formalising their earlier commitment.

The Games Poster

On Thursday 3rd September Sixty-five thousand spectators packed into the Estadi Olympic to witness the Opening Ceremony for the Barcelona Paralympic Games. The 3 hour ceremony commenced at 6.00pm with a kiss blown to the spectators by a girl atop a human pyramid formed by the Falcons de Vilafranca. At the centre of the infield throughout the ceremony was an olive tree – Mediterranean symbol of victory and wisdom. The parade of nations was followed by speeches from Pasqual Maragall, Mayor of Barcelona, José María Arroyo, President of the ONCE Foundation and Guillermo Cabezas, President of the ICC. Her Majesty Queen Sofia of Spain then declared the Games officially open. This was the cue for the Paralympic flag to enter the stadium carried by eight Spanish athletes accompanied by the Paralympic anthem. The Paralympic flame then entered the stadium carried by single arm amputee José Santos Poyatos who passed it to Puri Santamarta, who ran with her guide dog, Dan. The flame was then passed to Neus Àlvarez Costa, an athlete with cerebral palsy who passed it onto Bertrand de Five Pranger. Betrand pushed his wheelchair up the slope of the stage to pass the flame to Antonio Rebollo, the Paralympic archer who had lit the Olympic cauldron and who repeated the task with his bow and arrow to light the Paralympic cauldron. The formal part of the ceremony was then completed by José Manuel Rodríguez Ibáñez who took the oath on behalf of the athletes and an unnamed female official who took the oath on behalf of the officials. The ceremony then concluded with some spectacular entertainment that included a personal message from Stephen Hawking and concluded with a pyro-musical finale.

José Manuel Rodríguez Ibáñez taking the oath on behalf of the athletes

Un-named female official taking the oath on behalf of the officials

The Games Themselves

Barcelona was the first Paralympic Games where the whole Games was totally computerised making results and medal tables instantly available in three languages (English, Spanish, Catalan) on five hundred touch-screen terminals around the village and venues. Sherrill (1993) claims this added an extra layer of nationalism to the Games by making medal counts instantly available and by giving instant access to statistics on opponents.

The swimming pool at Montjuic

The sports events in Barcelona were spread across five areas as follows:

Montjuic Area:	Athletics, Football (7-a-side), Judo, Powerlifting, Swimming, Table Tennis, Volleyball (Sitting & Standing), Weightlifting, Wheelchair Fencing
Parc de Mar Area:	Boccia
Vall d'Hebron Area:	Archery, Cycling, Goalball, Tennis
Badalona Area:	Wheelchair Basketball
Molle del Vallès Area:	Shooting

Unlike Korea four years previously the Paralympians in Barcelona used the same village as their Olympic counterparts. They used approximately 60% of the Olympic village and had the same housing, dining hall and recreational facilities.

Athletes relaxing in the Games village

In order to try and maintain the increasing credibility and quality of competition at the Paralympic Games the Barcelona organising committee introduced strict rules and regulations on eligibility. Despite the controversy this caused at the time this ultimately led to a simplified and higher level of competition than ever before and allowed for athletes with different disabilities to compete in the same events. This was not without controversy, however, and led to either the deletion of events or meant that some athletes had to compete in events that they simply had no chance of winning. Cerebral Palsied athletes were particularly badly hit, partly because sport for cerebral palsied athletes was not as well developed as other groups and partly because of differing political power between the IOSDs within ICC meant some were in a stronger position than others when decisions on event eligibility were made. This particularly hit those in the most disabled categories. A campaign 'DeletedButNotDefeated' was started that eventually led to a one hour exhibition athletics event being allowed to take place in the daily afternoon break on Thursday 10th September. However, the stadium was virtually empty as no one was told the event was taking place and the loud speakers and electronic scoreboards were switched off for the break making information about winners very hard to access.

Wheelchair Tennis, which had been a demonstration event in Seoul four years earlier, became an official medal sport and was dominated by America and the Netherlands taking two gold medals each.

The Table Tennis venue

The growing recognition of the Paralympic Games was reinforced by the presence of Juan Antonio Samaranch, President of the International Olympic Committee at the Opening Ceremony.

The Outstanding Performers in Barcelona

Once again, for the third Games in a row the undoubted star of the show in Barcelona was Trischa Zorn (USA), a visually impaired swimmer, who won eight individual and two relay gold medals as well as two silver medals. Two other Americans, John Morgan and Bart Dodson, also put in outstanding performances in the pool and on the track respectively, both leaving Barcelona with eight gold medals a piece. These three alone won nearly one-third of the Americans table topping gold medal count. On the track Adeoye Ajibola of Nigeria, a single-arm amputee, stunned the watching crowd in the 100m event by winning in a world record 10.72 seconds. He then went on to win the 200m event, setting yet another world record.

The Winners Medal

The Games Closing Ceremony

On Monday 14th September the Closing Ceremony of the IX Paralympic Games commenced at 8.00pm with a firework display. The ceremony included a brief presentation from the City of Atlanta as hosts for the 1996 Paralympic Games following the lowering and handing over of the Paralympic flag to Andrew Fleming, President of the Atlanta Paralympic Organising Committee. The ceremony was attended by King Juan Carlos and Queen Sofia, along with Princess Cristina and 45,000 other spectators. The capacity had been reduced by 20,000 due the area needed for the performers' stage. The athletes from all the nations were gathered on the infield from the beginning of the ceremony.

Athletes at the closing ceremony in a packed stadium

The Final Medal Table

Rank	NPC	Gold	Silver	Bronze	Total
1	USA	75	52	48	175
2	Germany	61	51	59	171
3	Great Britain	40	47	41	128
4	France	36	36	34	106
5	Spain	34	31	42	107
6	Canada	28	21	26	75
Number of Countries winning a medal					55
% of participating countries winning a medal					66.3

Games Trivia

American quadriplegic track racer Wiley Clark had been training for years towards Paralympic victory in the men's T2 400m and 800m track races in Barcelona. However, just one day before his events began Wiley was hit by a van whilst crossing the street near the Paralympic village in Barcelona and suffered a fractured rib and femur. After a week in Vall d'Hebron Hospital he was airlifted home by the United States Air Force. Whilst in hospital in Barcelona he was able to watch his chief rival, Rick Reelie from Canada take gold medals in both of his events.

Thirty-one of the eighty two national teams competing in Barcelona took no female athletes with them and male athletes made up nearly seventy-seven percent of the participants, showing that there was still a long way to go in developing sport for women with disabilities.

The Korean Boccia team of Lim Shin-Hyuk, Lee Jin-Woo and Lee Ki-Yean initially won the bronze medal against Ireland. However, at the medal ceremony after receiving their medals from Jack Weinstein of CP-ISRA, for reasons unrecorded, the Korean boccia players removed the medals from around their necks and threw them and the flowers they were presented with to the floor. This was done in full view of the spectators, press and television. At the ICC meeting held on 13th September the committee voted to ban the Koreans from further competition for life. However, the letter that went out following the vote stated that the Korean athletes would be banned from the next Paralympic Games. Because of this administrative error and the fact it was discussed at the very last ICC meeting in Larnaca, Cyprus, it was decided to hand the matter over to the boccia committee of the International Paralympic Committee.

The first three positive doping tests ever recorded at a Paralympic Games occurred in Barcelona. They were a shot putter, a judo player and a wheelchair basketball player from the USA, David Kiley, whose positive test for a banned substance led to the disqualification the American men's wheelchair basketball team who had won the gold medal in Seoul and a request for the whole team to return their medals in order that they could be re-distributed to the Dutch team they had beaten in the final.

References

British Paralympic Association, undated, The Official Celebratory Brochure of the 1992 Paralympic Games in Barcelona, Madrid and Tignes (Author copy)

British Paralympic Association, undated, A Report on the Paralympic Games Barcelona '92 (Author facsimile copy)

British Wheelchair Sports Foundation, undated, Wheelpower Paralympic Special (Author copy)

Fundación ONCE, 1993, Paralímpics '92: Barcelona 1992 IX Paralympic Games Official Report, Enciclopèdia Catalana, Spain.

Great Britain Paralympic Team Barcelona Newsletter, Sunday 30th August – Saturday 12th September 1992 (Author facsimile copy)

Reynolds, J., Stirk, A., Thomas, A. & Geary, F., 1994, Paralympics – Barcelona 1992, in the British Journal of Sports Medicine, 28(1); p. 14-17.

Sainsbury, A.J., 1993, Barcelona Paralympics 1992 Team Managers Report (Author Copy)

Sherrill, C., 1993, Paralympics 1992: Excellence and Challenge, Palaestra Vol. 9(1); p. 25-42.

Chapter 17: Madrid, Spain 1992

Logos:		
	Confirmed Participating Nations	75
	Confirmed Participating Athletes	~1600*
	Number of Events	68
	Opening Ceremony	Tuesday 15th September (5.00pm)
	Closing Ceremony	Tuesday 22nd September (5.00pm)
Mascot: Andy	Officially Opened by	Queen Sofia of Spain
	Main Stadium	Palacio de los Deportes de Madrid (For Opening and Closing Ceremonies)
	Flame Lit by	Coral Bistuer (Olympic Taekwondo Champion)
	Athlete's Oath	All athletes together in unison
	Official's Oath	None Known

*This number is an approximation based upon available information as no complete set of results or entry lists is currently available

Participating Nations (75): Algeria, Argentina, **Aruba**, Australia, Austria, Belgium, **Bolivia**, Brasil, Bulgaria, Canada, Chile, China, Commonwealth of Independent States (Unified Team), Colombia, Croatia, **Curacao**, Czech and Slovak Federal Republic, Denmark, Dominican Republic, Ecuador, Egypt, **El Salvador**, Estonia, Faroe Islands, Fiji, Finland, France, Germany, **Ghana**, Great Britain, Greece, Guatemala, **Honduras**, Hungary, Iceland, India, Ireland, Italy, **Ivory Coast**, Japan, Jordan, Kenya, Lebanon, Lithuania, Luxembourg, Malta, Mexico, Morocco, Namibia, Netherlands, **Nicaragua**, Nigeria, Panama, **Paraguay**, Peru, Philippines, Poland, Portugal, Puerto Rico, Romania, **Saudi Arabia**, **Sierra Leone**, Singapore, South Africa, South Korea, Spain, **Sri Lanka**, **Surinam**, Sweden, Tunisia, Turkey, United States, Uruguay, Venezuela, Zimbabwe. **(Countries in bold are those appearing at a summer Paralympic Games for the first time)**

Sports (5): Athletics, Basketball, Indoor Football, Swimming, Table Tennis.

Impairment Groups (1): Intellectually Disabled.

Logos: The Games in Madrid actually used two logos. The first was the five tae guk design first used in Seoul and was, at that time, the logo for the International Paralympic Committee. The second, based upon the five Olympic colours, depicts an energetic figure with arms raised as a sign of joy, triumph and happiness at the opportunity to take part in these Games and break the ribbon of that was meant to depict the barriers that had thus far prevented athletes with intellectual disabilities from participating in the Games.

Mascot: The mascot for the Games, ANDY, was a stylised heart meant to represent the heartiness, solidarity and friendship that would preside over the Games and which would keep beating towards full and complete integration of athletes with an intellectual disability at the next Paralympic Games in Atlanta four years later.

The Selection of Madrid as the Host City

The International Association of Sports for Persons with a Mental Handicap, which later became the International Association of Sports for Persons with Intellectual Disability (INAS-FID), were accepted into membership of the International Co-ordinating Committee at their 10th meeting held in Gothenburg in 1986. Although events for athletes with an intellectual disability were added to the programme for the Winter Games in Tignes the same year it was decided that a separate summer Games, sanctioned by ICC, would be held in Madrid immediately after the Games in Barcelona as part of their gradual inclusion into the overall Paralympic framework. It is clear from the literature available regarding the Paralympic Games that the Games in Madrid are rarely, if ever, recognised as a Paralympic Games. Even the International Paralympic Committee website makes no mention of these Games. However, the contract between ICC and IPC regarding control of all the Games that occurred in 1992 specifically refers to the Paralympic Games in Tignes, Barcelona AND Madrid. The issue of the inclusion of athletes from INAS-FMH in the Barcelona Paralympic Games was discussed at the ICC meeting held in Copenhagen from 27-29 March 1989. Following discussion in which representatives of ISMGF stated that admission to a Paralympic competition would be detrimental to the sports movement for the disabled a vote was held in which CISS, CP-ISRA, INAS-FMH and ISOD voted in favour of the participation of intellectually disabled athletes in Barcelona, but ISMGF voted against and IBSA abstained. As the vote had to unanimous the matter was tabled for the next meeting. That meeting was held in Aylesbury, England on 30-31 July 1989. In between these two meetings ISMGF, ISOD and IBSA had either held General Assemblies or Executive Board meetings at which it had been decided not to support the full inclusion of intellectually disabled athletes in Barcelona, although IBSA would accept demonstration events. The vote ended 3 in favour of their inclusion and 3 against and so the motion was lost. A second vote for the inclusion of demonstration events ended with 3 in favour, 1 against and two abstentions, but as the vote needed to be unanimous the motion was once again lost. Before the next ICC meeting in Barcelona from 27-28 January 1990 Mr Vicente, President of INAS-FMH made a request for ICC to sanction a Games under the Paralympic flag at a different venue and time to the Games in Barcelona. Mr Vicente stated that they were to be held in Madrid. After some discussion and with the blessing of the Barcelona Organising Committee a vote was held and the motion was carried unanimously.

The Games Poster[7]

Although the author has a good idea of what the poster for these Games looks like, from a photograph where the poster is hanging on the wall in the background, no original colour version of the poster has been located. The poster has the five tae guk logo at the top followed by the words 'Paralimpiada' and 'Madrid '92' (on two separate lines). There is a large picture of the Games Mascot ANDY running with the Olympic torch and the bottom quarter is logos and names of sponsoring organisations.

The Games Opening Ceremony

On 15th September the Paralympic Torch arrived in Madrid from Barcelona. The flame was received in the Puerta del Sol by Joaquin Leguina, President of the Autonomous Community of Madrid, from Paralympic athlete Miguel Cano. From here Olympic medallist Blanca Fernandez Ochoa carried it to City Hall where it was handed over to the Mayor, José Alvarez del Manzano. From City Hall the flame was carried by student athletes from local schools before finally arriving at the site of the Opening Ceremony in the Palacio de Deportes. The Opening ceremony was presided over by Her Majesty Queen Sofia of Spain, Honorary President of the Games and she was joined by Elias Harawi, first lady of Lebanon, Danuta Walesa, first lady of Poland, Juan Antonio Samaranch, President of the

---

[7] If anyone has a copy of this poster or knows the whereabouts of a copy please e-mail parahist@hotmail.co.uk

IOC, Fernando Martin Vicente, President of the Organising Committee, Joaquin Leguina, José Alvarez del Manzano and representatives of ICC.

Following some singing and other cultural entertainment the parade of the participants commenced with each appearing in alphabetical order (in Spanish) with the exceptions of Greece, who came first, and Spain who came last. This was followed by the entry of the Paralympic flag, carried by four female Olympic field hockey players Somia Barri, Maria Isabel Martinez, Maria Angeles Rodriguez and Virginia Ramirez. The flag was raised to the strains of the Paralympic anthem composed by Luis Cobos and was immediately followed by the entry of the Olympic torch carried by Fermin Cacho, Olympic 1500m gold medallist. He handed it to Coral Bistuer, Olympic and World Taekwondo champion whose job it was to light the flame. All the athletes then recited the Paralympic oath together in unison as follows:

> "In the name of all participants I swear we came to these Paralympic Games as loyal athletes, respectful of the rules that govern them, wishing to participate in them with a Knightly spirit, for the greater glory of sport and for the honour of our nations."

The Games Themselves

A total of seventy-five nations from all five continents gathered in Madrid for the Games to compete in sixty-eight events spread over five sports. The countries with the largest teams were Great Britain (92), Spain (88), Poland (68), France (61), Brazil (58), Australia (52) and Japan (52) and those with the smallest teams were Estonia (3), Peru, Namibia (1) and Curaçao. These figures, mostly taken from DePauw and Rich (1993), have been used to approximate the total number of athletes who participated in Madrid. The Games in Madrid also appear to have been partly hit by the fact the Special Olympics were due to be holding games in Barcelona that year. This appears to have caused some conflict, at least at the national level, in some countries as to which event they should attend. In the USA, where Special Olympics started they appear to have chosen to attend the event in Barcelona and it was only due to a special personal invitation from the President of the Madrid Organising Committee, Fernando Vicente Martin, that a team of eight athletes represented the USA in athletics and swimming in Madrid from Lee County, Florida. In the UK, following discussions between Special Olympics UK and the UK Sports Association for Persons with a Mental Handicap (the term in use at that time) they decided to send a large team to Madrid instead. The venues for the sports competitions were as follows:

Ciudad de los Poetas:	Basketball
Consejo Superior de Deportes:	Football, Table Tennis
La Emerita Sports Complex, University of Madrid:	Football
Piscina Mundial '86:	Swimming
Palacio de los Deportes:	Basketball Final
Polideportivo Dehesa de la Villa:	Basketball
Pistas INEF, Universidad Politécnica de Madrid:	Athletics

The Outstanding Performers in Madrid

The Australian men's swimming team was totally dominant in the pool, with Joseph Walker being the undoubted star winning nine gold medals (five individual, 4 relay) from nine events and setting two world records. However, this feat was equalled in the women's swimming events where Sigrun Huld of Iceland also took five individual and four relay gold medals. In the table tennis George Zlat of Romania in the men's events and Zhan Luo of China in the women's events both went home with three gold medals from the singles, doubles and team events. On the track Lorena Milichi of Uruguay also won three gold medals from the 400m, high jump and 4 x 100m relay. She also took silver in the 100m and bronze in the 200m.

The Winners Medal

The Games Closing Ceremony

The closing ceremony for the Games commenced at 5.00pm on Tuesday 22nd September at the Palacio de los Deportes de Madrid with the men's Basketball final between host nation Spain and the Dominican Republic. At half time in this game the medals were awarded for the winners of the football tournament. At the end of the men's basketball final the medals were awarded to the winning teams in the men's and women's basketball tournament. Once the medals had been awarded the closing ceremony proper began with the sounds of Japanese traditional drummers and a rhythmic gymnastics exhibition. This was followed by the parade of the national flags which eventually filled the floor of the stadium. Once all the flags were in place the Paralympic flag was lowered and the flame extinguished accompanied by the strains of the Hymn of Joy. The Games then concluded with a farewell party for all the participants.

The Final Medal Table

Rank	NPC	Gold	Silver	Bronze	Total
1	Australia	13	10	9	32
2	Romania	10	6	7	23
3	Iceland	10	6	6	22
4	Sweden	9	11	10	30
5	Uruguay	5	4	5	14
6	Spain	5	1	7	13
12	Great Britain	2	4	5	11
Number of Countries winning a medal					26
% of participating countries winning a medal					34.7

Games Trivia

The first three athletes with an intellectual disability to win medals in the history of the Paralympic Games were Joseph Walker (AUS) (Gold), Damian Huber (ARG) (Silver) and Joshua Hoffer (AUS) (Bronze) in the men's 200m freestyle swimming. The medals were presented by Jerry Wolsh and Wim Zonneveld, honorary members of INAS-FMH

In order to accommodate all those individuals from all over Spain who failed to qualify for the Paralympic Games in Madrid the organising committee set up a parallel Games in Madrid at the same time where young people from 32 sports organisations from all over Spain participated in the same five sports. Stressing participation all entrants received prizes and gifts. They also had their own official Opening Ceremony.

References

British Paralympic Association, undated, The Official Celebratory Brochure of the 1992 Paralympic Games in Barcelona, Madrid and Tignes (Author copy)

DePauw, K.P. and Rich, S., 1993, Paralympics for the Mentally Handicapped. Palaestra. Vol. 9:p. 59–64.

Fundacion ANDE, 1992, Paralympics Madrid 92, No. 37 (Author facsimile copy)

Fundacion ANDE, 1992, Paralympics Madrid 92, No. 31 (March) (Author copy)

Paralympic Madrid 92 Newsletter Monday 14th – Tuesday 22nd September 1992 (IPC Archives)

Chapter 18: Lillehammer, Norway 1994

'No Limits'

Logo:	Confirmed Participating Nations	31
Paralympics '94 Lillehammer	Confirmed Participating Athletes	471 (381 Men, 90 Women)
	Number of Events	133
	Opening Ceremony	Thursday 10th March (6.30pm)
Mascot: Sondre 	Closing Ceremony	Saturday 19th March (6.30pm)
	Officially Opened by	HM Queen Sonja
	Stadium	Håkon Hall (for Opening & Closing Ceremonies)
	Flame Lit by	Helge Bjørnstad (Ice Sledge Hockey)
	Athlete's Oath	Cato Zahl Pedersen (Alpine Skier)
	Official's Oath	Unknown[8]

Participating Nations (31): Australia, Austria, **Belarus**, Belgium, **Bulgaria**, Canada, **Czech Republic**, Denmark, Estonia, Finland, France, Germany, Great

---

[8] If anyone knows who took the official's oath please e-mail parahist@hotmail.co.uk

Britain, **Iceland**, Italy, Japan, **Kazakhstan**, **Latvia**, Liechtenstein, **Lithuania**, Netherlands, New Zealand, Norway, Poland, **Russia**, **Slovakia**, South Korea, Spain, Sweden, Switzerland, United States. **(Countries in bold are those appearing at a winter Paralympic Games for the first time)**

Sports (5): Alpine, Biathlon, Cross Country, Ice Sledge Hockey, Ice Sledge Speed Racing.

Impairment Groups (6): Amputees, Blind and Visually Impaired, Cerebral Palsied, Intellectually Disabled*, Les Autres and Spinal Cord Injuries.

*Demonstration events were held for athletes with an intellectual disability in men's 10km Cross Country Classical Technique and Women's 5km Cross Country Classical Technique

Logo: The main illustration, depicting the sun people, aimed to evoke feelings of power, vitality, strength and energy, all of which are characteristics of disabled athletes. This was the last time the five tae-guks was used in connection with the Paralympic Games or the International Paralympic Committee.

Mascot: Following a competition, an illustrator by the name of Tor Lindrupsen won with his children's drawing of Sondre. Sondre is apparently a friendly teenage troll boy who is charming, good-natured, elegant and poised despite having had his left leg amputated above the knee. The name for the mascot was chosen in a separate competition and derives from the great skiing pioneer Sondre Nordheim.

Sondre the Lillehammer Mascot

The Selection of Lillehammer as the Host City

In line with the change to hold the Olympic Winter Games every two years after the Olympic Summer Games, the next Paralympic Winter Games were held in Lillehammer, Norway in 1994. On 21st October 1989 the Board of the Norwegian Sports Organisation for the Disabled decided to apply to host the sixth winter Paralympic Games to be held in Lillehammer as soon as possible after the winter Olympic Games that had been awarded to Lillehammer at the 94th IOC session in Seoul, South Korea on 15th September 1988. On 28th June 1990 the Lillehammer Paralympic Organising Committee held its first board meeting and on 15th July 1990 the Norwegian Sports Organisation for the Disabled was awarded the right to host the sixth winter Paralympic Games at the 2nd General Assembly of the International Paralympic Committee in Groningen, The Netherlands.

Date of Vote	Location	Candidate City	Voting Round		
			1	2	3
15/9/1988	Seoul, South Korea	Lillehammer, Norway	25	30	45
			19	33	39
		Ostersund, Sweden	23	22	-
		Anchorage, USA	17	-	-
		Sofia, Bulgaria			

On 12th June 1991, after nearly two years of preparations LPOC made an application to the Norwegian Parliament, which was adopted and funding of up to NOK 90million allocated. As part of the resolution from Parliament it was stipulated that LPOC should be set up as a limited company, as had been done with the Olympic Organising Committee, and that the company should be 51% owned by the Norwegian Government and 49% owned by the Norwegian Sports Organisation for the Disabled. It consisted of seven members of which four were appointed by the Government and three by the Norwegian Sports Organisation for the Disabled and held its first meeting on 21st August 1991. The members were as follows:

President: Gerhard Heiberg
Vice-President: Sverre Bergenholdt
Members: Magnhild Sundli Brennvall
                   Ingar Flugsrud
                   Aase Gudding Gresvig
                   Cato Zahl Pedersen
                   Carl E. Wang

Later on Stein Hamnes was appointed as an alternative representative for the Norwegian Sports Organisation for the Disabled and Odd Arve Lien, deputy mayor of the Municipality of Lillehammer was appointed as an observer.

The Games Poster

The Games Opening Ceremony

At the Opening Ceremony on 10 March at 6.30pm, the delegations were welcomed to Norway officially by Her Majesty (HM) Queen Sonja of Norway and the Games were opened as the Paralympic flame was lit by Helge Bjørnstad and the athlete's oath taken by Cato Zahl Pedersen. According to the Final Report of the organising committee the objectives of the opening and closing ceremonies were to:

- Present Norwegian culture based on breadth and quality; tradition and innovation and a meeting of Norwegian and international expression.
- Express the motto for the Lillehammer Paralympic Games – Vi flytter grenser/ No Limits.
- Create a unified performance for the audience including both ceremonial and cultural elements.

Performers were brought in from all five continents for the opening ceremony in order to represent the five tear-drop symbol, which was being used at a Paralympic Games for the very last time. A pop song, entitled "Shapes That Go Together" was especially written for the ceremony and performed by Norwegian group A-ha. According to the Official Report it was hoped that the song would be an international hit. In the end it reached #27 in the charts in the UK, and was in the charts for three weeks in total. It also reached #57 in Germany, #28 in Poland

and #15 in Japan. Around six hundred performers took part in a ceremony lasting two hours.

Raising the Paralympic flag

An Opening Ceremony Ticket

The Games Themselves

A total of 471 athletes from 31 nations took part in 133 medal events across five sports in Lillehammer. Once again demonstration events were held for athletes with intellectual disabilities in cross country skiing. This was also the first winter Paralympic Games to incorporate a torch relay. The Paralympic Torch Relay started as an offshoot of the Morgedal Flame when the Olympic torch relay arrived in Lillehammer on Friday 11th February 1994. From Lillehammer the 'offshoot' was transported to the Beitostølen Health Sports Centre, where it was kept until the Paralympic torch relay began on Friday 4th March. The relay passed through Fagernes, Geilo, Hønefoss, Oslo, Hamar and Øyer before arriving in Lillehammer on 10th March.

IPC President Dr Robert Steadward at the Lillehammer Games.

The 1050-meter-high mountain Hafjell, one of the toughest courses ever for athletes with disabilities, was the scene of the events in Alpine Skiing and Ice Sledge Hockey was added to the programme for the first time in which Sweden defeated Norway, 1-0, in sudden death in the gold-medal match. The main competitive venues for the Lillehammer Paralympic Games were:

Hafjell Alpine Centre: Alpine Events
Birkebeineren Ski Stadium: Biathlon, Nordic Events
Hamar Olympia Hall: Ice Sledge Racing
Kristin Hall: Ice Sledge Hockey

A guide leading a visually impaired skier in a cross country event

Demonstration Events for Intellectually Disabled Athletes

Women's 5km Cross Country
1. Anna Zetterström (SWE) 19.01.0
2. Pirjo Karppinen (FIN) 19.15.5
3. Terrylin Johnson (CAN)20.22.2
4. Jaana Mosorin (FIN) 20.26.1
5. Brita Hall (CAN) 21.45.6
6. Jirina Kamenikova (CZE) 22.01.4

Men's 10km Cross Country
1. Nils-Peter Kling (SWE) 30.36.8
2. Tuomo Kukkohovi (FIN) 31.35.3
3. Martin Bujnovsky (SVK) 32.01.0
4. Matti Haatainen (FIN) 32.40.1
5. Asko Takkunen (FIN) 33.32.0
6. Luboslav Matija (SVK) 34.51.8

The Outstanding Performers in Lillehammer

Lillehammer saw a return to form of Ragnhild Myklebust of Norway. After dominating the Cross Country and Ice Sledge Racing in Innsbruck in 1988 where she won five gold and two silver medals, she had a relatively modest Games in Tignes winning only two gold medals in the Cross Country events. However, in front of her home supporters Myklebust stormed to five gold, two silver and two bronze medals in the Biathlon, Cross Country Skiing and Ice Sledge Racing. Frank Hoefle of Germany was the most successful male skier in Lillehamme winning 4 gold and one silver medal in cross country and biathlon events. A further seven athletes left Lillehammer with four gold medals each.

The Winners Medal

A medal ceremony in Lillehammer

The Closing Ceremony

The closing ceremony on 19 March in Hakon's Hall was somewhat simpler than the opening ceremony in that only Norwegian performers were used, including soprano Sissel Kyrkjebo. There was a contribution from the next hosts, Nagano, and flag hand-over celebration to the Mayor of Nagano. The Ceremony was attended by the King and Queen of Norway.

The Final Medal Table

Rank	NPC	Gold	Silver	Bronze	Total
1	Norway	29	22	13	64
2	Germany	25	21	18	64
3	USA	24	12	7	43
4	France	14	6	11	31
5	Russia	11	11	8	30
6	Austria	7	16	12	35
Number of Countries winning a medal					24
% of participating countries winning a medal					77.4

Games Trivia

An 'offshoot' of the Paralympic flame was taken during the closing ceremony prior to the extinguishing of the flame and transported to Sarajevo together with the Paralympic flag as a flame of peace accompanied by fourteen athletes. This was a joint project with Peace Flame and garnered a large amount of media coverage.

A total of 49 drugs tests were carried out during the Lillehammer Paralympic Games. Lots were drawn for drug testing in the morning at the out-patients clinic. The samples were sent by courier from the transport section to Aker Hospital in Oslo. The Norwegian Confederation of Sport's anti-doping team was responsible for taking the blood samples.

Norwegian Ice Sledge Hockey player and leg amputee Helge Bjørnstad was winched up to light the Paralympic cauldron at the opening ceremony. The lighting went off without a hitch, but Bjørnstad admitted afterwards that he had been worried his prosthesis might fall off in the middle of the flame lighting.

References

Lillehammer Paralympic Organising Committee, 1994, The VI Paralympic Winter Games (Final Report) Aothor facsimile copy.

Chapter 19: Atlanta, USA 1996

'The Triumph of the Human Spirit'

Logo:	Confirmed Participating Nations	103
	Confirmed Participating Athletes	3259 (2469 Men, 790 Women)
	Number of Events	517
	Opening Ceremony	Thursday 15th August (8.00pm)
	Closing Ceremony	Sunday 25th August (8.30pm)
Mascot: Blaze	Officially Opened by	Vice President Al Gore
	Main Stadium	Centennial Olympic Stadium
	Flame Lit by	Mark Wellman (Paraplegic Cross Country Skier & Rock Climber)
	Athlete's Oath	Trisha Zorn (Swimmer)
	Official's Oath	Unknown[9]

---

[9] If you know who took the official's oath in Atlanta please e-mail parahist@hotmail.co.uk

Participating Nations (103): **Afghanistan**, Algeria, **Angola**, Argentina, **Armenia**, Australia, Austria, **Azerbaijan**, Bahrain, **Belarus**, Belgium, **Bermuda**, **Bosnia-Herzegovina**, Brasil, Bulgaria, Burkino Faso, Canada, Chile, China, Chinese Taipei, Colombia, Croatia, Cuba, Cyprus, **Czech Republic**, Denmark, Dominican Republic, Ecuador, Egypt, Estonia, Faroe Islands, Fiji, Finland, France, Germany, Great Britain, Greece, Honduras, Hong Kong, Hungary, Iceland, India, Indonesia, Iran, Ireland, Israel, Italy, Ivory Coast, Jamaica, Japan, Jordan, **Kazakhstan**, Kenya, Kuwait, **Kyrgyzstan**, Latvia, **Libya**, Lithuania, Luxembourg, Macao, **Macedonia**, Malaysia, **Mauritius**, Mexico, **Moldova**, Morocco, Netherlands, New Zealand, Nigeria, Norway, Oman, Pakistan, Panama, Peru, Poland, Portugal, Puerto Rico, **Qatar**, Romania, **Russia**, Saudi Arabia, Sierra Leone, Singapore, **Slovakia**, Slovenia, South Africa, South Korea, Spain, Sri Lanka, Sweden, Switzerland, Syria, Thailand, Tunisia, Uganda, **Ukraine**, United Arab Emirates, United States, Uruguay, Venezuela, Yugoslavia, **Zambia**, Zimbabwe. **(Countries in bold are those appearing at a summer Paralympic Games for the first time)**

Sports (17 + 2 Demonstration Sports): Archery, Athletics, Boccia, Cycling, Equestrianism, Football (7-a-side), Goalball, Judo, Lawn Bowls, Powerlifting, Sailing (Demonstration), Shooting, Swimming, Table Tennis, Volleyball (Sitting & Standing), Wheelchair Basketball, Wheelchair Fencing, Wheelchair Rugby (Demonstration), Wheelchair Tennis.

Impairment Groups (6): Amputees, Blind & Visually Impaired, Cerebral Palsied, Intellectually Disabled, Les Autres, Spinal Cord Injuries

Logo: Entitled 'Starfire' the logo for the Atlanta Paralympics was meant to represent the fulfilment of an athlete's dream. It may be interpreted as the star being the athlete and the fire being the passion that burns in the heart to fulfil their dreams. The fifth point of the star, revealed by the 'dynamic flow of the rings' represents the fulfilment of the athletes' quest.

Mascot: Blaze, an American Bald Eagle, is representative of the Phoenix that rose, renewed, from its own ashes, which may be interpreted as the rebirth of the human spirit through achievement in sport.

The Selection of Atlanta as the Host City

On 18th September 1990 at the IOC session in Tokyo, Japan Atlanta was awarded the right to host the summer Olympic Games of 1996. Bob Steadward the newly appointed President of the International Paralympic Committee (IPC) met with the Bid Committee for the Olympic Games in Atlanta on January 5th 1991 and was told that the Bid Committee had just completed a feasibility study on the possibility of hosting the 1996 Paralympic Games and were in the process of analysing the results. The Bid Committee became the Atlanta Organising Committee for the Olympic Games soon after. At the IPC Executive Board meeting in March 1992 held in Tignes, France representatives of the Atlanta Paralympic Organising Committee submitted a formal bid to host the 1996

Paralympic Games, which was accepted by the IPC board subject to the successful negotiation of the contract.

The Games Poster

Atlanta appears to be another host city where no real historical archive of the Games was saved. Despite contacting several people who worked at the Atlanta Games none could remember which poster was the main poster for the Games. The two shown above are the most likely candidates.

The Games Opening Ceremony

The opening ceremony for the Atlanta Paralympic Games commenced at 8.00pm on Thursday 15th August in the Centennial Olympic Stadium. Sixty-four thousand spectators packed the stadium, which commenced with a rendition of the 'Star Spangled Banner' by paraplegic soul singer Teddy Pendergrass. Actor Christopher Reeve, paralysed as a result of a horse-riding accident, acted as Master of Ceremonies in a star-studded evening that included performances from the likes of Aretha Franklin, Carly Simon, Lisa Minelli and Hall and Oates. A team of 14 US Army Parachuters targeted a child-formed 'Starfire' logo in the centre of the arena. The final parachutist, Dana Bowman, parachute adorned with the starfire logo was a double leg amputee as a result of a parachute accident two years previously. A trained American bald eagle circled the stadium before gliding down towards the American flag. Following the Parade of Nations the official part of the ceremony commenced. Speeches from Atlanta Paralympic Organising Committee (APOC) President Andrew Fleming and IPC President Robert Steadward were followed by one from US Vice-President Al Gore who declared the Games officially open. The culmination of the evening was when

Paralympian and Atlanta native Al Mead passed the Paralympic torch on to winter Paralympian and rock climber Mark Wellman, who with the flaming torch holstered to his legs hoisted himself up the last 98 feet of the 184 foot cauldron to light the flame that would burn throughout the Games, at which point the night sky exploded with fireworks.

The Canadian team in the opening parade.

The Games Themselves

A relatively indifferent attitude by the Olympic Organising Committee in Atlanta towards the Paralympic Games, especially during the Olympic/Paralympic Games transition period lead to a wide number of problems. This was especially true in the Paralympic village, which was the target of numerous complaints by participating delegations regarding the state of the rooms, the food, the transportation and many other aspects. Many of the behind the scenes organisational problems in Atlanta appear to have their roots in the refusal of the Atlanta Olympic Organising Committee to have anything to do with the organisation of the Paralympic Games. They were two totally separate Games with two totally separate organising committees – the last time this was to occur in the organisation of a Paralympic Games. Many of the problems that occurred in the Paralympic village appear to stem from the actions of the Olympic

Organising Committee who failed to carry out agreed handover procedures (including cleaning) and apparently went around ripping out appliances, plug sockets from walls and generally leaving the village in a total mess. They were also two days late handing the village over further adding to the Paralympic Organising Committee's problems. One other area of criticism for APOC was their handling of the 56 Intellectually Disabled athletes competing in the Games for the first time. No mention was made of them in any of the material produced to advertise the Games even when explaining classification. Worse still they were not even mentioned or introduced at the opening ceremony. Despite repeated official complaints to APOC management by Bernard Athos, President of INAS-FMH APOC officials refused to respond, until Athos went to the Atlanta press with his grievances. Once the Atlanta newspapers took up the story APOC apparently immediately apologised for their unintended oversight (Bailey, 2008).

However, the level of competition and organisation of the events was generally of a very high standard. Fifty-six athletes with an intellectual disability took part in the Games for the very first time in swimming and track and field. Wheelchair Rugby, won by the 'Wheelblacks' of New Zealand, and Sailing, won by Great Britain, appeared on the programme for the first time as demonstration events. In order to keep costs down the Paralympic Organising Committee used a wide range of public and private facilities spread around the city to host the different sports which in many ways added to the transportation problems that had plagued the city during the Olympic Games:

Alexander Memorial Coliseum	Volleyball (Standing)
Aqualand Marina – Lake Lanier	Yachting
Atlanta Metro College	Judo, Rugby
Centennial Olympic Stadium	Athletics
Clark – Atlanta University	Football, Lawn Bowls
Clayton State College	Volleyball (Sitting)
Emory University	Boccia
Georgia International Horse Park	Equestrian
Georgia State University	Goalball
Georgia Tech University	Swimming
Gwinnett Civic and Cultural Centre	Table Tennis
Marriott Marquis Hotel Ballroom	Powerlifting
Mercer University	Fencing
Morehouse College	Basketball (Preliminaries)
Stone Mountain Park	Archery, Cycling (Road & Track), Tennis
The Omni	Basketball
Wolf Creek Shooting Range	Shooting

The Georgia Tech University swimming pool

One important first from Atlanta, as had happened with the Olympic Games back in 1984 in Los Angeles, was that for the first time a corporate sponsorship programme was launched that marketed the Games as a commercially viable event. Twenty-six sponsors signed on at the Worldwide, Official Sponsor and Official Supplier levels. This programme resulted in more than two thirds of the cost of the Games being covered by sponsors. However, this wasn't without problems as attempts to charge for entry to all competitions resulted in almost empty stands for all but the opening and closing ceremonies. It was also a steep learning curve for the newly formed International Paralympic Committee in contract negotiation when all they received after the Games was a cheque for $725.000, whilst at the same time APOC was able to transfer the sum of $3,850.000 into a newly formed USA Disabled Athletes Fund.

A Cultural Paralympiad was included to showcase the works of artists with a disability across a wide variety of creative disciplines including dance, music, visual art, film and theatre. The idea behind the Cultural Paralympiad was to widen the appeal and impact of the Games and to draw parallels between excellence in sport and in the arts.

The Outstanding Performers in Atlanta

Chantal Petitclerc (CAN) lining up for the women's T53 100m race in which she took the gold medal

Outstanding performances in the swimming pool by Beatrice Hess (FRA) with six gold and one silver medal and Alwin de Groot (NED) with five gold, two silver and one bronze medal put them at the top of the list of individual medal winners. Priya Cooper (AUS), Walter Wu (CAN) and Yvonne Hopf (GER) also won five gold medals each in the pool. On the track Louise Sauvage (AUS) took gold in all track events from 400m to 5000m.

The Winners Medal

The Games Closing Ceremony

The closing ceremony on Sunday 25th August commenced in the Centennial Olympic Stadium at 8.30pm with a Mardi Gras style parade, fireworks and F-18 fighter jet flyby. Speeches followed from APOC President Andrew Fleming, IPC President Robert Steadward, Mayor of Atlanta Bill Campbell and US Attorney General Janet Reno who had the honour of handing over the Paralympic flag to the representatives of the next host city of Sydney, Australia. Under the leadership of Master of Ceremonies Casey Kasem the Atlanta Paralympic Closing Ceremony concluded with entertainment from yet another plethora of stars including Chubby Checker, Bo Diddley, The Four Tops and Jerry Lee Lewis.

The Final Medal Table

Rank	NPC	Gold	Silver	Bronze	Total
1	USA	47	46	65	158
2	Australia	42	37	27	106
3	Germany	40	58	51	149
4	Great Britain	39	42	41	122
5	Spain	39	31	36	106
6	France	35	29	31	95
Number of Countries winning a medal					60
% of participating countries winning a medal					58.3

Games Trivia

Organisers of the Atlanta Paralympic Games had to pay $1million to get the Games broadcast on American television. This is in stark contrast to the $456million paid to the organisers of the Atlanta Olympic Games by NBC for the rights to broadcast them on American television.

Live coverage of the Paralympics was all but impossible in 11 out of the 14 sporting venues in Atlanta as only one camera and crew was available at each. Only athletics, swimming and Basketball had sufficient cameras to provide live coverage.

The Iraqi wheelchair basketball team, who were to be their country's sole competitors at the Games, failed to arrive in Atlanta despite being expected right up until the last minute. It is claimed that this was due to a lack of available hard currency to pay for the expenses of the team whilst in Atlanta due to the sanctions in place that prevented Iraq selling their oil following their invasion of Kuwait, but it may have been due to the fact that their very first Games was due to be against the USA.

References

Atlanta Paralympic Organising Committee, 1997, The triumph of the human spirit: The Atlanta Paralympic experience, Disability Today Publishing Group; Ontario, Canada

British Paralympic Association, 1996, Official Guide and Team Handbook, BPA; Croydon, UK

British Paralympic Association, 1997,The BPA Official Games Report: Atlanta 1996, BPA; Croydon, UK

British Wheelchair Sports Foundation, 1997, Wheelpower Paralympic Atlanta Special, BWSF; Stoke Mandeville, UK

Sherrill, C., 1997, Paralympic Games 1996: Feminist and other concerns: What's your excuse? Palaestra, Vol. 13(1): p. 32-38

Chapter 20: Nagano, Japan 1998

'Paralympics – Catch the Excitement'

Logo:		Confirmed Participating Nations	31
PARALYMPICS NAGANO'98		Confirmed Participating Athletes	561 (440 Men, 121 Women)
		Number of Events	122
		Opening Ceremony	Thursday 5th March (7.00pm)
Mascot: Parabbit		Closing Ceremony	Saturday 14th March (6.30pm)
		Officially Opened by	Crown Prince Naruhito
		Stadium	M-Wave
		Flame Lit by	Naoya Maruyama (Alpine Skier)
		Athlete's Oath	Naoya Ryuei (Alpine Skier)
		Official's Oath	Takashi Takano (Ice Sledge Hockey Referee)

Participating Nations (31): **Armenia**, Australia, Austria, Belarus, Bulgaria, Canada, Czech Republic, Denmark, Estonia, Finland, France, Germany, Great

Britain, **Iran**, Italy, Japan, Kazakhstan, Netherlands, New Zealand, Norway, Poland, Russia, Slovakia, **Slovenia**, **South Africa**, South Korea, Spain, Sweden, Switzerland, **Ukraine**, United States.**(Countries in bold are those appearing at a winter Paralympic Games for the first time)**

NB. Klimenti Epelman (Chef De Mission) and Vladimir Ryabov (Slalom Forerunner) of Krgyzstan both took part in the Opening Ceremony, but no Krgyzstani athletes actually participated in any of the events.

Sports (5): Alpine, Biathlon, Cross Country, Ice Sledge Hockey and Ice Sledge Racing.

Impairment Groups (6): Amputees, Blind and Visually Impaired, Cerebral Palsied, Intellectually Disabled, Les Autres and Spinal Cord Injuries.

Logo: The logo design selected for the Nagano 1998 Winter Paralympics was designed by Sadahiko Kojima following the announcement of a national competition. It represents a simplified form of the Chinese character 'naga' for Nagano. It also symbolises a rabbit jumping and playing in snow or on ice with the swift movements that are characteristic of rabbits. This figure was combined with the Games details and the former IPC logo of three tae-guks.

Mascot: The mascot chosen for the Games was based upon the same rabbit emblem selected for the logo. A national competition was held to name the mascot and following 10,057 entries which suggested 3,408 different names the winning name chosen was Parabbit.

The Selection of Nagano as the Host City

The decision on the host city for the winter Olympic Games of 1998 was made in at the 97th IOC session in Birmingham, UK on 15th June 1991 when the Games were awarded to Nagano, Japan. The voting was as follows:

Date of Vote	Location	Candidates	Voting Round				
			1	2	3	4	5
15/6/1991	Birmingham, United Kingdom	Nagano, Japan	21		30	36	46
		Salt Lake City, USA	15	59	27	29	42
		Ostersund, Sweden	18		25	23	-
		Jaca, Spain	19		5	-	-
		Aosta, Italy	15	29	-	-	-

Following a presentation at the IPC General Assembly in Berlin, Germany on 10th September 1993 Nagano was formally selected to host the 7th winter Paralympic Games in 1998. The contract was finally signed on 7th March 1994, just prior to the winter Paralympic Games in Lillehammer.

The Games Poster

The Games Opening Ceremony

The opening ceremony took place in the M-Wave stadium. The opening and closing ceremonies were produced by Joe Hisaishi, a composer and producer born in the Nagano prefecture. The theme for the opening ceremony was 'Hope' because, according to the Official Report, the Nagano Paralympic Games marked the first winter Games to be held in Asia and the last Paralympic Games of the twentieth century. The theme apparently originated from a Frederic Watts painting entitled 'HOPE' in which a girl who is blind is sitting on a devastated earth listening to the music of a harp with only one string. The painting is meant to express hope generating from despair and difficulty.

Athletes at the Opening Ceremony in the M-Wave stadium

The opening ceremony began at 7.00pm with the ceremonial part of the programme including the entrance of the delegations, messages from the NAPOC President Goro Yoshimura and IPC President Robert Steadward, followed by His

Imperial Highness Crown Prince Naruhito declaring the Games officially open. The Paralympic flame, which was ignited at the Tokyo Metropolitan Yoyogi Park and carried by 754 relay runners to the M-Wave was passed finally to Japanese Alpine athlete Naoya Maruyama to light a specially constructed tower at the centre of the stadium. However, after the opening ceremony and in order for the flame to burn continuously throughout the Games a cauldron was set up outside the stadium and lit by persons related to the Dosojin Fire Festival. In addition, mini-cauldrons were set up and lit in Yamanouchi Town and Nozawa Onsen Village.

Opening Ceremony Ticket from Nagano

The artistic part of the programme consisted of four themes (Hope, Fire, Chaos, Finale) depicted by live music and dance performances. The overall theme was that of struggle, but not between good and evil, rather the co-existence of what appear to be in opposition – light and shade; static and dynamic; young and old; people with and without disabilities.

The Games Themselves

A total of 561 athletes from 31 nations took part in 122 medal events across five sports in Nagano. For the first time ever in a winter Paralympic Games the number of female participants was over one hundred. From an attendance and media coverage perspective the Nagano Paralympic Games were highly successful. A total of 151,376 spectators attended the Games, including 15,634 for the Opening and Closing Ceremonies and 1,468 media representatives covered the Games. The official Games website recorded a total of 7.7 million hits during the course of the Games, with 1 million hits coming on the first and second days of competition alone. Norway repeated its success at the 1994 Lillehammer Games by topping the medal table with 18 gold medals. Germany was second with 14 gold medals, followed closely by the USA with 13 gold medals. The main sports venues in Nagano were:

Mt. Higashidate and Mt Nishidate Ski Areas: Alpine Skiing
Kamishiro, Hakuba Village: Cross Country Skiing
Nozawa Onsen Ski Area: Biathlon
M-Wave: Ice Sledge Racing
Aqua Wing: Sledge Hockey

Ice sledge racing in the M-Wave stadium.

The Outstanding Performers in Nagano

Once again it was Ragnhild Myklebust from Norway who topped the table of individual medal winners with five gold medals in the Cross Country Skiing and Biathlon events. Magda Amo (ESP) and Rolf Heinzmann (SUI) in the Alpine Skiing events, Valeri Kouptchinski (RUS) in the cross country skiing and Knut Lundstroem (NOR) in the Ice Sledge Racing all left Nagano with four gold medals apiece.

Ragnhild Myklebust in action

The Winners Medal

The Closing Ceremony

The closing ceremony once again took place in the M-Wave stadium commencing at 6.30pm with the entrance of the athletes, officials and dignitaries followed by a dance of joy called Bangaku performed by citizens of Nagano. Again the ceremony consisted of a mixture of the ceremonial (speeches, lowering and handover of the IPC flag to the Mayor of Salt Lake City) and artistic (Dance of Joy: Dragon God and Lions, Dengaku: Dancing for All, Presentation by Salt Lake City Organisers). The ceremony concluded with a singer, Susan Osborn, appearing on stage with two children and singing the "Sukiyaki Song", the lyrics of which tell the story of a man who looks up and whistles while he is walking so that his tears won't fall. The verses of the song describe his memories and feelings. The two children who entered with Susan Osborn then extinguished the Paralympic flame to complete the ceremony.

The Final Medal Table

Rank	NPC	Gold	Silver	Bronze	Total
1	Norway	18	9	13	40
2	Germany	14	17	13	44
3	USA	13	8	13	34
4	Japan	12	16	13	41
5	Russia	12	10	9	31
6	Switzerland	10	5	8	23
Number of Countries winning a medal					21
% of participating countries winning a medal					67.7

Games Trivia

From mid-January, the producer of the Closing Ceremony made announcements in newspapers and over the Internet calling for people to make and donate origami cranes, which are believed to ensure the realisation of one's prayers, in order to decorate the venue. The total number of cranes easily surpassed the initial goal of a million set by the organisers and by the closing ceremony they had amassed 7.5 million cranes from 350,000 groups and individuals.

Paper cranes hanging from the stadium roof during the closing ceremony.

A total of 52 doping tests were carried out at the Nagano Paralympic Games covering all events and using the same sampling kits as had been used at the Olympic Games. Doping Control Stations were supported by volunteers recruited from among doping control staff at the Olympic Games and students of the School of National Rehabilitation Centre for the Disabled, with samples being sent to the only IOC accredited laboratory in Japan for analysis.

References

Nagano Paralympic Organising Committee, 1998, 1998 Winter Paralympic Games Nagano Official Report, NPOC, Nagano.

Chapter 21: Sydney, Australia 2000

'Without Limits'

Logo:	Confirmed Participating Nations	121 + 2 'Independent Paralympic Athletes'
PARALYMPIC GAMES SYDNEY 2000 ™©	Confirmed Participating Athletes	3882 (2891 Men, 991 Women)
	Number of Events	551
	Opening Ceremony	Wednesday 18th October (8.00pm)
	Closing Ceremony	Sunday 29th October (7.30pm)
Mascot: Lizzie	Officially Opened by	Sir William Deane (Governor General of Australia)
	Main Stadium	Stadium Australia
	Flame Lit by	Louise Sauvage (Athlete)
	Athlete's Oath	Tracey Cross (Swimmer)
	Official's Oath	Mary Longden (Equestrian Referee)

Participating Nations (121) + Individual Paralympic Athletes (2): Algeria, Angola, Argentina, Armenia, Australia, Austria, Azerbaijan, Bahrain, **Barbados**, Belarus, Belgium, **Benin**, Bermuda, Bosnia-Herzegovina, Brasil, Bulgaria, Burkino Faso, **Cambodia**, Canada, Chile, China, Chinese Taipei, Colombia,

Costa Rica, Croatia, Cuba, Cyprus, Czech Republic, Denmark, Ecuador, Egypt, El Salvador, Estonia, Faroe Islands, Fiji, Finland, France, Germany, Great Britain, Greece, Honduras, Hong Kong, Hungary, Iceland, India, Indonesia, Iran, Iraq, Ireland, Israel, Italy, Ivory Coast, Jamaica, Japan, Jordan, Kazakhstan, Kenya, Kuwait, Kyrgyzstan, **Laos**, Latvia, Lebanon, **Lesotho**, Libya, Lithuania, Macao, Macedonia, **Madagascar**, Malaysia, **Mali**, **Mauritania**, Mexico, Moldova, **Mongolia**, Morocco, Netherlands, New Zealand, Nigeria, Norway, Oman, Pakistan, **Palestine**, Panama, Papua New Guinea, Peru, Philippines, Poland, Portugal, Puerto Rico, Qatar, Romania, Russia, **Rwanda**, **Samoa**, Saudi Arabia, Singapore, Slovakia, Slovenia, South Africa, South Korea, Spain, Sri Lanka, Sweden, Switzerland, Syria, Thailand, **Tonga**, Tunisia, Turkey, **Turkmenistan**, Uganda, Ukraine, United Arab Emirates, United States, Uruguay, **Vanuatu**, Venezuela, **Vietnam**, Yugoslavia, Zambia, Zimbabwe + Individual Paralympic Athletes (Pereira, Alcino; Lukas, Mateus).**(Countries in bold are those appearing at a summer Paralympic Games for the first time)**

Sports (19): Archery, Athletics, Basketball (Intellectual Disability), Boccia, Cycling, Equestrianism, Football (7-a-side), Goalball, Judo, Powerlifting, Sailing, Shooting, Swimming, Table Tennis, Volleyball (Sitting & Standing), Wheelchair Basketball, Wheelchair Fencing, Wheelchair Rugby, Wheelchair Tennis.

Impairment Groups (6): Amputees, Blind & Visually Impaired, Cerebral Palsied, Intellectually Disabled, Les Autres, Spinal Cord Injuries
Logo: The Sydney 2000 Paralympic Games logo embodies the vitality of Sydney, the spirit of Australia and the ability and achievement of the Paralympic athlete. The logo depicts a dynamic human form — represented by three graphic shapes — leaping triumphantly forward and "breaking through" towards the Paralympic Games in 2000. It also portrays the Paralympic torch and echoes the sails of Sydney's greatest landmark, the Opera House. The logo is cast in three of the unique colours of Australia: the rich blue of Sydney Harbour, the warm red of the earth, and the lush green of the forest. **Mascot**: The Mascot for the Sydney 2000 Paralympic Games was Lizzie, the frill-necked lizard, which was chosen to carry the Paralympic messages of performance, power and pride. Lizzie's strength, determination and attitude symbolise all Paralympians. Lizzie's frill is shaped as the map of Australia with its green and gold colours, while her body is the red ochre colour of the land.

The Selection of Sydney as the Host City

On 23rd September 1993 at the 101st IOC Session in Monte-Carlo, Monaco Sydney was elected as the Olympic host city for the 2000 Olympic Games. At the 10th IPC Executive Committee meeting on the 9th, 12th and 13th September 1993 held in Berlin, Germany the Executive Committee decided, based upon presentations and site visits that four of the five Olympic candidates (Beijing, Berlin, Manchester, Sydney) were capable of hosting a Paralympic Games and that this information would be forwarded to the IOC. However, it was decided that the evaluations should be sent to the IOC without attaching any kind of ranking of the candidates as it was felt it would place IPC in an awkward position should their number one choice not be elected. It was also felt that future bidding cities might think that IPC had no impact upon the IOC decision making process, which could undermine future bids. The fifth city not mentioned by IPC was Istanbul, Turkey.

The Games Poster

The Games Opening Ceremony

The Opening Ceremony for the Sydney Games took place on Wednesday 18th October and commenced at 8.00pm with the national anthem of Australia. The whole ceremony had a distinctly Aboriginal feel to it and began with sections called 'The Quest' and 'Celebration'. It comprised over 6000 performers with Australian actor Bryan Brown acting as Ceremonies Narrator for the evening. The Parade of Nations included Atajan Begniyazov, Turkmenistan's only competitor at the Games, who handed his crutches to a friend before performing handstand press ups to wild applause from the crowd. For an encore he walked 20m on his hands.

Addresses were given by Dr John Grant, President of the Sydney Paralympic Organising Committee (SPOC) and Dr Robert Steadward, President of the International Paralympic Committee (IPC) before the Governor-General of Australia, Sir William Deane, officially declared the Games open. This was followed by the entrance and raising of the IPC flag after which Tracey Cross, a blind swimmer, took the oath on behalf of the athletes. Mary Longden, an Equestrian Referee, then took the oath on behalf of the Officials:

> 'In the name of all judges and officials, I promise that we shall officiate the Paralympic Games with complete impartiality, respecting and

abiding by the rules which govern them, in the true spirit of sportsmanship'

The Paralympic torch then entered the stadium carried by Katrina Webb and made its way to one of Australia's star athletes, Louise Sauvage, who had the honour of lighting the cauldron. The ceremony then concluded with a concert by some of Australia's biggest musical stars including Kylie Minogue, Yothu Yindi, Billy Thorpe, Christine Anu, Taxiride and Vanessa Amorosi before ending with a grand firework finale.

The Games Themselves

From the very beginning the organisers of the Sydney Paralympics worked on the principle that all the core services necessary for the Paralympic Games would be organised and delivered by the same staff that delivered those services for the Olympic Games. This approach helped overcome many of the problems that had been encountered by the Atlanta Paralympic Organising Committee in dealing with their Olympic counterparts and assisted them greatly in delivering on their promise to provide the best possible environment for athletes with a disability to compete in. Seven different venues were used to host the nineteen sports that made up the Paralympic programme in Sydney:

Anne Clark Netball Centre, Lidcombe:	Volleyball (Sitting & Standing)
Dunc Gray Velodrome, Bass Hill:	Cycling
Equestrian Centre, Horsely Park:	Equestrian
Exhibition Halls, Darling Harbour:	Judo, Wheelchair Fencing
Sailing Marina, Rushcutters Bay:	Sailing
Shooting Centre, Cecil Park:	Shooting
Sydney Olympic Park:	Archery, Athletics, Basketball (Wheelchair & Intellectually Disabled), Boccia, Football, Goalball, Powerlifting, Swimming, Table Tennis, Wheelchair Rugby, Wheelchair Tennis.

The swimming pool at Sydney Olympic Park

Huge crowds flocked to the Paralympics everyday swelled by a policy of providing free day tickets to schools to bring classes of children to the Paralympics. In total some 340,000 school children attended the Paralympics and this provided an excellent opportunity to reinforce the major schools education project that ran alongside the Olympic and Paralympic Games. In total 1.16 million tickets were sold. As well as the 121 nation delegations that competed there was also a delegation of two independent athletes from East Timor taking part who received rapturous encouragement from the spectators whenever they competed. Sailing and Wheelchair Rugby were upgraded to full medal sports. The Sydney Games also saw the introduction for the first time of female powerlifting, which was dominated by athletes from China and Nigeria. However powerlifting was also responsible for the dramatic rise in positive doping tests in Sydney. A total of 630 tests were carried out, which returned 11 positive outcomes. Of these 10 were in powerlifting. The eleventh positive test was an American track athlete.

For the first time ever, people around the world could watch Paralympic events live on the internet via the WeMedia website. On October 27, 2000, just before the Games ended IPC signed a multi-million dollar deal with WeMedia covering six-years of worldwide television broadcast and Internet Webcast rights to the next three Paralympic Games. The President of the IPC said of WeMedia 'They have employed the most sophisticated technology, including live captioning for the deaf and hard of hearing, in order to make these Games accessible to all people. I anticipate even greater success in Salt Lake City, Athens, and Turin.'

The Outstanding Performers in Sydney

The big medal winners once again came in the swimming pool. Beatrice Hess of France topped the list of individual medal winners for the second Games running taking home seven gold medals. She was closely followed by fellow swimmers Mayumi Narita (JPN) with six gold and one silver medal and Alwin Houtsma (NED) with five gold, two silver and one bronze. On the track it was two female wheelchair athletes who reigned supreme. Tanni Grey-Thompson (GBR), in a repeat of her successes in Barcelona eight years earlier, won four gold medals in the 100m, 200m, 400m and 800m in the T53 category and in the T52 category Lisa Franks (CAN) also took home four gold medals from the 200m, 400m, 800m and 1500m. In clearly demonstrating the progress of many nations relatively new to the Paralympic Games Mohamed Allek of Algeria took home three gold medals in the T37 100m, 200m and 400m, setting a Paralympic record in the 100m and a world record in the 400m in the process.

The Winners Medal

The Closing Ceremony

The closing ceremony for the Sydney Games took place on Sunday 29th October, commencing at 7.30pm with a ceremony that was, in true Australian tradition, informal, irreverent and one big party! The athletes entered the stadium en masse with nations inter-mingled and took centre stage for a ceremony that was an explosion of fire, nostalgia, emotion and irreverence. The Paralympic flag was handed over to the Athens Paralympic Organising Committee to the strains of the Millennium Choir, performing Mikis Theodoraki's 'Axion Esti, Tis Dikiosinis Helie Noite'. IPC President Dr Robert Steadward was unstinting in his praise of the Sydney Paralympic Games and declared them the best Games ever. The ceremony ended to the sounds of Judith Dunham and the Seekers singing 'the carnival is over' and the Sydney Paralympic flame was finally extinguished plunging the crowd into momentary darkness.

Strengthening IPC – IOC Relations

In the mid to late nineteen nineties in the wake of the Salt Lake City bidding scandal the IOC set up the IOC 2000 Commission on Ethics and Reform whose job it was to make recommendations aimed at reforming not only the bidding process, but also to try and repair some of the damage done to the image of the Olympic movement. As part of this process the then IPC President, Dr Robert Steadward, was one of only twelve individuals from outside the Olympic movement invited to sit on this commission. This appointment was the start of a much closer working relationship between the IOC and IPC, which culminated in two important events occurring at the Sydney 2000 Olympic and Paralympics Games. Firstly at the 111th IOC Session in Sydney, Dr Steadward was elected as an IOC member, thus strengthening the credibility and profile of the Paralympic movement. Then at the Sydney Paralympic Games Dr Steadward and Juan Antonio Samaranch, the then President of the IOC signed a general memorandum of understanding, which included representation of the IPC on IOC Commissions as well as financial assistance for the Paralympic movement from the IOC. This was followed about eight months later by the signing of a much more detailed co-operative agreement between the two organisations, dated 19th June 2001, which provided for the following benefits for the IPC and the Paralympic Games:

- A full seven years for the preparation of the Paralympic Games.
- Full support of the host city and the OCOG for the organisation of the Paralympic Games.
- A financial guarantee of viability for the Paralympic Games.
- Increased support for Paralympic athletes and team officials through travel grants, the elimination of entry fees and free provision of accommodation and ground transport.
- Increased support for technical officials through free travel, accommodation and ground transport.
- Support for the administration of the IPC.

(IOC-IPC Formal Agreement dated 19th June 2001)

Most of the proposals of this second agreement were not due to come into force until Beijing 2008. However, Athens 2004 and Torino 2006 voluntarily chose to implement many of the actions outlined in the agreement such as the concept of having a single organising committee for both Games. On 25th August 2003 the new Presidents of the two organisations, Dr Jacques Rogge (IOC) and Sir Philip Craven (IPC), signed an amendment to the 2001 agreement, which transferred broadcasting and marketing responsibilities of the 2008, 2010 and 2012 Paralympic Games to the host organising committees. In return the organising committees were to pay IPC US$9 million for the 2008 Games and US$14 million for the 2010 and 2012 Games.

The Sydney 2000 Paralympic Games Eligibility Scandal.

On October 21st 2000 the Spanish intellectually disabled basketball team won the gold medal at the Sydney Paralympic Games beating Russia 87 – 63 in the final. This victory capped Spain's best ever performance at a Summer Paralympic Games winning 107 medals and finishing third in the medal table. However, triumph was to turn into disaster in late November when Carlos Ribagorda, a member of the gold medal winning basketball team and also a journalist with a Madrid based business magazine, Capital, wrote an article chronicling long term and widespread fraud and cheating within intellectually disabled sport in Spain. The pinnacle of his revelations was that 10 of the 12 gold medal winning Spanish basketball players actually had no intellectual disability at all and had been deliberately recruited to increase the strength of the team in order to win medals and thus guarantee future funding. It also turned out that this was not a new occurrence, but had been going on for a number of years. In later transpired that four members of the Spanish intellectually disabled basketball team that had won the gold medal at the World Championships in Brazil also had no disability. The potential cheating was apparently not restricted to the sport of basketball either.

One member of Spain's intellectually disabled track and field team, two swimmers and one table tennis player were suspected of not having a disability and went on to win medals.

At the centre of the growing storm was Fernando Vicente Martin a former Madrid councillor who held numerous prominent positions in the world of disability sport. The father of a disabled daughter, he was an International Paralympic Committee Executive Board member, Vice-President of the Spanish Paralympic Committee, President of INAS-FID and President of the Spanish Sports Federation for the Intellectually Disabled (Feddi). He was also founder and President of the National Association of Special Sports (Ande), a charitable body for the intellectually disabled, which received generous state subsidies and was a major sponsor of the Madrid Paralympic Games for the Intellectually Disabled in 1992. Initially Vicente Martin denied any wrongdoing and claimed that all of the Spanish athletes were intellectually disabled, albeit many of them were very near the upper limits of the qualification criteria (maximum IQ of 75). According to Nash (2001) in an article in the Independent newspaper in the UK Martin Vicente initially denounced Ribagorda's article as the lies of a 'handicapped person who had gone mad'. The Spanish Paralympic Committee launched a full investigation in November 2000 and concluded not only that fraud had been committed in Sydney, but that Fernando Vicente Martin was the man responsible for the events that had occurred. In January the Spanish Paralympic Committee expelled him and in February IPC suspended him and he quit as President of INAS-FID.

As a result of the Spanish Paralympic Committee's findings the International Paralympic Committee set up an investigation commission in December 2000 to examine the allegations consisting of Andre Noel Chaker, a lawyer specialising in sports legislation; Dr Donald Royer of the IPC Legal Committee; Dr Lutz Worms, a specialist in sports medicine and Thomas Reinecke, IPC Chief Operating Officer. In January the Commission requested specific information for investigative purposes from INAS-FID including the INAS-FID Registration cards for the 244 athletes who had participated in Sydney. In the end, according to issue 1 of The Paralympian (2001) the INAS-FID Secretariat forwarded 230 of the 244 Registration Cards. Fourteen cards were, therefore, missing and it later transpired that 11 cards provided were for athletes not accredited to compete in Sydney. These were excluded from the investigation. After careful scrutiny of the remaining 219 cards it was found that 157 (72%) were found to be invalid in that one or more of the primary requirements was found to be incomplete or missing. The commission concluded that the eligibility verification of the forms at both national and international level had been seriously mismanaged and administered. To make matters worse it was found that 94 of the 132 possible medals for intellectually disabled events at the Sydney Games were awarded to athletes amongst the 157 cards deemed to be invalid, however, it should be pointed out that just because a card had been deemed invalid it did not automatically bring into question the athlete's eligibility.

Based upon these findings, on 29th January, 2001, the IPC Management Committee suspended INAS-FID, it's President Fernando Vicente Martin and all athletes with an intellectual disability from all IPC activities. This decision was later upheld and endorsed at the IPC Executive Committee held in Salt Lake City on 9th March, 2001, where they approved five resolutions relating to the case:

I. The IPC IC findings have proven beyond doubt that the process of assessment, verification and certification of intellectually disabled athletes was not properly carried out, supervised or audited. The IPC determined that the President and Technical Officer of INAS-FID, Mr. Fernando Martín Vicente and Mr. Felipe Gutiérez Garcia respectively, are primarily responsible for this serious violation. Consequently, it was decided that both be expelled from IPC with immediate effect.

II. IPC demanded that the membership of INAS-FID review their eligibility criteria and process and implement a new mechanism following the recommendation of the IPC IC, which clearly defines the eligibility process, qualification and accreditation of assessors and standard documentation to the full satisfaction of IPC.

III. IPC requests the National Paralympic Committees whose athletes submitted inaccurate or invalid documentation at the XI Paralympic Summer Games Sydney 2000 to review the status of their athletes by an independent investigation committee similar to that conducted by the Spanish Paralympic Committee, and to produce a findings report for the IPC IC within the next three (3) months, but no later than May 31, 2001.

All medals won by athletes who do not meet the international eligibility standards should be returned to IPC via the respective National Paralympic Committee.

IV. IPC urges INAS-FID to admit their responsibility and accountability with regard to the current violations, and to rectify their policy and leadership at the upcoming General Assembly scheduled for April 2001, including the expulsion from their executive positions on the INAS-FID Executive Committee, members who voted in favor of the motion of confidence for Mr. Fernando Martin Vicente at the last INAS-FID Executive Committee meeting.

V. Until and unless INAS-FID has resolved the above issues to the satisfaction of the IPC Executive Committee, the membership of INAS-FID will remain suspended indefinitely. INAS-FID may produce their new policy, and results of their investigation, to IPC at any time for consideration.

However, and as proof of respect to athletes with an intellectual disability, according to the definitions provided by the World Health Organisation and the American Association of Mental Retardation, the IPC Executive Committee accepts that competitions and events sanctioned by the IPC and involving athletes with an intellectual disability may continue to be planned and organised, including the VIII Paralympic Winter Games Salt Lake City 2002. Intellectually disabled athletes may obtain provisional recognition from IPC, if their eligibility is duly proven and verified by a new eligibility committee appointed by INAS-FID and IPC.

(The Paralympian, 2001/1; p.3)

By late 2002 IPC and INAS-FID were still working together and making some progress towards the establishment of a new, more robust, eligibility system that encompassed stringent verification procedures. However, both sides agreed that the new system still did not meet the necessary criteria. Unfortunately, by early to mid 2003 it was decided that the new system was still not reliable enough and events for athletes with an intellectual disability were removed from the programme for Athens 2004. This situation remained the same some five years further on. Athletes with an intellectual disability did not appear in the Beijing 2008 Paralympic Games. However, at a joint meeting of a working group of members from both IPC and INAS-FID held during the Games in Beijing it appears that significant progress was made leading to a very positive sounding press release being issued. It laid out the outline of the new classification and testing system for athletes with an intellectual disability, which was piloted in early 2009. At the 14th IPC General Assembly held in Kuala Lumpur, Malaysia on 22nd and 23rd November 2009 it was decided to allow athletes with an Intellectual Disability to compete at the Paralympic Games from 2012.

The Final Medal Table

Rank	NPC	Gold	Silver	Bronze	Total
1	Australia	63	39	47	149
2	Great Britain	41	43	47	131
3	Canada	38	33	25	96
4	Spain	38	30	38	106
5	United States	36	39	34	109
6	China	34	22	17	73
Number of Countries winning a medal					68
% of participating countries winning a medal					55.7

Games Trivia

The Paralympic village was officially opened on 11th October by Australia's first female Paralympian Daphne Hilton (nee Ceeney) who had competed in the very first Paralympic Games in Rome, 1960.

The Paralympic Bronze medals for the Sydney Games were produced by the Perth Mint and the Royal Australian Mint who melted down the recently defunct 1 cent and 2 cent coins and adding one percent silver to create the bronze medals.

Tickets for the Sydney Paralympic Opening and Closing Ceremonies sold out completely. Tickets for the Sydney Olympic Closing Ceremony did not sell out!

When the two Independent Paralympic Athletes, Mateus Lucas and Alcino Pereira, from East Timor were entering the Paralympic Village through one of the security check points Police Senior Constable Barry Parrish noticed whilst checking their bags that they had nothing in them. With the help of friends and local businesses Barry collected donations including clothing, toiletries, travel bags and other personal items to give to the athletes in order to make their stay more comfortable and a lot warmer.

Sydney Paralympic Games supporters Australia Post encouraged village residents to send home lots of postcards and other mail by offering personalised stamps – complete with a photograph of the sender.

Nearly one thousand competitors in Sydney elected six new members of the IPC Athletes' Commission from eleven candidates. The successful candidates were Ahraf Eid Maraey (EGY) Ljiljana Ljubisic (CAN), Hamish MacDonald (AUS), Rose Atieno Olang (KEN), Enrique Sanchez-Guijo (ESP) and James Thomson (USA).

References

British Paralympic Association, Undated, The Golden Games - The British Paralympic Association Official Games Report: Sydney 2000, BPA; Croydon, UK

British Paralympic Association, 2000, The Official British Paralympic Association Team Handook and Guide, BPA; Croydon, UK

Brown, M. (Ed), Undated, Mind, Body, Spirit: Sydney 2000 Paralympic Games – The Official Souvenir Book, News Custom Publishing; Southbank, Australia

Casman, R. & Darcy, S., 2008, Benchmark Games: The Sydney 2000 Paralympic Games, Walla Walla Press; Petersham, Australia

Craft, D.H., 2001, Impressions from Australia: The Sydney 2000 Paralympic Games, Palaestra, Vol. 17(1) (http://www.palaestra.com/sydneyparalympics.html) accessed 17-7-2011.

Darcy, S., 2003, The Politics of Disability and Access: the Sydney 2000 Games experience, Disability and Society, Vol. 18(6): p. 737-757.

Sydney Paralympic Organising Committee, 2000, Sydney 2000 Paralympic Games Opening Ceremony Programme, SPOC; Sydney, Australia (Author Copy)

Sydney Paralympic Organising Committee, 2000, Sydney 2000 Paralympic Games Opening Ceremony Media Guide, SPOC; Sydney, Australia (Author Copy)

Sydney Paralympic Organising Committee, 2000, Paralympic Village Newspaper Editions 1-20 (11 – 30 October) (Author Copies)

Sydney Paralympic Organising Committee, undated, Sydney 2000 Paralympic Games- Post Games Report, SPOC; Sydney, Australia

Woods, M., 2006, Personal Best: Ten lessons to help you achieve your true
potential, Capstone; Chichester, UK

Chapter 22: Salt Lake City, USA 2002

'Awaken the Mind – Free the Body – Inspire the Spirit'

Logo:	Confirmed Participating Nations	36
	Confirmed Participating Athletes	416 (329 Men, 87 Women)
	Number of Events	92
	Opening Ceremony	Thursday 7th March (7.00pm) (Rice-Eccles Stadium)
Mascot: Otto	Closing Ceremony	Saturday 16th March (7.30pm) (Olympic Medal Plaza)
	Officially Opened by	George W. Bush (via video)
	Stadium	Rice-Eccles Stadium
	Flame Lit by	Muffy Davis, Chris Waddell (Alpine Skiers)
	Athlete's Oath	Sarah Billmeier (Alpine Skier)
	Official's Oath	Scott Brinkman (Ice Sledge Hockey Official)

Participating Nations (36): **Andorra**, Armenia, Australia, Austria, Belarus, Bulgaria, Canada, **Chile**, **China**, **Croatia**, Czech Republic, Denmark, Estonia, Finland, France, Germany, Great Britain, **Greece**, **Hungary**, Iran, Italy, Japan, Kazakhstan, Netherlands, New Zealand, Norway, Poland, Russia, Slovakia, South Africa, South Korea, Spain, Sweden, Switzerland, Ukraine, United States.

(**Countries in bold are those appearing at a winter Paralympic Games for the first time)**

Sports (4): Alpine, Biathlon, Cross Country and Ice Sledge Hockey.

Impairment Groups (5): Amputees, Blind and Visually Impaired, Cerebral Palsied, Les Autres and Spinal Cord Injuries.

Logo: The logo for the Salt Lake Paralympics can be split into three distinct parts making up the whole. The sphere at the top represents both the global unity of the Paralympic Movement and also the head of the Paralympic athlete, which the overall logo appears to depict. The two broad fluid lines represent the athlete in motion with the three tae-guks, the former IPC logo, beneath the athlete.

Mascot: The Salt Lake organisers chose the otter as the official mascot for the Games because they considered it to embody vitality and agility. The otter also had a long historical connection with the region stretching back to ancient Indian tribes who believed it to be one of the most powerful of all animals. Having been nearly hunted to extinction in the early twentieth century, the river otter was successfully reintroduced to Utah in 1990.

Otto the Salt Lake City Paralympic mascot with athletes

The Selection of Salt Lake City as the Host City

The decision on the host city for the winter Olympic Games of 2002 was made at the 104th IOC session in Budapest, Hungary on 16th June 1995 when the Games were awarded to Salt Lake City, USA. The voting was very short and one-sided as follows:

Date of Vote	Location	Candidates	Voting Round
			1
6/16/1995	Budapest, Hungary	Salt Lake City, USA	54
		Ostersund, Sweden	14
		Sion, Switzerland	14
		Quebec City, Canada	7
		Graz, Austria	
		Jaca, Spain	
		Poprad-Tatry, Slovakia	
		Sochi, Russia	
		Tarvisio, Italy	

The Games Poster

The Games Opening Ceremony

On March 7th at 7.00pm a sell-out crowd of 46,000 spectators welcomed 36 nations to Rice-Eccles Stadium for the opening ceremony of the Salt Lake 2002 Paralympic Winter Games. The Opening Ceremony was a celebration of

Paralympic Sport based on the Games' theme "Awaken the Mind – Free the Body – Inspire the Spirit". The fact that a rainstorm began halfway through the ceremony did little to dampen the enthusiasm of those present, who were treated to a start-studded line-up for the cultural and entertainment portion of the ceremony including the likes of Stevie Wonder, violinist Vanessa-Mae, Donny Osmond, Country singer Wynonna Ryder and teenage Country singer Billy Gilman.

Eric Weihenmeyer, the first blind man to successfully climb Mount Everest, carried the Paralympic torch to the podium - guided by his dog – and passed it to Muffy Davis and Chris Waddell, the best American sit-skiers, who jointly lit the Paralympic cauldron. The athlete's oath was taken by a further alpine skier, Sarah Billmeier.

A giant ice crystal rises from the centre of the arena

The Games Themselves

A total of 416 athletes from 36 nations took part in 92 medal events across four sports in Salt Lake. This was actually a drop in participant numbers from Nagano four years earlier, but an increase in the number of nations participating with delegations from Andorra, Chile, China, Croatia, Greece and Hungary competing in a winter Paralympic Games for the very first time. Ice sledge racing was also dropped from the programme. Due to an overly high demand for certain events the organising committee had to raise the overall number of tickets available by 23,000 and in the end managed to sell an unprecedented 211,790 tickets, which amounted to 85% of all available tickets.

A total of 836 accredited media representatives reported from the Salt Lake Games for written press, photography, non-rights holding broadcasters and more than 30 broadcasters. Following months of negotiations, a live, worldwide television signal of all sports was secured. Originally only a 30-minute international highlight package was scheduled to take place. The main sports venues in Salt Lake were:

E Center:	Ice Sledge Hockey
Snow Basin:	Alpine Skiing
Soldier Hollow:	Biathlon and Cross Country Skiing

A total of 97 doping control tests were carried out in Salt Lake City resulting in the the one and only known positive test at a winter Paralympic Games to date when German Nordic Skier Thomas Oelsner tested positive after winning two gold medals in men's standing biathlon events.

Soldier Hollow – venue for the Biathlon and Cross Country Skiing events

The Outstanding Performers in Salt Lake City

For the fourth time in five Games Ragnhild Myklebust of Norway was the star performer in Salt Lake once again capturing five gold medals in the Cross Country Skiing and Biathlon events. Martin Braxenthaler (GER), Gerd Schoenfelder (GER), Michael Milton (AUS), Sarah Will (USA) in the alpine events and Verena Bentele (GER) in the Biathlon and Cross Country Skiing events all left Salt Lake with four gold medals each.

The Winners Medal

The Closing Ceremony

The closing ceremony took place in the Olympic Medal Plaza in downtown Salt Lake City in front of 20,000 athletes and spectators. In linking the closing ceremony to the opening ceremony, Muffy Davis and Chris Waddell, who lit the Paralympic flame, gave a speech at the closing ceremony thanking the volunteers for all their hard work. Canadian alpine skier Lauren Woolstencroft and Norwegian ice sledge hockey player Eskil Hagen were awarded the Whang Youn Dai Overcome prize and the Paralympic flag was passed on to the Mayor of Torino, Italy – hosts for the 2006 winter Games. The ceremony ended with a concert by rhythm and blues singer Patti Labelle, the extinguishing of the Paralympic flame and a huge fireworks display.

The Final Medal Table

Rank	NPC	Gold	Silver	Bronze	Total
1	Germany	17	1	15	33
2	USA	10	22	11	43
3	Norway	10	3	6	19
4	Austria	9	10	10	29
5	Russia	7	9	5	21
6	Canada	6	4	5	15
Number of Countries winning a medal					22
% of participating countries winning a medal					61.1

Games Trivia

The weight of not just a nation, but an entire continent was resting on the shoulders of Bruce Warner, who was not only the only competitor from South Africa at the Salt Lake Games, but the only competitor from the entire African content. His best finish was ninth in the men's slalom LW2.

References

Salt Lake 2002 Paralympic Winter Games Commemorative book, No publisher details. (Author copy)
Salt Lake 2002 Paralympic Winter Games Paralympic Record Newsletter (Nos. 1-19) (Author Copies)
The Paralympian,2002, Paralympic Games/ Salt Lake City, No. 2, p.2.

Chapter 23: Athens, Greece 2004

Logo:	Confirmed Participating Nations	135
ATHENS 2004 PARALYMPIC GAMES	Confirmed Participating Athletes	3808 (2643 Men, 1165 Women)
	Number of Events	520
	Opening Ceremony	Friday 17th September (8.30pm)
	Closing Ceremony	Tuesday 28th September (8.30pm)
Mascot: Proteus	Officially Opened by	Konstantinos Stefanopoulos (President of the Hellenic Republic)
	Main Stadium	Olympic Stadium
	Flame Lit by	Georgios Toptsis (Athlete)
	Athlete's Oath	Maria Kalpakidou (Swimmer)
	Official's Oath	Vlassis Tamvakieras (Athletics Official)

Participating Nations (135): Afghanistan, Algeria, Angola, Argentina, Armenia, Australia, Austria, Azerbaijan, Bahrain, **Bangladesh**, Barbados, Belarus, Belgium, Benin, Bermuda, Bosnia-Herzegovina, **Botswana**, Brasil, Bulgaria, Cambodia, Canada, **Cape Verde**, **Central African Republic**, Chile, China, Chinese Taipei,

Colombia, Costa Rica, Croatia, Cuba, Cyprus, Czech Republic, Denmark, Dominican Republic, Ecuador, Egypt, El Salvador, Estonia, Ethiopia, Faroe Islands, Fiji, Finland, France, Germany, Ghana, Great Britain, Greece, Guatemala, **Guinea**, Honduras, Hong Kong, Hungary, Iceland, India, Indonesia, Iran, Iraq, Ireland, Israel, Italy, Ivory Coast, Jamaica, Japan, Jordan, Kazakhstan, Kenya, Kuwait, Kyrgyzstan, Latvia, Lesotho, Libya, Liechtenstein, Lithuania, Macao, Macedonia, Malaysia, Mauritania, Mauritius, Mexico, Moldova, Mongolia, Morocco, Namibia, **Nepal**, Netherlands, New Zealand, Nicaragua, **Niger**, Nigeria, Norway, Oman, Pakistan, Palestine, Panama, Peru, Philippines, Poland, Portugal, Puerto Rico, Qatar, Romania, Russia, Rwanda, Samoa, Saudi Arabia, **Senegal**, **Serbia and Montenegro**, Singapore, Slovakia, Slovenia, South Africa, South Korea, Spain, Sri Lanka, Sudan, Surinam, Sweden, Switzerland, Syria, **Tajikistan**, Tanzania, Thailand, Tonga, Tunisia, Turkey, Turkmenistan, Uganda, Ukraine, United Arab Emirates, United States, Uruguay, **Uzbekistan**, Venezuela, Vietnam, Zimbabwe. **(Countries in bold are those appearing at a summer Paralympic Games for the first time)**

Sports (19): Archery, Athletics, Boccia, Cycling, Equestrianism, Football (5-a-side), Football (7-a-side), Goalball, Judo, Powerlifting, Sailing, Shooting, Swimming, Table Tennis, Volleyball (Sitting), Wheelchair Basketball, Wheelchair Fencing, Wheelchair Rugby, Wheelchair Tennis.

Impairment Groups (5): Amputees, Blind & Visually Impaired, Cerebral Palsied, Les Autres, Spinal Cord Injuries

Logo: The logo aims to embody the strength and determination of the Paralympic athlete. It features the profile of an athlete - male or female - looking forward, symbolising optimism for the future. At the same time, this human face attempts to reflect the individual's willpower and determination to succeed in all pursuits. The face's lines are smooth, its colour a warm and bright orange - harbinger of the great celebration to come.

Mascot: The creator of Proteas, Spyros Gogos, was asked to create a mascot that would express the four values of the Athens Paralympics: strength, pursuit, inspiration and celebration. In addition, he tried to create a mascot expressing the Greek nature of the competitions and a differentiation from mascots of previous Games. Proteas' name is connected with the Greek adjective "protos", meaning "first in rank" or "excellent". The notion of excellence is something the mascot shares with Paralympians, who succeed in achieving ever-higher standards of performance.

The Selection of Athens as the Host City

Athens was selected as the host city for the 2004 Olympic and Paralympic Games at the 106th IOC Session held in Lausanne, Switzerland on 5th September 1997 beating Rome, Cape Town, Stockholm and Buenos Aires in the process.

The Games Poster

The Games Opening Ceremony

The Opening Ceremony of the Athens 2004 Paralympic Games took place on Friday 17th September. The ceremony began with 150 children entering the stadium and approaching a tree standing in the centre. The tree was meant to symbolise the Tree of Knowledge and passed its light and wisdom to the children. This was followed by fireworks that lit up the Athens night sky. Konstantinos Stefanopoulos, President of the Hellenic Republic and Sir Philip Craven, President of IPC then entered the stadium. The official part of the ceremony then began with the Parade of Athletes. Following speeches by Sir Philip and Gianna Angelopoulos-Daskalaki, President of the Athens Organising Committee for the Olympic Games the President of the Hellenic Republic officially declared the Games open.

The Chinese team, hosts of the next Paralympic Games in 2008, during the Parade of Athletes

Following the entry and hoisting of the Paralympic Flag swimmer Maria Kalpakidou took the oath on behalf of the athletes and athletics official Vlassis Tamvakieras took the oath on behalf of the officials. There was then an artistic performance entitled 'A Journey to the Sun' before the ceremony concluded with the lighting of the Paralympic flame by Greek athlete Georgios Toptsis.

The Games Themselves

The nineteen Paralympic sports that occurred in Athens took place over ten different Paralympic venues spread around the city of Athens:

Agios Kosmos Olympic Sailing Centre:	Sailing
Ano Liosia Olympic Hall:	Boccia, Judo
Athens Olympic Sports Complex:	Athletics, Swimming, Wheelchair Basketball, Wheelchair Tennis
Faliro Coastal Zone Olympic Complex:	Goalball
Galatsi Olympic Hall:	Table Tennis
Helliniko Olympic Complex:	Archery, Football (5-a-side, 7-a-side), Sitting Volleyball, Wheelchair Fencing, Wheelchair Rugby
Markopoulo Olympic Equestrian Centre:	Equestrian
Markopoulo Olympic Shooting Centre:	Shooting
Nikaia Olympic Weightlifting Hall	Powerlifting
Vouliagmeni Olympic Centre:	Cycling

The Athens Paralympic Village

A clear indication of the growing awareness and importance of the Paralympic Games was the fact that Athens 2004 saw the participation of eleven countries in their first ever Games. It was claimed by some that hosting the Games in a country where there is no tradition of sport for persons with a disability and, in some ways, a great ignorance of the needs of persons with a disability was a risk, but the organisers and the Greek people rose well to the challenge.

IOC President Jacques Rogge and IPC President Sir Philip Craven at the cycling venue

Athens saw the introduction of Judo for women in which Germany came out on top and also Sitting Volleyball for women in which China beat the Netherlands. Football (5-a-side) for the visually impaired was also added to the programme and, like their able-bodied team has done in the World Cup on so many occasions before, it was Brazil who edged out Argentina in the final via a penalty shoot out.

Bill Morgan (CAN) in the men's up to 81kg judo

A total of 3,103 media representatives including 68 broadcasters were present in Athens to cover the Games. A total of 617 hours broadcast in 25 countries and right across Europe were watched by a record number of viewers all over the world. In Germany highlights of the Athens Paralympic Games broadcast on

Sunday 19 September, were watched by nearly 1.5 million viewers. In Great Britain, the BBC attracted around 2 million viewers for their first Sunday Paralympic special, whereas 634,000 persons watched the summary broadcast in Spain on the same day. Italian television reported an average of 600,000 viewers for their daily broadcasts of Paralympic highlights.

The Paralympic Flame was lit on September 9th and began its journey in front of the Acropolis. A total of 705 torchbearers carried the Paralympic flame 410km through 54 municipalities of Greece. The route took in places of historical significance such as the theatre of Herod Atticus, the temples of Poseidon at Cape Sounion and the Temple of Artemis in Vravrona.

A new record number of 1,829 athletes (~48%) voted for the IPC Athletes' Committee's summer Games representatives during the Games. The successful candidates were Robert Balk (USA), Konstantinos Fykas (GRE), Beatrice Hess (FRA), Ljiljana Ljubisic (CAN), Rutger Sturkenboom (NED) and Ana Garcia-Arcicollar Vallejo (ESP).

The Outstanding Performers in Athens

Japanese swimmer Mayumi Narita went one better than her six gold medals in Sydney by winning seven gold and one bronze medal in Athens making her the most successful athlete at the Games. Canadian wheelchair athlete Chantal Petitclerc was crowned 'Queen of the Track' taking five gold medals and setting three world records in the 100m, 200m, 400m, 800m and 1500m in the T54 category. In the shooting Jonas Jacobsson of Sweden proved himself to be the top marksman at the Paralympics taking home four gold medals.

The Winners Medal

Paralympic Gold Medal from Athens 2004

The Games Closing Ceremony

Following some excellent competition the Athens Games were sadly marred by a tragic accident. The Athens 2004 Organising Committee decided to cancel the artistic and entertainment portions of the Closing Ceremony, due to a tragic road accident that claimed the lives of seven high school students who were traveling to Athens to attend the Paralympic Games. As well as the seven schoolchildren who were killed over 30 more were injured, when their bus collided with a truck on the Athens-Lamia E75 National Highway. The bus had left the village of Farkadona, near Trikkala, in Thessaly, central Greece about 300km north of Athens to bring the students to watch the second-to-last day of the Paralympic Games. The accident happened at about 10am between the towns of Kammena Vourla and Aghios Konstantinos, in the Prefecture of Phthiotis. The site of the accident is known as the "Maliakos Horseshoe", a 180-degree curve around the Maliakos Gulf and is considered the most dangerous part of the E75 Highway. It had previously been the site of several other serious accidents. In the end the Closing Ceremony consisted only of the protocol segments such as the entry of athletes, the speech by the IPC President Sir Philip Craven, the handover of the Paralympic Flag to the Beijing Organising Committee and the extinguishing of the Paralympic Flame. Sir Philip dedicated the Athens 2004 Paralympic Games to the memory of the children and their families. Ticket holders who decided not to attend the Closing Ceremony were refunded the amount they had paid.

The Final Medal Table

Rank	NPC	Gold	Silver	Bronze	Total
1	China	63	46	32	141
2	Great Britain	35	30	29	94
3	Canada	28	19	25	72
4	Australia	26	38	36	100
5	United States	27	22	39	88
6	Ukraine	24	12	19	55
Number of Countries winning a medal					75
% of participating countries winning a medal					55.6

Games Trivia

The Athens 2004 Paralympic Games was the first major competition to have the revised IPC Anti-Doping Code applied. It was launched in January 2004 and was in full compliance with the World Anti-Doping Authority (WADA) code.

Twelve year old Jessica Long, a double leg amputee from the USA won three gold medals in the pool. Long was born in a Siberian orphanage and later adopted by an American family. She had both legs amputated at 18 months old, but made the US Paralympic team after competing for only two years.

References

Athens 2004, 2004, Official Programme: Opening Ceremony Paralympic Games Athens 2004 (Author Copy)

Athens 2004, 2004, Paralympic Family Guide (Author Copy)

Athens 2004, 2005, Official Report of the XXVIII Olympiad (Vol.2) The Paralympic Games; p. 476-513

British Paralympic Association, 2004, Athens 2004 Team Handbook and Guide, BPA; Croydon, UK (Author Copy)

The Paralympian, 2004, Official Newsletter of the International Paralympic Committee, Issue 3 (2004) (Author Copy)

Chapter 24: Torino, Italy 2006

'Passion Lives Here'

Logo:	Confirmed Participating Nations	38
torino 2006 paralympic games	Confirmed Participating Athletes	474 (375 Men, 99 Women)
	Number of Events	58
	Opening Ceremony	Friday 10th March (Stadio Comunale)
Mascot: Aster	Closing Ceremony	Sunday 19th March (Piazza Castello)
	Officially Opened by	Carlo Azeglio Ciampi (President of the Italian Republic)
	Stadium	Stadio Olimpico
	Flame Lit by	Silvia Battaglio (Visually Impaired Child), Aroldo Ruschioni (4 Summer Sports)
	Athlete's Oath	Fabrizio Zardini (Alpine Skier)
	Official's Oath	Mauro Scanacapra (Ice Sledge Hockey Referee)

Participating Nations (38): Andorra, Armenia, Australia, Austria, Belarus, Belgium, Bulgaria, Canada, Chile, China, Croatia, Czech Republic, Denmark,

Finland, France, Germany, Great Britain, Hungary, Iran, Italy, Japan, Kazakhstan, Latvia, **Mexico**, **Mongolia**, New Zealand, Norway, Poland, Russia, Slovakia, Slovenia, South Africa, South Korea, Spain, Sweden, Switzerland, Ukraine, United States. **(Countries in bold are those appearing at a winter Paralympic Games for the first time)**

Sports (5): Alpine, Ice Sledge Hockey, Biathlon, Cross Country, and Wheelchair Curling.

Impairment Groups (5): Amputees, Blind and Visually Impaired, Cerebral Palsied, Les Autres and Spinal Cord Injuries.

Logo: The three graphic shapes at the top of the logo aim to symbolise the human figure and their soaring motion aims to convey energy, joy and the desire to reach ever higher. The IPC logo at the bottom represents both the Paralympic movement as well as its motto of Mind, Body and Spirit. Finally the logo colours of blue, green and red, being the colours of the IPC logo were reinterpreted to depict the distinguishing colour of Italian sport, as well as the colour of snow and ice (blue), nature and the Italian landscape (green) and passion, which expresses vitality, enthusiasm and willpower (red).

Mascot: Designed by Pedro Albuquerque, Aster the snowflake aims to depict the originality of Paralympic athletes, rather than focusing upon their disabilities. The complexity and originality of a snow flake expresses through its limits an original way of practicing sport at the highest competition level.

The Selection of Torino as the Host City

The decision on the host city for the winter Olympic Games of 2006 was made at the 109th IOC session in Seoul, South Korea on 19th June 1999 when the Games were awarded to Turin in Italy. As with the vote for the 2002 winter Olympic Games the vote was very quick and short with just one round of voting needed to decide the winner.

Date of Vote	Location	Candidates	Voting Round
			1
19/6/1999	Seoul, South Korea	Turin, Italy	53
		Sion, Switzerland	36
		Helsinki, Finand	-
		Klagenfurt, Austria	-
		Poprad-Tatry, Slovakia	-
		Zakopane, Poland	-

The Games Poster

I have, so far, been unable to locate an official Torino 2006 Winter Paralympic Games poster similar to the one used at the Torino 2006 Winter Olympic Games. However, the following posters were also used in Torino to advertise the individual Paralympic sports.

Wheelchair Curling   Ice Sledge Hockey   Biathlon

Cross Country Skiing   Alpine Skiing

The Games Opening Ceremony

The opening ceremony of the ninth winter Paralympic Games took place in the Stadio Comunale, which had also hosted the opening ceremony for the Olympic Games several weeks earlier. Around 25,000 spectators were in attendance. The ceremony itself was divided into nine artistic and official segments as follows: 1, Our Games –a movie shown before the countdown that explained the key points of the evening and overall story behind the ceremony; 2, History of an Idea – Skaters and flag-wavers greeted the President of the International Paralympic Committee and other dignitaries; 3, Differences among Equals – artistic section involving drummers, dancers and other performers; 4, Beyond all Limits, Beyond all Barriers – Italian Paralympic and Olympic archer, Paula Fantato and a visually impaired young athlete deliver messages to the crowd; 5, Athletes' Parade – athletes from 38 countries enter the stadium; 6, The Music of the Heart – tells a story about athletes from every corner of the world; 7, Forty Nations, a Single Voice – despite the fact that only 38 nations took part this section included the official speeches, the official opening of the Games by the President of the Italian Republic, Carlo Azeglio Ciampi, the entry of the Paralympic flag and the taking of the athletes' and officials' oaths; 8, The Shape of the Flame – the arrival of the Paralympic flame and the lighting of the cauldron by Silvia Battaglio, a visually impaired child and Aroldo Ruschioni, who took part in four summer Paralympic sports in the 1960s; 9, The Sound of Light – a combination of fire and music designed as an homage to the perfection of all athletes.

The Games Themselves

A total of 474 athletes from 38 nations took part in 58 medal events across five sports in Torino. Mexico and Mongolia competed in a winter Paralympic Games for the very first time. Wheelchair Curling was added to the programme. A total of 162,974 tickets were sold during the Games. Several competitions, including the finals of the Ice Sledge Hockey and Wheelchair Curling, as well as the Opening Ceremony, were sold out. The main competitive venues for the Torino winter Paralympic Games were as follows:

Sestriere Borgata:	Alpine skiing
Cesana - San Sicario:	Cross-country skiing and biathlon
Central Torino Esposizioni:	Ice sledge hockey
Pinerolo:	Wheelchair Curling

Alpine skiing, Cross-country skiing and Biathlon athletes were housed in the Paralympic village in Sestriere. Ice Sledge Hockey and Wheelchair Curling athletes were accommodated in the Paralympic village in Turin.

A record number of media representatives covered the Games, with 1,037 written press, photographers, rights holding broadcasters and non-rights holding broadcasters present. The Host Broadcaster, International Sports Broadcasting (ISB) provided more than 130 hours of live coverage and had 303 staff on site. A number of European Broadcasting Union (EBU) broadcasters extended their coverage with Internet broadband streaming and mobile technology.

www.ParalympicSport.TV

Although media coverage of the Paralympic Games was on the increase the disparity between levels of coverage, especially television coverage, led IPC to introduce its own internet based free-view television service that provided a sustainable global media platform with which to reach audiences around the world. Sponsored by VISA and Samsung, the system allows IPC to satisfy additional demand where only limited coverage is available or to provide coverage where none exists. It was first introduced at the Torino 2006 Winter Paralympic Games and was an instant hit, broadcasting over 150 hours of live sport. The five key objectives of ParalympicSport.TV (PSTV) are:

- To create a sustainable global media platform to reach out to current and potential fans.
- To turn the weakness caused by a lack of mainstream media coverage into a strength as PSTV is often the only coverage available.

- To satisfy additional demand in areas where only limited coverage is available.
- To Communicate IPC's vision.
- To make coverage easily accessible in order to allow for maximum exposure.

Fans from 110 countries took advantage of this service in Torino, watching an average of just under four and a half hours of sport. It is interesting to note from the table below that the country that had the greatest percentage of viewers in Torino was the USA, who have been deprived of any live coverage at all of Paralympic sport by the US networks up to and including the London 2012 summer Paralympic Games, although this is set to change for Sochi 2014.

Torino, 2006		
Rank	Country	%
1	United States	21%
2	Italy	15%
3	Canada	11%
4	Germany	8%
5	Japan	7%
6	France	5%
7	Netherlands	5%
8	United Kingdom	5%
9	Belgium	4%
10	Spain	3%

Percentage audience by nation of the Torino Winter Paralympic Games on ParalympicSport.TV

The Outstanding Performers in Torino

Ukranian athlete Olena Iurkovska led the medal tally taking four gold, one silver and a bronze medal in biathlon and cross country sitski events. For the men German veteran Martin Braxenthaler took home three gold medals in the alpine sitski events.

The Winners Medal

A medal ceremony in progress

The Closing Ceremony

The Closing Ceremony, held on 19 March, took place in Piazza Castello, and the theme of the event was spring time – the transition from the dark and cold of winter to a time of warmth and excitement. It was supposed to be a metaphor for the change experienced by the city of Torino as a result of hosting both the Olympics and Paralympics. Three hundred artists were involved in the Ceremony, most of them from Torino-based companies.

The Final Medal Table

Rank	NPC	Gold	Silver	Bronze	Total
1	Russia	13	13	7	33
2	Germany	8	5	5	18
3	Ukraine	7	9	9	25
4	France	7	2	6	15
5	USA	7	2	3	12
6	Canada	5	3	5	13
Number of Countries winning a medal					19
% of participating countries winning a medal					50.0

Games Trivia

A new record number of 381 athletes voted for the IPC Athletes' Council's winter representative candidates during the Games. The newly elected members included Katarzyna Rogowiec from Poland, Hans Burn from Switzerland and Eskil Hagen from Norway.

Vancouver's Mayor Sam Sullivan accepted the Paralympic Flag on behalf of Canada at the Turin Paralympic Games Closing Ceremony. Whistler Mayor Ken Melamed then had the honour of carrying the flag back to Canada, where he and Vancouver's Mayor participated in a public flag-raising ceremony in Whistler on Friday 24th March. This was the first time in history that two Mayors from the next host Olympic region had participated in a Paralympic flag handover.

At the Closing Ceremony of the Torino 2006 Paralympic Winter Games, Ukranian athlete Olena Iurkovska was awarded the Whang Youn Dai Overcome Prize that acknowledges the overcoming of adversities through the pursuit of excellence.

A total of 242 doping control tests were carried out in Torino. All produced negative results.

References

Breaking all Limits, Opening Ceremony Programme for the Torino Winter Paralympic Games (Author copy)
International Paralympic Committee website (http://www.paralympic.org/paralympic-games/torino-2006)

Chapter 25: Beijing, China 2008

'One World, One Dream'

Logo:	Participating Nations	146
	Participating Athletes	4011 (2628 men, 1383 women)
	Number of Events	472
	Opening Ceremony	Saturday 6th September (8.00pm)
	Closing Ceremony	Wednesday 17th September (8.00pm)
Mascot: Fu Niu Lele	Officially Opened by	Hu Jintao – President of the People's Republic of China
	Stadium	'Bird's Nest' National Stadium
	Flame Lit by	Hou Bin (Field Athlete)
	Athlete's Oath	Wu Chunmiao (Track Athlete)
	Official's Oath	Hao Guohua (Goalball Judge)

Participating Nations (146 Nations): Afghanistan, Algeria, Angola, Argentina, Armenia, Australia, Austria, Azerbaijan, Bahrain, Bangladesh, Barbados, Belarus, Belgium, Benin, Bermuda, Bosnia-Herzegovina, Brasil, Bulgaria, Burkino Faso,

Burundi, Cambodia, Canada, Cape Verde, Central African Republic, Chile, China, Chinese Taipei, Colombia, Costa Rica, Croatia, Cuba, Cyprus, Czech Republic, Denmark, Dominican Republic, Ecuador, Egypt, El Salvador, Estonia, Ethiopia, Faroe Islands, Fiji, Finland, France, **Gabon**, **Georgia**, Germany, Ghana, Great Britain, Greece, Guatemala, Guinea, Haiti, Honduras, Hong Kong, Hungary, Iceland, India, Indonesia, Iran, Iraq, Ireland, Israel, Italy, Ivory Coast, Jamaica, Japan, Jordan, Kazakhstan, Kenya, Kuwait, Kyrgyzstan, Laos, Latvia, Lebanon, Lesotho, Libya, Lithuania, Luxembourg, Macao, Macedonia, Madagascar, Malaysia, Malta, Mauritius, Mexico, Moldova, Mongolia, **Montenegro**, Morocco, Myanmar, Namibia, Nepal, Netherlands, New Zealand, Niger, Nigeria, Norway, Oman, Pakistan, Palestine, Panama, Papua New Guinea, Peru, Philippines, Poland, Portugal, Puerto Rico, Qatar, Romania, Russia, Rwanda, Samoa, Saudi Arabia, Senegal, **Serbia**, Singapore, Slovakia, Slovenia, South Africa, South Korea, Spain, Sri Lanka, Surinam, Sweden, Switzerland, Syria, Tajikistan, Tanzania, Thailand, **Timor-Leste**, Tonga, Tunisia, Turkey, Turkmenistan, Uganda, Ukraine, United Arab Emirates, United States, Uruguay, Uzbekistan, Vanuatu, Venezuela, Vietnam, Zambia, Zimbabwe. **(Countries in bold are those appearing at a summer Paralympic Games for the first time)**

Sports (20): Archery, Athletics, Boccia, Cycling, Equestrianism, Football (5-a-side), Football (7-a-side), Goalball, Judo, Powerlifting, Rowing, Sailing, Shooting, Swimming, Table Tennis, Volleyball (Sitting), Wheelchair Basketball, Wheelchair Fencing, Wheelchair Rugby, Wheelchair Tennis.

Impairment Groups (5): Amputees, Blind & Visually Impaired, Cerebral Palsied, Les Autres, Spinal Cord Injuries

Logo: Dubbed 'Sky, Earth and Human Beings' and unveiled during a grand ceremony at the China Millennium Monument on July 13, 2004 in Beijing, the logo for the Beijing 2008 Paralympic Games is in the form of an athlete in motion. It is intended to embody the tremendous efforts that persons with a disability have to make in sport as well as in everyday life. It is typically Chinese in its form and style and the three colours used represent the sun (red), the sky (blue) and the earth (green). They are also intended to reflect the integration of heart, body and spirit, which are at the core of Chinese culture as well as the Paralympic Games.

Mascot: The Official Mascot of the Beijing 2008 Paralympic Games, Fu Niu Lele, was unveiled at a grand ceremony at the foot of the Great Wall on September 6th 2006, marking exactly two years to the opening ceremony of the Paralympic Games. "Fu" means "blessing", "Niu" means "cow" and "Lele" means "happiness". A modern cartoon figure in traditional Chinese colours Fu Niu Lele was designed by Wu Guanying, Professor at the Academy of Art and Design at Tsinghua University and apparently derives its inspiration from the farming and cultivation culture prevalent in ancient Chinese civilisation. Fu Niu Lele aims to symbolise the indomitable spirit of Paralympians and their resolve to be self-reliant. It also aims to symbolise the harmonious co-existence between man and nature.

The Selection of Beijing as the Host City

Beijing was elected as the host city for the 2008 Olympic and Paralympic Games at the 112th IOC Session held in Moscow, Russia on 13th July 2001 beating Toronto, Paris, Istanbul and Osaka in the process.

The Games Poster

The Games Opening Ceremony

The Opening Ceremony for the Beijing 2008 Paralympic Games commenced at 8.00pm on Saturday 6th September with entry of the President of the People's Republic of China, Hu Jintao and the President of IPC Sir Philip Craven and aimed to showcase the chosen Paralympic theme of 'Transcendence, Integration, Equality'. The Parade of Athletes was marred slightly by a protester who ran onto the track and was seen by the author to kick out at one of the athletes. They were, however, quickly removed by security.

Protester being removed from the track during the Parade of Athletes

Following artistic presentations in three chapters entitled Journey of Space, Journey of Time and Journey of Life, the President of BOCOG, Liu Qi, and the President of IPC, Sir Philip Craven gave speeches of welcome before Hu Jintao, President of the People's Republic of China officially declared the Games open. Following the entrance and hoisting of the IPC Flag and the oaths on behalf of the athletes (Wu Chunmiao (Track Athlete)) and the official's (Hao Guohua (Goalball Judge)) the Paralympic Torch entered the stadium. The honour of lighting the cauldron went to Hou Bin, gold medallist in the men's F42 high jump at the previous three Paralympic Games. The single leg amputee using a wheelchair for the ceremony hoisted himself, his wheelchair and the Paralympic torch to base of the stadium roof before lighting the cauldron. He can just be seen in the photo below as a white dot at the base of the cauldron.

Hou Bin lights the cauldron

The Games Themselves

The Beijing 2008 Paralympic Games saw a record 1.82 million tickets sold, with an additional 1.62 million tickets provided to children, education and community groups. The Opening and Closing Ceremony were sold out events, in addition to all Swimming events and most of the Athletics events. The games were spread over three regions of China with the sailing in Qingdao and the equestrian events in Hong Kong. Adaptive rowing, which made its debut on the Paralympic programme and the remaining sports were spread over various venues in Beijing:

Adapted rowing – the newest sport on the Paralympic programme

Beijing Institute of Technology Gymnasium: Goalball
Beijing Olympic Green: Archery, Athletics, Boccia, Football
                                                      (5-a- side, 7-a-side), Swimming,
                                                      Wheelchair Basketball, Wheelchair
                                                      Fencing, Wheelchair Tennis
Beijing Science and Technology University
Gymnasium: Wheelchair Basketball, Wheelchair
                                                      Rugby
Beijing Shooting Range Hall: Shooting
Beijing University of Aeronautics and
Astronautics Gymnasium: Powerlifting
Beijing Workers Gymnasium: Judo
China Agricultural University Gymnasium: Sitting Volleyball
Laoshan Velodrome: Cycling
Peking University Gymnasium: Table Tennis
Shunyi Olympic Rowing – Canoeing Park: Rowing
Hong Kong: Equestrianism
Qingdao: Sailing

Two iconic venues in Beijing at night – the water cube and the bird's nest

The Beijing 2008 Paralympic Games had the largest number of rightsholding broadcasters in the history of the Paralympic Games with a total of 64 rightsholders covering more than 80 countries worldwide, from all five continents. The total broadcasting time increased by 200 percent compared to the Athens 2004 Paralympic Games and the worldwide audience watching the Beijing Games was more than twice as high totaling 3.8 billion cumulated viewers. Although media coverage of the Games is on the increase the disparity between levels of coverage, especially television coverage, led IPC to introduce its own internet based free view television service that provided a sustainable global media platform with which to reach audiences around the world (www.ParalympicSport.TV (PSTV)). Sponsored by VISA and Samsung, this system allows IPC to satisfy additional demand where only limited coverage is available or to provide coverage where none exists. It was first introduced at the Torino 2006 Winter Paralympic Games and was an instant hit, broadcasting over 150 hours of live sport. By increasing awareness of Paralympic sport PSTV should eventually impact upon traditional media coverage by increasing interest amongst audiences. It has received extremely positive audience feedback and has provided great promotion for the movement. It has also overcome the issue of time difference as spectators are now able to watch their chosen events at a time that suits them from any place in the world. In Beijing fans from 166 countries took advantage of the service. It is interesting to note that the country that had the greatest percentage of viewers in both Torino and Beijing was the USA, who had been deprived of any live coverage at all of either event by the US networks. In Beijing American viewers made up 14% of all viewings followed by Canada (9%) and France and the United Kingdom (8%). In addition IPC also added a YouTube channel to their media coverage of the Beijing Games.

The Games saw a total of 279 new World records set, and a total of 339 Paralympic records broken. Nearly half of the new World Records came in the swimming pool where the men's competition saw 83 new World records and 124 Paralympic records broken and the women's competition saw 55 new World records set and 83 Paralympic records broken.

Over a period of ten days a Paralympic Torch Relay comprising 850 Torchbearers took two routes designed to encompass both 'Ancient' and 'Modern' China. The "Ancient China" route went through the historic cities of Xi'an, Hohhot, Changsha, Nanjing and Luoyang and the "Modern China" route went through Shenzhen, Wuhan, Shanghai, Qingdao and Dalian with the Torch Lighting having taken place at the Temple of Heaven.

The impact of the Beijing Paralympic Games upon Chinese attitudes towards disability cannot be overlooked. This is perhaps best summed up by Sun and Le Clair (2011) who quote from an editorial in the China Daily Newspaper dated 6-7 September 2008:

> "Just look around, you rarely see a person with a disability, although statistics show that there are more than one million disabled people in Beijing. That means one in 15 citizens. Yet on the streets you hardly see any such persons. This fact indicates the lack of facilities to make them more mobile....We must learn to be more considerate, and take the

needs of disabled people into account when planning buildings, streets, and other infrastructure"

(Sun and Le Clair, 2011; p.121)

A record number of 3,539 athletes (~89%) in all three Paralympic Villages (Beijing, Hong Kong, Qingdao) voted for six of the 14 candidates running for the IPC Athletes' Council up from approximately 48% of all accredited athletes who voted at the Athens 2004 Paralympic Games. The athletes elected to the IPC Athletes' Council in Beijing were Teresa Perales (ESP), Marketa Sidkova (CZE), Yu Chui Yee (HKG), Heinz Frei (SUI), Robert Balk (USA) and David Smetanine (FRA).

The Outstanding Performers in Beijing

Two swimmers and a track athlete won 5 gold medals each in Beijing. Matthew Cowdrey of Australia won 5 gold and 3 silver medals in the S9 class swimming competitions. Fresh from finishing 16th in the Olympic 10km open water event Natalie du Toit of South Africa took 5 gold medals in the women's S9 class competitions. Chantal Petitclerc of Canada repeated her amazing feat of four years earlier in Athens by taking gold medals in the women's T54 100m, 200m, 400m, 800m and 1500m. Jonas Jacobsson of Sweden competing in shooting at his eighth summer Paralympic Games took three more gold medals in the SH1 category taking his total shooting medals won since Arnhem in 1980 to 16 gold, 1 silver and 8 bronze.

The Winners Medal

Paralympic Gold medal from Beijing 2008

The Games Closing Ceremony

The Closing Ceremony for the Beijing 2008 Paralympic Games commenced at 8.00pm on Wednesday 17th September with an invitation for all spectators present to write a postcard sending their blessings to their friends and family around the world and to hand it to the 'postmen' spread around the stadium for posting. The President of the People's Republic of China, Hu Jintao and the President of IPC, Sir Philip Craven then took their seats in the stadium. The flags of all the delegations were then paraded into the stadium followed by the athletes of all nations mixed together. Following presentations to representatives of the volunteers by the newly elected members of the IPC athletes' Commission the flags of the nations exited the stadium and the artistic portion of the ceremony began. The sections of this performance had titles such as Red leaves of fragrant hill, Sowing, Watering, Harvest, Celebration and Mail it to the future where the athletes and performers got to fill out their postcards. Speeches were then given by the President of BOCOG, Liu Qi and the President of IPC, Sir Philip Craven after which the flag of Great Britain was raised and their national anthem was played as the hosts of the next Paralympic Games in London 2012. The IPC flag was then lowered and presented to the Mayor of London, Boris Johnson. The Paralympic flame was then extinguished and the ceremony ended with a huge fireworks display.

The Mayor of London, Boris Johnson receives the Paralympic flag on behalf of London 2012

The Final Medal Table

Rank	NPC	Gold	Silver	Bronze	Total
1	China	89	70	52	211
2	Great Britain	42	29	31	102
3	United States	36	35	28	99
4	Ukraine	24	18	32	74
5	Australia	23	29	27	79
6	South Africa	21	3	6	30
Number of Countries winning a medal					76
% of participating countries winning a medal					52.1

Games Trivia

Identical twins Carmen and Ramona Brussig from Germany both won medals in the women's judo in Beijing. Carmen, 15 minutes older than Ramona, won a bronze medal in the 48 kg weight class on her Paralympic debut. Twenty-four hours later her sister Ramona took silver in the 57 kg weight class, having taken gold in Athens four years earlier.

Having won the individual women's class 10 table tennis event in Athens aged just fifteen Natalie Partyka of Poland qualified for and played in both the Olympic and Paralympic table tennis events in Beijing. In the Olympics she lost a five set thriller to the world number 10 in the women's team event, but at the Paralympics she swept all before her beating the home favourite Fan Lei in straight sets in the final.

The only other person to compete in both the Olympic and Paralympic Games in Beijing was Natalie du Toit from South Africa who competed as a swimmer.

In her fifth Paralympic Games 53 year old Barbara Buchan from the USA won her first Paralympic gold medal when she won the women's 3 km individual pursuit LC3-4/ CP3 category setting a new world record in the process and becoming the oldest cycling champion at the Beijing Games.

References

Beijing Organising Committee for the Olympic Games, 2008, Official programme for the Opening Ceremony of the Beijing 2008 Paralympic Games, BOCOG; Beijing, China

Beijing Organising Committee for the Olympic Games, 2008, Official programme for the Closing Ceremony of the Beijing 2008 Paralympic Games, BOCOG; Beijing, China

Beijing Organising Committee for the Olympic Games, 2008, Transendence, Integration, Equality: Supplement on Paralympic Games, BOCOG; Beijing, China

Beijing Organising Committee for the Olympic Games, 2008, The Official BOCOG Newsletter, Issue No. 29 (June 2006), BOCOG; Beijing, China

Beijing Organising Committee for the Olympic Games, 2008, The Official BOCOG Newsletter, Issue No. 33 (September 2006), BOCOG; Beijing, China

Beijing Organising Committee for the Olympic Games, 2008, Village Life – Paralympic Village Newsletters Nos 1-12 (6th – 17th September) (Author copies)

China Daily Newspaper – The Paralympian, Issues 4-8 & 10 (Author copies)

ParalympicsGB, 2008, Beijing Team Handbook, ParalympicsGB; London, UK

Sun, S & Le Clair, J.M., 2011, Legacies and Tensions after the 2008 Beijing Paralympic Games, in Legg, D. & Gilbert, K. (Eds), Paralympic Legacies, Commonground Publishing Ltd; Champaign, IL.

Chapter 26: Vancouver, Canada 2010

'With Glowing Hearts'

Logo:	Confirmed Participating Nations	44
	Confirmed Participating Athletes	502 (381 Men, 121 Women)
	Number of Events	64 events
	Opening Ceremony	Friday 12th March (6.00pm) (BC Place Stadium)
Mascot: Sumi	Closing Ceremony	Sunday 21st March (7.00pm) (Whistler Medals Plaza)
	Officially Opened by	Michaëlle Jean (Governor General of Canada)
	Stadium	BC Place Stadium
	Flame Lit by	Zach Beaumont (Amputee Non-athlete)
	Athlete's Oath	Hervé Lord (Sledge Hockey)
	Official's Oath	Linda Kirton (Curling Official)

Participating Nations (44): Andorra, **Argentina**, Armenia, Australia, Austria, Belarus, Belgium, **Bosnia & Herzgovina**, Bulgaria, Canada, Chile, China, Croatia, Czech Republic, Denmark, Finland, France, Germany, Great Britain,

Greece, Hungary, Iceland, Iran, Italy, Japan, Kazakhstan, Mexico, Mongolia, Netherlands, New Zealand, Norway, Poland, **Romania**, **Russian Federation**, **Serbia**, Slovakia, Slovenia, South Africa, South Korea, Spain, Sweden, Switzerland, Ukraine, United States. **(Countries in bold are those appearing at a winter Paralympic Games for the first time)**

Sports (5): Alpine, Ice Sledge Hockey, Biathlon, Cross Country, and Wheelchair Curling.

Impairment Groups (5): Amputees, Blind and Visually Impaired, Cerebral Palsied, Les Autres and Spinal Cord Injuries.

Logo: The Vancouver 2010 Paralympic Winter Games Emblem represents the spirit of the Host Region, the Paralympic athlete's journey and the harmony that exists between the athlete, their sport and the environment. The emblem captures the image of Vancouver and Whistler's lush coastal forests, dramatic mountains and majestic sky — a natural theatre that will inspire Paralympians as they reach the pinnacle of sport and human achievement in 2010.

The emblem also reflects the athletes' mountainous inner strength and personal transformation as they push themselves to new heights in the pursuit of excellence. A dynamic human form is created by the valley, mountains and sun of the West Coast. This design honours the harmonious relationship by suggesting that the athlete and mountain are one.

Mascot: Sumi is an animal spirit who lives in the mountains of British Columbia. Like many Canadians, Sumi's background is drawn from many places. He wears the hat of the orca whale, flies with the wings of the mighty thunderbird and runs on the strong furry legs of the black bear. Sumi's name comes from the Salish word "Sumesh" which means "guardian spirit." Sumi takes his role very seriously. He works hard to protect the land, water and creatures of his homeland.

Transformation is a common theme in the art and legend of West Coast First Nations. Transformation represents the connection and kinship between the human, animal and spirit world. Revered animals, such as the orca whale, the bear and the thunderbird, are depicted in transformation through masks, totems and other forms of art. The orca is the traveller and guardian of the sea. The bear often represents strength and friendship. And the thunderbird — which creates thunder by flapping its wings — is one of the most powerful of the supernatural creatures.

The Selection of Vancouver as the Host City

The decision on the host city for the winter Olympic Games of 2002 was made at the 115th IOC session in Prague, Czech Republic on 2nd July 2003 when the Games were awarded to Vancouver in Canada.

Date of Vote	Location	Candidates	Voting Round	
			1	2
2/07/2003	Prague, Czech Republic	Vancouver, Canada	40	56
		PyeongChang, South Korea	51	53
		Salzburg, Austria	16	-
		Andorra la Vella, Andorra		
		Berne, Switzerland		
		Harbin, China		
		Jaca, Spain		
		Sarajevo, Bosnia-Herzegovina		

The Games Poster

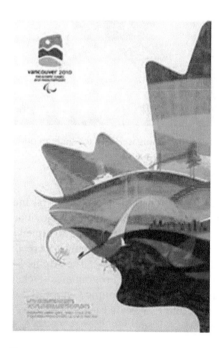

The Games Opening Ceremony

The Opening Ceremony took place on Friday 12th March in BC Place Stadium in Vancouver starting at 6.00pm. A sell-out crowd of 60,000 viewed the Opening Ceremony, which had a theme of "One Inspires Many" and featured over 5000 local performers, including hip-hop dancer Luca "Lazylegz" Patuelli. The 2 hours live ceremony was produced by Vancouver-based Patrick Roberge Productions Inc. The Games were officially opened by Michaëlle Jean, Governor General of Canada, with the athlete's oath being taken by Hervé Lord, a Canadian Ice Sledge Hockey player and the oath on behalf of the officials being taken by Linda Kirton, a curling official.

Over 600 torchbearers carried the flame during the Vancouver 2010 Paralympic Torch Relay. The Paralympic Torch visited eleven communities all over Canada in ten days, culminating in a 24 hour long circular relay through downtown Vancouver before being handed to 15-year old amputee snowboarder Zach Beaumont to light the Games Cauldron.

Paralympic cauldron burning in BC Place stadium during the Games.

The Games Themselves

A total of 502 athletes from 44 nations took part in 64 medal events across five sports in Vancouver. Argentina, Bosnia and Herzogovina, Romania, Serbia and The Russian Federation competed in a winter Paralympic Games for the very first time. The three largest delegations in Vancouver were the USA (50 athletes), Canada (45 athletes) and Japan (41 athletes). The Alpine Skiing Super Combined event was added to the Paralympic Programme. Ticket sales in Vancouver reached a new record for a winter Paralympic Games of 230,000 compared to the 162,974 tickets sold in Torino four years earlier. The main competition venues in Vancouver were as follows:

Doug Mitchell Thunderbird Sports Centre, Vancouver: Ice sledge hockey
Vancouver Olympic/Paralympic Centre, Vancouver: Wheelchair curling
Whistler Creekside, Whistler: Alpine Skiing
Whistler Paralympic Park, Whistler: Biathlon, Cross
    Country Skiing

The athletes and officials were accommodated in two Paralympic Villages, in Vancouver and Whistler, which accommodated a total of around 1,350 participants. 6,100 volunteers ensured the Games ran smoothly.

Nearly 1,200 media representatives covered the Games, which was an increase of 12 per cent from the previous Paralympics Games in Torino. 1.6 billion viewers in 22 countries followed the Vancouver 2010 Paralympic Games worldwide with Japan having the biggest audience at around 538 million viewers, followed by Germany, which had nearly 400 million viewers. Alpine skiing was the most popular sport amongst viewers, with a total audience of more than 690 million. In addition the IPCs own online television channel, www.ParalympicSport.TV, provided more than 437,000 live streams during the Games.

Wheelchair Curling in action in Vancouver

Ice Sledge Hockey semi-final match USA v Norway

Sell-out crowds at the Ice Sledge Hockey

The Outstanding Performers in Vancouver

Germany's Verena Bentele (Cross-Country Skiing & Biathlon) and Canadian Alpine Skier Lauren Woolstencroft topped the individual medal tally winning five gold medals each. German Alpine Skiier Gerd Schoenfelder and Russia's Cross-Country Skier Irek Zaripov did almost as well, winning four gold medals and one silver medal from the five events that they each entered.

The Winners Medal

Medal ceremony for the Cross Country Skiing Men's 20 km standing event

The Closing Ceremony

Athletes paraded through cheering supporters lining Whister's Village Stroll on their way to the Closing Ceremony, which took place on Sunday 21st March commencing at 7.00pm. The Canadian national anthem 'O Canada' was sung by Whistler's Ali Milner whilst 125 skiers skied down Whistler Mountain. Winnipeg-born singer Chantal Kreviazuk then performed 'Today's A Greatest Day' in honour of the athletes and Canadian Inuit throat-singer Tania Tagaq performed as Paralympian Kelly Smith was tossed in the air on a traditional Inuit blanket. Sir Philip Craven, President of IPC then awarded the 2010 Whang Youn Dai Achievement Award to Colette Bourgonje of Canada and Takayuki Endo of Japan after which Sir Philip declared the Vancouver Games 'the best winter Paralympic Games ever'. After the Paralympic flag lowering ceremony the mayors of Vancouver and Whistler, Gregor Robertson and Ken Melamed, handed over the Paralympic flag to Sir Philip who entrusted it to the Mayor of Sochi Anatoly Pakhomov in readiness for the next winter Games in four years time.

The Final Medal Table

Rank	NPC	Gold	Silver	Bronze	Total
1	Germany	13	5	6	24
2	Russia	12	16	10	38
3	Canada	10	5	4	19
4	Slovakia	6	2	3	11
5	Ukraine	5	8	6	19
6	USA	4	5	4	13
Number of Countries winning a medal					21
% of participating countries winning a medal					47.7

Games Trivia

A record number (for a winter Games) of 403 athletes in both the Vancouver and Whistler Paralympic Village elected three of the six candidates running for the IPC Athletes' Council. The successful candidates were Katarzyna Rogowiec (POL), Todd Nicholson (CAN) and Eskil Hagen (NOR).

Brian McKeever of Canada became the first athlete to be selected for a winter Paralympic and winter Olympic Games team in the same year. However, in the end, he did not actually compete at the Olympic Games, where he was due to compete in the men's 50 km cross-country race, but the Canadian team coach replaced him with a skier who did well at an earlier event. At the Paralympics, he competed in Cross-country skiing and Biathlon.

A total of 444 doping tests were conducted during the Vancouver 2010 Paralympic Winter Games, with 221 in-competition and 223 out-of-competition tests.

References

International Paralympic Committee website
        (http://www.paralympic.org/paralympic-games/vancouver-2010)

Chapter 27: London, UK 2012

'Inspire a Generation'

Logo:	Participating Nations	164
	Participating Athletes	4237 (2736 Men, 1501 Women)
	Number of Events	503 in 20 Sports
	Opening Ceremony	Wednesday 29th August (7.30pm)
	Closing Ceremony	Sunday 9th September (7.30pm)
Mascot: Mandeville	Officially Opened by	Her Majesty Queen Elizabeth II
	Stadium	The Olympic Stadium
	Flame Lit by	Margaret Maughan (Archery Gold Medalist – Rome 1960)
	Athlete's Oath	Liz Johnson (Swimming)
	Official's Oath	Richard Allcroft (Wheelchair Rugby)
	Coach's Oath	David Hunter (GBR Equestrian Team Leader)

Participating Nations (164): Afghanistan (1), Albania (1), Algeria (33), **Andorra (1)**, Angola (4), **Antigua and Barbuda (1)**, Argentina (63), Armenia (2), Australia (161), Austria (32), Azerbaijan (21), Bahrain (2), Barbados (1), Belarus (30), Belgium (42), Benin (1), Bermuda (1), Bosnia and Herzegovina (13), Brazil (189), **Brunei (1)**, Bulgaria (8), Burkina Faso (2), Burundi (1), Cambodia (1), **Cameroon (1)**, Canada (149), Cape Verde (1), Central African Republic (1), Chile (7), China (282) Colombia (39), **Comoros (1)**, Costa Rica (2), Côte d'Ivoire (4), Croatia (25), Cuba (23), Cyprus (3), Czech Republic (46), Denmark (28), **DR Congo (2)**, **Djibouti (1)**, Dominican Republic (2), Ecuador (2), Egypt (40), El Salvador (1), Estonia (3), Ethiopia (4), Faroe Islands (1), Fiji (1), Finland (35), France (156), Gabon (1), **Gambia (2)**, Georgia (2), Germany (145), Ghana (4), Great Britain (288), Greece (61), Guatemala (1), **Guinea-Bissau (2)**, Haiti (2), Honduras (1), Hong Kong (28), Hungary (33), Iceland (4), India (10), Indonesia (4), Iran (79), Iraq (19), Ireland (49), Israel (25), Italy (99), Jamaica (3), Japan (116), Jordan (9), Kazakhstan (7), Kenya (13), Kuwait (6), Kyrgyzstan (1), Laos (1), Latvia (8), Lebanon (1), Lesotho (1), **Liberia (1)**, Libya (2), Lithuania (11), Macau (2), Macedonia (2), Madagascar (1), Malaysia (22), Mali (1), Malta (1), Mauritania (2), Mauritius (2), Mexico (81), Moldova (2), Mongolia (6), Montenegro (1), Morocco (30), **Mozambique (2)**, Myanmar (2), Namibia (5), Nepal (2), Netherlands (91), New Zealand (24), Nicaragua (2), Niger (2), Nigeria (29), **North Korea (1)**, Norway (22), Oman (2), Pakistan (2), Palestine (2), Panama (2), Papua New Guinea (2), Peru (1), Philippines (9), Poland (100), Portugal (30), Puerto Rico (2), Qatar (1), Romania (5), Russia (183), Rwanda (14), Samoa (2), **San Marino (1)**, Saudi Arabia (4), Senegal (1), Serbia (13), Sierra Leone (1), Singapore (8), Slovakia (33), Slovenia (22), **Solomon Islands (1)**, South Africa (62), South Korea (88), Spain (142), Sri Lanka (7), Suriname (1), Sweden (59), Switzerland (25), Syria (5), Chinese Taipei (18), Tajikistan (1), Tanzania (1), Thailand (50), Timor-Leste (1), Tonga (1), Trinidad and Tobago (2), Tunisia (31), Turkey (69), Turkmenistan (5), Uganda (2), Ukraine (150), United Arab Emirates (15), United States (216), Uruguay (1), Uzbekistan (10), Vanuatu (1), Venezuela (27), Vietnam (11), **Virgin Islands (1)**, Zambia (2), Zimbabwe (2) **(Countries in bold are those appearing at a summer Paralympic Games for the first time)** (Numbers in brackets after each country are the team size)

Sports (20): Archery, Athletics, Boccia, Cycling, Equestrianism, Football (5-a-side), Football (7-a-side), Goalball, Judo, Powerlifting, Rowing, Sailing, Shooting, Swimming, Table Tennis, Volleyball (Sitting), Wheelchair Basketball, Wheelchair Fencing, Wheelchair Rugby, Wheelchair Tennis.

Impairment Groups (6): Amputees, Blind & Visually Impaired, Cerebral Palsied, Intellectually Disabled, Les Autres, Spinal Cord Injuries.

Logo: For the first time ever the logo for the London Paralympic Games had the same core design as its Olympic counterpart, which was part of London's commitment to hosting a truly integrated Paralympic Games. Designed by international brand consultant Wolff Olins and launched on 4th June 2007 by Sebastian Coe, Chairman of the London Organising Committee, the logo is based upon the number 2012 – the year of the Games. The four original colours of the London 2012 identity – pink, blue, green and orange – were apparently inspired by the worlds of media, communications and fashion. The colours were chosen to communicate the spirit of the London 2012 Games: energetic, spirited, bright and youthful. All four colours are depicted in the Paralympic version of the logo.

Mascot: Mandeville, named after Stoke Mandeville Hospital where the Paralympic movement has its origins, was designed by London based creative agency iris. Mandeville was unveiled, along with its Olympic counterpart, Wenlock, on 19th May 2010. The three spikes on Mandeville's head are meant to represent the three Paralympic agitos.

The Selection of London as the Host City

London was elected as the host city for the 2012 Olympic and Paralympic Games at the 117th IOC Session held in Singapore on 6th July 2005 beating Moscow, New York, Madrid and Paris in the process.

The Games Poster

Unlike previous Games there was no official single poster, which previously had usually been a combination of the Games logo and the dates for the Games. Instead, the London Organising Committee commissioned twelve leading British artists to create images that celebrated London's hosting of the Games. Six were commissioned to create images for the Olympic Games and six for the Paralympic Games, which are shown below.

Tracey Emin	Michael Craig-Martin	Sarah Morris
'Birds'	'GO'	'Big Ben'

Bob & Roberta Smith   Gary Hume   Fiona Banner
'Love'   'Capital'   'Superhuman Nude'

The Games Opening Ceremony

The opening ceremony was held on 29 August at the Olympic Stadium and was inspired by William Shakespeare's play *The Tempest* and themed around the concept of 'Enlightenment'. It featured appearances by world renowned theoretical physicist Stephen Hawking, along with actors Ian McKellen and Nicola Miles-Wildin playing the roles of Prospero and Miranda – characters from *The Tempest*.

Part of the London Paralympic Closing Ceremony themed around 'enlightenment'

The ceremony also featured a performance by leading UK disabled theatre company Graeae, who played their version of the polio survivor Ian Dury's 1981 protest song 'Spasticus Autisticus'.

UK disabled theatre group performing 'Spasticus Autisticus'

The Games were officially opened by Her Majesty Queen Elizabeth II, before Royal Marine Joe Townsend, who lost both of his legs after stepping on a land mine on duty in Afghanistan and who hopes to compete in the Rio 2016 Paralympic Games, delivered the flame to the Olympic Stadium via a zipline from the ArcelorMittal Orbit tower. He passed the flame to Gret Britain five-a-side football captain David Clarke, who then passed it to the final torch bearer of the London 2012 Paralympic Games, Margaret Maughan, who won Great Britain's very first gold medal at the first Paralympic Games in Rome in 1960 and who lit the Paralympic cauldron for London 2102.

Royal Marine Joe Townsend

Rome Paralympic Medalist Margaret Maughan

The Games Themselves

London saw a record 4237 participants from 164 nations take part in 503 events spread over 20 sports. In addition a record 2.7 million tickets were sold for the Games with most events and sessions selling out. There were also 251 new world records and a further 314 Paralympic Games records set, strongly suggesting that Paralympic sports have not yet reached their peak in performance terms. The 20 sports were spread over eight venues with eight of the sports occurring on the Olympic Park and the rest elsewhere as follows:

Olympic Park Venues

Aquatics Centre:	Swimming
Basketball Arena:	Wheelchair Basketball, Wheelchair Rugby
Copperbox:	Goalball
Eton Manor:	Wheelchair Tennis
Olympic Stadium:	Athletics
Riverbank Arena:	Football (5-a-side), Football (7-a-side)
Velodrome:	Cycling (Track)

The Velodrome in the Olympic Park

Non-Olympic Park Venues

Brands Hatch:	Cycling (Road)
Eton Dorney:	Rowing
Excel Centre:	Boccia, Judo, Powerlifting, Table Tennis, Volleyball (sitting), Wheelchair Fencing.
Greenwich Park:	Equestrianism
North Greenwich Arena:	Wheelchair Basketball
Royal Artillery Barracks:	Archery, Shooting
Weymouth and Portland:	Sailing

Around seventy thousand volunteers assisted with the running of London 2012 and they were widely hailed for their friendliness, helpfulness and sense of fun.

The London 2012 volunteers were universally hailed for their helpfulness and sense of fun

The Outstanding Performers in London

As is often the case at the summer Paralympic Games the leading male and female medal winners were both swimmers. Jacqueline Freney of Australia won eight gold medals and Daniel Dias of Brazil won six gold medals. On the track Great Britain's David Weir and USA's Martin Raymond won four gold medals each. Weir won the T54 800m, 1,500m, 5,000m and marathon and 18 year old Raymond won the T52 100m, 200m, 400m and 800m. In cycling Britain's Sarah Storey also won four gold medals, joining Dame Tanni Grey-Thompson as the most successful British female Paralympian and second on the all-time British list behind swimmer Mike Kenny.

The Winners Medal

The Games Closing Ceremony

The closing ceremony was held on 9th September at the Olympic Stadium. The show opened with Lance Corporal Rory McKenzie, who is supported by the Help For Heroes charity, proclaiming to the crowd that 'We have all been touched by the triumphs and drama of the Paralympics....Let the love that the Paralympics has kindled in our hearts burn brightly as we come together as one, for the Festival of the Flame'. The bulk of the closing ceremony revolved around a live performance by British rock band Coldplay set to sequences representing the four seasons, along with performances by superstar singers Rihanna and American rapper Jay-Z.

Coldplay and Rihanna during Paralympic Closing Ceremony performance

The Royal family was represented by His Royal Highness Prince Edward the Earl of Wessex and his wife. Paralympians Michael McKillop of Ireland, and Kenya's Mary Nakhumicha Zakayo were given the Whang Youn Dai award for those exemplifying the spirit of the Games. To mark its hosting of the 2016 Summer Paralympics, the Paralympic flag was passed from Boris Johnson, Mayor of London to Eduardo Paes, Mayor of Rio de Janeiro, whilst representatives of the Rio 2016 team provided a samba-inspired performance to give a taste of the next Games in four years' time.

Representatives of Rio 2016 provide a samba inspired introduction to what lies ahead in 4-years time

LOCOG chief Sebastian Coe and IPC president Philip Craven both congratulated London for its successful hosting of the Paralympics; Coe was proud that both the Olympics and Paralympics in London could be labeled 'Made in Britain'. Sir Phillip, perhaps unsurprisingly proclaimed the London 2012 Paralympic Games 'the greatest Paralympic Games ever.'

Lord Sebastian Coe and Sir Philip Craven giving closing ceremony speeches

British Paralympic gold medalists Ellie Simmonds and Jonnie Peacock shared the honour of extinguishing the Paralympic cauldron, sharing its final flame on torches to others throughout the stadium to represent its eternal spirit. The ceremony ended with a spectacular firework display over the Olympic Stadium and Park, providing a fitting finale to the London 2012 Olympic and Paralympic Games.

The Final Medal Table

Rank	NPC	Gold	Silver	Bronze	Total
1	China	95	71	65	231
2	Russia	36	38	28	102
3	Great Britain	34	43	43	120
4	Ukraine	32	24	28	84
5	Australia	32	23	30	85
6	United States	31	29	38	98
Number of Countries winning a medal					75
% of participating countries winning a medal					45.7

Torch Relay

Prior to the Stoke Mandeville Flame Ceremony held on Tuesday 28th August, National Flames had been created at the summit of the highest peaks in the four home nations - Scafell Pike (England), Snowdon (Wales), Ben Nevis (Scotland) and Slieve Donard (Northern Ireland). The four individual Flames were then placed in miner's lanterns and transferred to the nation's capital cities (London, Belfast Edinburgh and Cardiff) where Paralympic celebrations took place.

London 2012 Paralympic Lantern

The four national flames are combined to form the Paralympic Flame

The individual lanterns were then brought together at Stoke Mandeville where they were used to light four torches. The flames from these four torches were then combined together in a cauldron at the Stoke Mandeville event to form the Paralympic Flame.

IPC President Sir Philip Craven was among the first five Torchbearers to carry the London 2012 Paralympic Flame on a 92-mile journey to the Olympic Stadium in a 24-hour torch relay that involved 580 Torchbearers working in teams of five. Sir Philip was joined by four British Paralympic legends – Baroness Susan Masham of Ilton, Caz Walton, Sally Haynes and Jane Blackburn. Plans are currently underway to make Stoke Mandeville the home of the flame lighting ceremony for all future Paralympic Games.

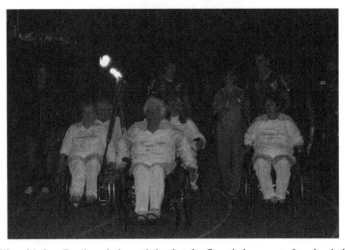

Sir Philip with four Paralympic legends begins the flame's journey to London led off by Sally Haynes.

Media Coverage

The London 2012 Paralympic Games were shown in more countries than ever before and attracted their biggest ever international audience. In the UK rights holder Channel 4, who won the rights in a first ever competitive bidding situation with the BBC, screened over 150 hours of live coverage, achieving record audiences. More than 11.2 million watched the Opening Ceremony, which was Channel 4's biggest audience for a decade and most days the channel enjoyed the biggest audience share of all the main UK television channels. Channel 4's coverage reached 39.9 million people, which amounts to over 69% of the UK population. According to the figures released by the International Paralympic Committee the London Paralympic 2012 Games were watched by a cumulative international audience of 3.4 billion (excluding the host nation), which is an increase of around 37 per cent on the last summer Games in Beijing. The London 2012 Games were broadcast in over 115 countries and the number of hours broadcast outside the host market grew by 82 per cent on 2008 to over 2,500 hours of content. The only real negative was the continued lack of interest in the Paralympic Games by the American television networks, with the US Olympic and Paralympic rights holder NBC showing only five-and-a-half hours of highlights, no live coverage, and no coverage at all of the opening and closing ceremonies.

Social media also played a massive role in spreading interest in Paralympic sport. A report published by Twitter revealed that the hashtag #Paralympics topped the table for the most trending UK sport event of 2012 beating off stiff competition from the Olympic Games and many leading Premiership football clubs. Around 50 leading athletes also took part in the Samsung Bloggers project which saw them record and post video blogs from behind the scenes before, during and after the London 2012 Games. Over 600 video blogs were uploaded and were viewed by over 300,000 people.

Games Trivia

In Wheelchair Tennis, Dutch sensation Esther Vergeer was reduced to tears winning her fourth Paralympic gold medal and 470th consecutive match.

Claims were made that the London Paralympic Games had a significant impact on British society. Research ahead of the Closing Ceremony found:

- 1 in 3 UK adults changed their attitude towards people with an impairment.
- 65% agree the Paralympics delivered a breakthrough in the way people with an impairment are viewed in the country – up from a 40% expectation in June 2010.
- Eight out of ten (81%) British adults thought the Paralympics had a positive impact on the way people with an impairment are viewed by the public.
- The Paralympic Games is about ability, not disability – and are about what people can do, not what they can't do.

As part of the inclusion and showcasing of British culture and Iconic British products minture radio-controlled models of the Mini were used in the athletics field events to transport throwing implements back to the the throwing circle or run up.

Models of the iconic British Mini used to transport field implements

References

Village Life, Daily Newsletter from the London 2012 Paralympic Games Village
        Issues 1-13 (Author copies)
Official Programme, London 2012 Paralympic Games (Author copy)
The Official Paralympic Games Daily Programme Issues 1-11 (Author copies)

Chapter 28: Toward a Single Worldwide Organisational Body for International Disability Sport.

The Games in New York, 1984 were the first summer Games to benefit from the centralised control of a single international body – the International Co-ordinating Committee of Sports for the Disabled (ICC). As far back as 1960, recognising the need to organise international sports for disability groups other than paraplegics the International Working Group on Sports for the Disabled was set up under the aegis of the World Veterans Federation whose headquarters was in Paris. Unfortunately, due to language difficulties and differences of opinion the organisation failed and was dissolved in 1964. In its place the International Sports Organisation for the Disabled (ISOD) was founded at a meeting in Paris in 1964. ISOD remained under the patronage of the World Veterans Federation until 1967, when it became an independent organisation and its headquarters were transferred to Stoke Mandeville. In the same year the British Limbless Ex-Servicemen's Association (BLESMA) organised the first ever international sports competition for amputees at Stoke Mandeville. Guttmann, now Sir Ludwig Guttmann after being knighted by the Queen for services to the disabled in 1966, became President of both ISMGF and ISOD and this dual role would play a major part in bringing the disability groups together in one Games. Initially ISOD represented a number of disability groups and together with ISMGF assisted in the organisation of the Paralympic Summer Games in Toronto, 1976 and Arnhem, 1980. They also initiated the first ever Winter Paralympic Games in Örnsköldvik, Norway in 1976.

However, by the mid- nineteen seventies there was a desire amongst the membership of ISOD to develop individual international sports organisations for the different disability groups within ISOD and in 1978 an international group governing cerebral palsy sport and recreation ceded from ISOD at an international seminar and games held in Edinburgh. This developing situation lead Sir Ludwig to raise the question at the ISOD General Assembly in Madrid in March, 1977, as to exactly what the future role of ISOD should be, which lead to the preparation of a discussion document, presented in November, 1978 by Joan Scruton, Secretary General of ISOD and ISMGF. In it she raised the possibility of ISOD taking on the role of an overall umbrella organisation that would become the co-ordinating committee for sport for all disabled and in Olympic years would act as an overall organising body representing all the relevant individual sports organisations. This is something the IOC had also been pushing for in its dealings with the disability sport movement as its representatives found it quite confusing trying to deal with such a wide variety of organisations.

Following a report in April 1979 by Guillermo Cabezas, Vice President of ISOD, and Ariel Fink, Vice President of ISMGF, on the setting up of a single federation a Study Group was set up consisting of representatives from all interested parties. The group held three meetings in July 1979, June 1980 (Arnhem), and December 1980 (Stoke Mandeville), which came up with several drafts of ideas for a new organisation. In the end the recommendations of the Study Group were rejected. However, it was recognised that the united efforts of the different disability organisations represented within the Study Group were the basis for further mutual co-operation. Therefore, at the ISOD General Assembly in December 1981, the new President of ISOD, following the death of Sir Ludwig, Mr Avronsaart, invited the three other international sports organisations to a meeting in order to discuss the establishment of a Co-operative Committee.

With the International Blind Sports Association (IBSA) having been founded in Paris in 1981, there were four different International Organisations for Sport for the Disabled (IOSD's) represented at the founding meeting on March 11th 1982 in Leysin, Switzerland during the Second World Championships in Winter Sports for the Disabled:

- International Stoke Mandeville Games Federation (ISMGF)
- International Sports Organisation for the Disabled (ISOD)
- International Blind Sports Association (IBSA) (1981)
- Cerebral Palsied – International Sports and Recreation Association (CP-ISRA) (1978)

After lengthy discussion it was unanimously agreed that the four international organisations should form a co-operative committee, with the chairmanship of future meetings of this co-operative committee rotating amongst the Presidents of the four member organisations. At the second meeting of the committee on 28th July 1982 at Stoke Mandeville it was agreed that the name for the new co-operative committee should be The International Co-ordinating Committee (ICC). This was later amended at the fifth meeting of ICC in 1984 to The International Co-ordinating Committee of World Sports Organisations for the Disabled.

International Co-ordinating Committee Meetings 1982 – 1993

	Date(s)	Venue	Chairperson	Represented
ICC1	Mar 11 1982	Leysin, Switzerland	M. Avronsart (ISOD)	CP-ISRA, IBSA, ISOD, ISMGF
ICC2	Jul 28 1982	Aylesbury, UK	A. Cameron (CP-ISRA)	CP-ISRA, IBSA, ISOD, ISMGF
ICC3	Jan 25 1983	Aylesbury, UK	H. Pielasch (IBSA)	CP-ISRA, IBSA, ISOD, ISMGF
ICC4	Jul 28 1983	Aylesbury, UK	R. Jackson	CP-ISRA, IBSA,

			(ISMGF)	ISOD, ISMGF
ICC5	Jan 20-21 1984	Innsbruck, Austria	G. Cabezas (ISOD)	CP-ISRA, IBSA, ISOD, ISMGF
ICC6	Jun 14 1984	New York, USA	A. Cameron (CP-ISRA)	CP-ISRA, IBSA, ISOD, ISMGF
ICC7	Feb 3 1985	Arnhem, Netherlands	J. Bromann (IBSA)	CP-ISRA, IBSA, ISOD, ISMGF
ICC8	Aug 4-5 1985	Aylesbury, UK	J. Grant (ISMGF)	CP-ISRA, IBSA, ISOD, ISMGF
ICC9	Feb 14-16 1986	Barcelona, Spain	G. Cabezas (ISOD)	CP-ISRA, IBSA, ISOD, ISMGF
ICC10	Aug 6-7 1986	Gothenburg, Sweden	A. Klapwijk (CP-ISRA)	CP-ISRA, IBSA, ISOD, ISMGF
ICC11	Jan 30-31 1987	Copenhagen, Denmark	J. Bromann (IBSA)	CISS, CP-ISRA, IBSA, INAS-FMH, ISOD, ISMGF
ICC12	Aug 2-3 1987	Aylesbury, UK	J. Grant (ISMGF)	CISS, CP-ISRA, IBSA, ISOD, ISMGF
ICC13	Jan 22-23 1988	Innsbruck, Austria	G. Cabezas (ISOD)	CISS, CP-ISRA, IBSA, INAS-FMH, ISOD, ISMGF
ICC14	Jun 19-20 1988	Aylesbury, UK	A. Klapwijk (CP-ISRA)	CISS, CP-ISRA, IBSA, INAS-FMH, ISOD, ISMGF
ICC15	Jan 27-29 1989	Copenhagen, Denmark	J. Bromann (IBSA)	CISS, CP-ISRA, IBSA, INAS-FMH, ISOD, ISMGF
ICC16	Jul 30-31 1989	Aylesbury, UK	J. Grant (ISMGF)	CISS, CP-ISRA, IBSA, INAS-FMH, ISOD, ISMGF
ICC17	Jan 27-28 1990	Barcelona, Spain	G. Cabezas (ISOD)	CISS, CP-ISRA, IBSA, INAS-FMH, ISOD, ISMGF
ICC18	Oct 6 1990	Aylesbury, UK	J. Weinstein (CP-ISRA)	CISS, CP-ISRA, IBSA, INAS-FMH, IPC, ISOD, ISMWSF
ICC19	Feb 16 1991	Barcelona, Spain	F. Vicente (INAS-FMH)	CP-ISRA, IBSA, INAS-FMH, IPC, ISOD, ISMWSF
ICC20	Aug 3 1991	London, UK	J. Grant (ISMGF)	CP-ISRA, IBSA, INAS-FMH, IPC, ISOD, ISMWSF
ICC21	Mar 21 1992	Tignes, France	J. Bromann (IBSA)	CP-ISRA, IBSA, IPC, ISOD, ISMWSF
ICC22	Aug 30 1992	Barcelona, Spain	G. Cabezas (ISOD)	CP-ISRA, IBSA, INAS-FMH, IPC, ISOD, ISMWSF
ICC23	Sep 13 1992	Barcelona, Spain	G. Cabezas (ISOD)	CP-ISRA, IBSA, IPC, ISOD, ISMWSF
ICC24	Mar 24-25 1993	Larnaca, Cyprus	E. Dendy (CP-ISRA)	CP-ISRA, IBSA, INAS-FMH, IPC, ISOD, ISMWSF

ICC and National Representation.

Following an ICC seminar held in the Netherlands in February 1985 recommendations were made that a further seminar be held, to which national members were invited, in order to discuss a possible future structure of ICC to include national representation. This seminar was finally held in Arnhem, The Netherlands from 12-15 March 1987. As well as representation from the six IOSD's the seminar was also attended by representatives from thirty-nine voting countries and one hundred and six national and international disability sports organisations in total. The main recommendation to come out of the seminar was that their had to be a change in the existing ICC structure and that any future structure must include; a, national representation, b, representation from and the continued existence of the IOSD's, c, regional representation and d, representation from the athletes. An ad-hoc committee was appointed to formulate a constitution for the new organization to replace ICC. It was voted that the ad-hoc committee should consist of the six representatives of the IOSD's, one elected representative from each of the Continental Associations, three athlete representatives and a representative of IFSD. Following nominations and votes for the continental and athlete representatives the final line up for the ad-hoc committee was as follows:

Member Representation	Name
CISS Representative	Mr Jerald M. Jordan
CP-ISRA Representative	Mr Jack Weinstein
IBSA Representative	Mr Jens Broeman
INAS-FMH Representative	Mr Joseph Paul Kieboom
ISMGF Representative	Mr Ariel Fink
ISOD Representative	Mr Guillermo Cabezas
Africa	Dr Nabil Salem (Egypt)
Americas	Mr Hugh Glynn (Canada)
Asia	Mr York Chow (Hong Kong)
Europe	Mr Carl Wang (Norway) (Chairman)
Middle East	Mr Akram Massarweh (Jordan)
Oceania	Mr Kevin Cosgrove (Australia)
Athlete Representative	Dr Ann Trotman (United Kingdom)
Athlete Representative	Mr Dick Bryant (USA)
Athlete Representative	Mr Marc De Meyer (Belgium)
IFSD	Mr W. van Zijll

The work of the ad-hoc committee was funded by IFSD and they held meetings in July, 1987 (Arnhem), October, 1987 (Cairo) and April, 1988 (Deventer). The new constitution proposed by them was circulated to the member nations and then discussed at a hearing during the Seoul Paralympic Summer Games in 1988. The hearing that occurred in Seoul was actually a very turbulent and highly charged affair with many representatives actually leaving the meeting, partly in frustration. However, it was finally agreed that draft recommendations for the new constitution should be submitted to the ad-hoc committee by December 21st 1988 and that a final draft constitution would be circulated to national and international organisations by March 1ˢᵗ 1989. This final draft was finally discussed and voted upon at a General Assembly held in Dussledorf, Germany on 21-22 September 1989.

The Formation of the International Paralympic Committee.

The General Assembly in Dussledorf did not start well for the IOSD's when it was decreed that only national organisations had the right to speak and vote. However, after some strenuous lobbying from the floor the decree was overturned and the IOSD's were finally given both speaking and voting rights. Part of the reason for these initial problems was possibly the fact that a neutral Chairperson, Dr Wilf Preising, was selected to Chair the Assembly, but lacked a knowledge and experience of the political rivalries inherent within international disability sport at the time. There followed many hours of, sometimes acrimonious, debate and argument and just when it appeared that an agreement would never be reached a series of motions from the floor by Jens Bromann (Denmark), York Chow (Hong Kong) and André Raes (Belgium) enabled the assembly to come to an agreement. Originally the new organisation was to have been called the International Confederation of Sports Organisations for the Disabled (ICSOD), but following a vote it was decided that it should be called the International Paralympic Committee (IPC) instead. The key objective of the newly formed IPC was decreed as being the only world multi-disability organisation with the right to organise Paralympic and multi-disability World Games, as well as World Championships. Following a further vote the structure of the proposed Executive Committee was enlarged from twenty to twenty-three members with the addition of an extra regional representative, splitting Asia into east and west, a Technical Officer and a Medical Officer. Prior to voting for the new Executive Board it was decreed that no one standing for a position could, if elected, also hold a position on the Executive Board of one of the IOSD's. This ruling caused several candidates to withdraw from the elections. The six IOSD's and the forty-one countries that were represented by various NOSD's are recognised as the founding members of the International Paralympic Committee. These were:

> Australia, Austria, Belgium, Bulgaria, Canada, Cyprus, Czechoslovakia, Denmark, Egypt, Faroe Isles, Finland, France, Germany, Greece, Hong Kong, Hungary, Iceland, Iran, Iraq, Ireland, Israel, Italy, Jordan, Kenya, Korea, Kuwait, Luxembourg, Malta, Morocco, Netherlands, New Zealand, Norway, Poland, Portugal, Spain, Sweden, Switzerland, USSR, UK, USA, Venezuela

The ICC – IPC Handover of Responsibilities.

IPC held their first Executive Committee meeting in Duisburg, Germany on 23ʳᵈ September 1989, the day after the General Assembly had closed. One of their first orders of business was to inform the IOC, IFSD, ICC and the United Nations (UN) of their existence and objectives. With the contracts already having been signed by ICC for the Winter and Summer Paralympic Games to be held in

Tignes, Barcelona and Madrid in 1992 IPC were unsure exactly as to when full authority should be passed from ICC to IPC. At the first ICC meeting held after the General Assembly in January 1990 in Barcelona the general consensus was that the meeting in Dussledorf had been very badly organised and chaotic and that a large part of the world, in particular the Far East and South Pacific Regions, had had no opportunity to vote. However, both the IPC Executive and ICC meetings agreed that there should be reciprocal invitations for members of each organisation to attend each others meetings in order to facilitate the transfer. Indeed, after some initial discussion the new President and Secretary General of IPC, Bob Steadward and Andre Raes, were invited to join the ICC meeting in Barcelona. After two sessions of discussion regarding the outcomes of Dussledorf it was voted on and agreed that the transition of responsibility from ICC to IPC would be postponed until the first meeting of ICC after the General Assembly of IPC to held in conjunction with the Assen World Games for he Disabled in June 1990 and that in the meantime ICC was to extend an invitation to the President and Secretary General of IPC to attend ICC meetings as observers. At the second IPC General Assembly, which was held in Groningen rather than Assen, it was proposed by Jens Bromann, President of IBSA, that an agreement be drawn up between ICC and IPC regarding the transfer of authority. A meeting was held between the six Presidents of the IOSD's and the IPC President on 5th October 1990 in Aylesbury, UK to draw up the agreement and it was signed the next day by all concerned at eighteenth meeting of ICC. The outcome of the agreement was that ICC would continue to be responsible for the 1992 Winter and Summer Paralympic Games, but that from that day forward IPC would assume immediate control over all other world multi-disability (more than one federation) games. On completion of the 1992 Paralympic Games ICC and IPC would then issue a joint communique spelling out the final transfer of power from ICC to IPC.

This is not to say that the relationship between ICC and IPC was always easy throughout this period. In February 1990 Guillermo Cabezas, as President of ISOD, wrote to Bob Steadward, President of IPC, complaining about the actions of his Technical Officer, who had already begun sanctioning events and proposing to take over control of some events in the name of IPC despite no agreement having been reached between IPC and ICC on this matter. A further issue arose in May 1991 when IPC were approached by the New Zealand Kiwi Marketing Board offering sponsorship of sixteen European nations attending the 1992 Winter and Summer Paralympic Games in return for exclusive use of reference to the Games for the promotion of fresh fruit products. Andre Raes, Secretary General of IPC, wrote to ICC asking that they confirm their agreement to this and would not grant any similar sponsorship in the fresh fruit sector. Communication between the two organisations during this period became quite acerbic and hint at a certain lack of trust between the two organisations, with IPC accusing ICC of a lack of co-operation on the matter and ICC accusing IPC of a lack of full disclosure of the facts and a desire to grab all of the 125,000 deutschmarks being offered by the New Zealand Kiwi Marketing Board for themselves. Despite last ditch efforts to find a solution to the situation by the time ICC met for their twentieth meeting in London in August 1991 the proposed deal had collapsed, but the ICC President protem still felt it necessary to have it recorded in the minutes of the meeting that the ICC Executive Committee would accept no blame whatsoever in the collapse of the deal.

Following the successful completion of the Winter and Summer Paralympic Games of 1992, ICC held their twenty-third and final meeting at the Sandy Beach Hotel, Larnaca, Cyprus from 24th-25th March 1993. At the meeting Jens Bromann moved that all residual funds after the winding up of ICC should be transferred to IPC. The motion was seconded by Bob Steadward, President of IPC. Although the motion was lost, after some discussion Bob Steadward proposed that each of the IOSD's (CP-ISRA, IBSA, ISMWSF, and ISOD) receive ten thousand dollars with the remainder being transferred to IPC. INAS-FMH were not to receive the payment as they were in debt to ICC for a similar amount for sanction fees from the Madrid Games. This motion passed with a majority of five for to one against. It was also agreed that the President of IPC and the President protem of ICC produce a statement that would be read out at the IPC General Assembly in Berlin later that year as well as being published on the front page of the Fall issue of the IPC newsletter and would include a vote of thanks to ICC members. At the IPC General Assembly in Berlin in September Miss Elisabeth Dendy, on behalf of ICC, handed over a cheque for forty thousand dollars to IPC and, whilst reminding those present that the IOSD's were an integral part of IPC, wished them all the best for their future endeavours. In response Bob Steadward thanked the Presidents and Secretary Generals of the IOSD's for their commitment over the previous twelve years.

The IPC Executive Board and Structure 1989 -1993.

Despite the ruling that no one standing for a position could, if elected, also hold a position on the Executive Board of one of the IOSD's, following a vote at the second IPC General Assembly in Groningen in July, 1990 this ruling was waived in the case of Dr Michael Riding who was allowed to act as both Medical Officer for IPC and Chairman of the ISMGF Medical Committee. Ten members of the new Executive Committee were elected immediately at the Dussledorf General Assembly. These were as follows:

Position	Name
President	Dr Robert Steadward (Canada)
First Vice-President	Mr Reiner Krippner (Germany)
Second Vice-President	Zauba A. Al-Rawi (Iraq)
Secretary General	André Raes (Belgium)
Treasurer	André Auberger (France)
Technical Officer	Hans Lindstrom (Sweden)
Medical Officer	Dr Michael Riding (Canada)
Member at Large	Valentin Dikui (Russia)
Member at Large	Il Mook Cho (Korea)
Member at Large	Miss Elizabeth Dendy (United Kingdom)

The six Regional Representatives were to be elected by nations within their own zones and by the spring of 1990 when the first IPC newsletter was released the six newly elected Regional Representatives were noted as follows:

Region	Name
Africa	Nabil Salem (Egypt)
Americas	Jim Leask (Canada)
East Asia	York Chow (Hong Kong)
Europe	Carl Wang (Norway)
Oceania	Barbara Worley (Australia)
West Asia	Akram Massarweh (Jordan)

For the period covering Executive Committee meeting number two (November 1989) to number five (May 1991) there were actually two Regional Representatives for Africa. The second representative was Chedlya Rachid (Morocco) Apparently, the results of the elections within the African Region held in Dussledorf to appoint their Regional Representative had been contested afterwards. Contradictory letters from the African Confederation, alternatively appointing Dr Salem and then Mrs Rachid, were received by IPC. At the fifth Executive Committee meeting the President decided to appoint someone to attend the next African Confederation meeting and report back. Although no outcome of this visit appears in the minutes only Dr Salem appeared at Executive Board meetings from then on. Jim Leask was replaced by James Neppl (USA) as Americas representative from the fifth Executive Committee meeting onwards. Yasuhiro Hatsuyama (Japan) replaced Dr York Chow as the East Asia Representative from meeting three onwards. Barbara Worley, having failed to make the second meeting due to travel problems was replaced by Eric Russell (Australia) for meetings three to eight and then George Dunstan for the remaining two meetings before the election of the new board.

The rest of the Executive Committee consisted of the six Presidents of the IOSD's;

IOSD	Name
CISS	Jerald Jordan
CP-ISRA	Jack Weinstein
IBSA	Jens Bromann
ISMWSF	John Grant
ISOD	Guillermo Cabezas
INAS-FID	Fernando Martin Vicente

and the Athletes Representative, Mr Martin Mansell (United Kingdom) who was elected at the General Assembly of Athletes held at the Assen World Games for the Disabled in July, 1990 and attended his first Executive Committee meeting in Brugge in November 1990. In all this Executive Board held ten meetings during its term of office:

Meeting	Date	Venue
EC 1	23rd September 1989	Duisburg, Germany
EC 2	30th November–1st December 1989	Brugge, Belgium
GA 2	15th-16th July 1990	Groningen, Netherlands
EC 3	15th & 17th July 1990	Groningen, Netherlands
EC 4	16th-17th November 1990	Brugge, Belgium
EC 5	9th-10th May 1991	Lillehammer, Norway
EC 6	1st & 3rd November 1991	Budapest, Hungary
GA 3	2nd-3rd November 1991	Budapest, Hungary
EC 7	29th-31st March 1992	Tignes, France
EC 8	5th-6th December 1992	Manchester, UK
EC 9	18th-21st March 1993	Lillehammer, Norway
EC 10 (Pt 1)	9th September 1993	Berlin, Germany
GA 4	10th-12th September 1993	Berlin, Germany

Following their election the first Executive Committee of IPC had many issues that needed sorting in order to build up the organisation on a firm footing. One of the first was to work on the constitution that was circulated and discussed in draft form at the Dussldorf General Assembly. This work was completed at the Brugge Executive Committee meeting and presented to the membership in time for the second General Assembly in Groningen. Following discussion and voting on forty amendments proposed by the membership IPC's first official constitution was accepted and registered in Belgium, where IPC had its first offices. At the Brugge Executive Committee the President also signed the contract for the 1994 Paralympic Winter Games in Lillehammer, Norway. This was the very first Paralympics Games over which IPC had sole authority.

When IPC was created all of the national members of the IOSD's became members of IPC. This meant that IPC had to communicate with up to six different organisations within any one country. This also meant that at a General Assembly each country, as well as the IOSD's had up to six votes to cast. This made communication between IPC and its membership both difficult and costly and so in order to try and overcome these difficulties IPC decreed that a National Contact Association (NCA) be formed in each country that had organisations that were members of IPC. This was either an umbrella body that had already been formed within a country covering all national associations in that country, such as the British Paralympic Association in the UK, or a national association selected by IPC where an umbrella body did not exist. A selected NCA within a particular country could change if the majority of existing national associations, who were in membership of IPC, decided accordingly. The job of the NCA was to try and co-ordinate all the relevant associations within their country, distribute information provided by IPC and to collect membership fees. However, initially this method lead to many problems due to the fact that there was much fighting between national associations in some countries, many of whom refused to communicate with each other, and so often information was not forwarded by the NCA to other organisations within their country. Gradually as the system settled down NCA's were pushed to form National Paralympic Committees (NPC's), which would be constitutional rather than administrative organisations. In Spring

1991 IPC had a list of 109 NCA's, but as of April 1992 the actual membership in the six regions of IPC totalled only fifty-six nations broken down as follows:

Region	Member Nations
Africa	7
Americas	5
East Asia	8
Europe	32
Middle East	2
South Pacific	2

The constitution accepted at the Groningen General Assembly allowed for the setting up of seven named standing committees within the IPC structure. These were a Sports Technical Committee, Sports Committees for each IPC sport, a Sports Science and Medical Committee, an Athletes' Committee, a Financial Committee, a Legal Committee and a Nominating Committee. One of the first committees to be set up on an interim basis was the Sports Technical Committee, later renamed the Sports Council Executive Committee, set up in 1990 and consisting of the following members:

Name	Affiliation
Hans Lindström	IPC Technical Officer
Michael Riding	IPC Medical Officer
Birgitta Blomquist	Swimming/ Ice Sports
André Deville	Switzerland
Ted Fay	Nordic Skiing
Pieter Joon	Volleyball
Jerry Johnston	Alpine Skiing
Donald Royer	Canada
Jean Stone	Secretary

The aim of the Sports Technical Committee was to maintain the operative functions needed for the supervision and operation of multi-disability competitions within the rules set down in the IPC constitution.

Interim Chairpersons for each IPC Sports Committee had been selected by the Fall of 1991 and at the Barcelona Paralympic Summer Games of 1992 elections took place for these positions. At the time there were twelve sports that were considered to be IPC sports and eight that were considered non-IPC sports with Paralympic status.

	Sport	Interim Chair	Chair Elected 1992
IPC Sports	Alpine Skiing	Jerry Johnston (CAN)	Jack Benedick (USA)
	Archery	Charles Drouin (CAN)	Jean vanden Dungen (NED)
	Athletics	Chris Cohen (GBR)	Chris Cohen (GBR)
	Cycling	Fredrik Kveil (NOR)	Fredrik Kveil (NOR)
	Equestrian	Birck Jacobsen (DEN)	Birck Jacobsen (DEN)
	Ice Sports	Thor Kleppe (NOR)	Thor Kleppe (NOR)
	Lawn Bowling	Bob Lowe (GBR)	
	Nordic Skiing	Ted Fay (USA)	Ted Fay (USA)
	Powerlifting	Pol Wautermartens (BEL)	Pol Wautermartens (BEL)
	Shooting	Fred Jansen (NED)	Fred Jansen (NED)
	Swimming	Birgitta Blomquist (GER)	Birgitta Blomquist (GER)
	Table Tennis	Tony Teff (GBR)	Tony Teff (GBR)
Non-IPC Sports With Paralympic Status	Boccia		Howard Bailey (GBR)
	Fencing		Alberto Martinez Vasallo (ESP)
	Goalball		Jim Leask (CAN)
	Judo		Bruno Carmeni (ITA)
	Soccer		Bob Fisher (GBR)
	Wheelchair Basketball		Phil Craven (GBR)
	Wheelchair Tennis		Ellen DeLange (GBR)
	Volleyball		Pieter Joon (NED)

What really stands out in the names and particularly the countries of these chairmen is the total dominance of Europe and North America. Of the nineteen named Chairmen elected in 1992 they only came from ten different countries and six of the Committee Chairman were British. This is possibly a reflection of the different states of development of disability sport around the world at the time as well as Britain's rich history as the birthplace of the Paralympic Games. The Chairmen of these twenty sports along with the IPC Technical and Medical Officers, the IOSD Technical Officers and the elected members of Sports Council Executive Committee (SCEC) came together to form the IPC Sports Council. At the 1992 Sports Council Meeting held in October in Northampton, UK, the following individuals were elected by the Sports Council to replace the interim appointees on the SCEC (formerly the Sports Technical Committee):

Name	Role
Fred Jansen (NED)	Summer Sports Representative
Ted Fay (USA)	Winter Sports Representative
Thor Kleppe (NOR)	Member at Large
Donald Royer (CAN)	Member at Large
Pol Wautermartens (BEL)	Member at Large

Jean Stone retained her place on the SCEC as Technical Secretary and Martin Mansell was added as Athletes' Representative and acted as Treasurer for the Committee.

Following an approach by Mr J.W. Masman, Chairman, and Mr Jaap Brouwer, Director, of Recreational Sports Development and Stimulation – Disabled International (RESPO DS DI), which was involved in the promotion and support of sports with a particular recreational value for persons with a disability, especially in developing countries, IPC moved to set up its first Development Committee comprised of André Raes (IPC Secretary General), Pieter Joon (Netherlands) and Horst Strokhendl (Germany). Their role was to define policies, initiate programmes and to work closely with RESPO DS DI in that the area of development.

At the 1992 Executive Committee meeting in Tignes Mr Einfeld was appointed interim Chairman of the IPC Legal Committee, with Bernard Atha (GBR) also being appointed to the committee until such time as proper elections could be held at the 1993 General Assembly in Berlin.

The final major structural issue initiated by the IPC Executive Committee in their first term of office began in early 1991 when they began to look at the possibility of establishing Regional Paralympic Committees in the six regions. The first of these was EUROCOM, representing the European region, with Carl Wang (Norway) being the first President.

The IPC Executive Board and Structure 1993–1997

At the Berlin General Assembly in September 1993 there were forty-seven nations plus the six IOSD's giving a total of two hundred and forty seven votes to be cast. Of the ten new members of the Executive Committee five were elected by acclamation as there was no other candidate standing. However, at the first Executive Board meeting held immediately after the elections in Berlin there was a dispute over the election of Dr Nabil Salem as second Vice-President due to the fact that the African Region had not as yet elected a new regional representative and so Dr Salem, effectively held two positions on the board. As it was the responsibility of the African region to fill this position the President stated that Dr Salem would continue in his roll as second Vice-President, with only one vote on the board, and the role of African regional representative would be filled by an elected individual in time for the next meeting.

Position	Name
President	Dr Robert Steadward (Canada) *
First Vice-President	Jens Bromann (Denmark)
Second Vice-President	Nabil Salem (Egypt)
Secretary General	André Raes (Belgium) *
Treasurer	André Auberger (France) *
Technical Officer	Hans Lindström (Sweden) *
Medical Officer	Dr Michael Riding (Canada) *
Member at Large	Marie Little (Australia)
Member at Large	Dr York Chow (Hong Kong)
Member at Large	Colin Rains (United Kingdom)

* Elected by acclamation (No other candidate)

In the end the following individuals were elected by their relevant regions to fill the role of Regional Representative on the Executive Board for the next four years:

Region	Name
Africa	Rachid Miskouri (Algeria)
Americas	Dick Loiselle (USA)
East Asia	Dr Yasuhiri Hatsuyama (Japan)
Europe	Carl Wang (Norway)
Middle East	Akram Massarweh (Jordan)
South Pacific	George Dunstan (Australia)

The role of athletes' representative was once again filled by Martin Mansell as the Chair of the Athletes' Commission.

	Name
Athletes' Representative	Martin Mansell (United Kingdom)

The newly elected, or in some cases re-elected Presidents of the IOSD's on the second IPC Executive Board were as follows:

IOSD	Name
CISS	Jerald Jordan
CP-ISRA	Elisabeth Dendy
IBSA	Enrique Sanz
ISMWSF	Donald Royer
ISOD	Guillermo Cabezas
INAS-FID	Bernard Atha

The second IPC Executive Board once again held ten meetings during its term of office. There was also an extraordinary General Assembly held in Atlanta in 1996 to discuss the outcomes of a special task force that was set up in this period to investigate the structure of IPC.

Meeting	Date	Venue
EC 10 (Pt 2)	12th-13th September 1993	Berlin, Germany
EC 11	7th-10th March 1994	Lillehammer, Norway
EC 12	18th-20th November 1994	Paris, France
EC 13	28th-30th April 1995	Atlanta, USA
EC 14	5th November 1995	Tokyo, Japan
GA 5	8th-9th November 1995	Tokyo, Japan
EC 15	3rd-5th March 1996	Cairo, Egypt
EC 16	12th-14th August 1996	Atlanta, USA
GA 6	16th-17th August 1996	Atlanta, USA
EC 17	24th-26th January 1997	Lille, France
EC 18	22nd-23rd May 1997	Nagano, Japan
EC 19 (Pt 1)	4th-5th November 1997	Sydney, Australia
GA 7	6th-7th November 1997	Sydney, Australia

At the first Executive Board meeting in Berlin three new committees were established. These were a constitution committee with Jens Bromann (NED) as Chair and Bernard Atha (GBR) as a member, a membership committee with Dr Salem (IPC 2nd Vice-President) as Chair who would work alongside the Secretary General and the regions and a development committee consisting of André Raes (IPC Secretary General), Donald Royer (ISMWSF President), Colin Rains (IPC Member at Large) and one athlete. At the same meeting the make-up of the IPC Sports Science Committee was agreed for the following four years.

Name	Specialism
Gudrun Doll-Tepper (GER)	Chair
Trevor Williams (GBR)	Sociology
Yagesh Bhambani (CAN)	Psychology
Michael Ferrara (USA)	Sports Medicine
Colin Higgs (CAN)	Biomechanics
Claudine Sherrill (USA)	Psychology

However, it was also made clear that no IPC money was to be made available for research.

At the twelfth Executive Board meeting in Paris in November 1994 it was decided that a Congress, to be held in conjunction with the 1995 General Assembly in Tokyo, would be held to discuss the future of IPC and the role of the IOSD's and their relation to IPC. Following the Congress twelve individuals were nominated at the General Assembly in Tokyo for a Task Force to study the discussions held during the Congress and make recommendations to be discussed and voted on at an Extraordinary General Assembly to be held in conjunction with the 1996 Atlanta Paralympic Games. Following an election by secret ballot the following were elected to the Task Force:

Name	Country
York Chow (Chair)	Hong Kong
Donald Royer	Canada
Brendan Burkett	Australia
Helen Manning	Canada
Phil Craven	United Kingdom

The Task Force produced a list of recommendations for the Assembly in Atlanta as well as requesting input and feedback on draft recommendations from the nations prior to Atlanta. However, of the more than eighty voting nations present in Atlanta only twenty-four took the opportunity to respond. Amongst the recommendations were a much smaller Executive Committee of ten members (President, First Vice-President, Vice President (Strategy and Planning), Vice-President (Games Liaison), Secretary General, Treasurer, Chairman of the Sports Council, Chairman of the Sports Science and Medical Committee, A summer and a Winter Sports Representative) and the introduction of a small Management Committee that would report to the Executive Board twice a year. In the end this motion was amended following discussion to include representation of the five IOSD's, the six regions and an athletes' representative bringing the total for the new Executive Board to twenty-two. However, it is noted in the minutes of the sixteenth Executive Board minutes that many nations expressed disappointment with this result and that it was rumoured that a new motion from the nations would be bought to the 1997 General Assembly to reduce the number of Executive Board members.

A further Task Force recommendation that was adopted was that the number of votes be reduced to one per member. This decision, along with a couple of other decisions on technical matters lead to threats of a total withdrawal from IPC of the International Blind Sports Association (IBSA). IBSA claimed, amongst other things, that the voting reduction would lead to less voting representation of blind and visually impaired athletes. A meeting was held in May 1997 between IPC and IBSA to discuss the possible implementation of an IPC-IBSA agreement on sports technical matters and eventually the threat of withdrawal was withdrawn.

One organisation that did withdraw from IPC during this four year period, however, was CISS, who had decided at their thirty-fourth Congress to no longer remain a member of IPC. This had followed several years of uncertainty by CISS over whether IPC actually had anything useful to offer the deaf sports community, which regularly had several thousand competitors at its World Games and, as such, was far to large to integrate as a whole into the Paralympic Games. However, it was agreed that IPC and CISS would continue to cooperate on issues that impacted both organisations and the IOC agreed to continue to fund CISS, despite their being outside of the single disability sport umbrella organisation that IOC wished to deal with.

The IPC Executive Board and Structure 1997–2001.

Delegates from seventy-three nations and five IOSD's, attended the Seventh General Assembly in Sydney, Australia in November 1997 to elect the third IPC

Executive Committee. Each with one vote following the reduction in number of votes at the previous years Extraordinary General Assembly in Atlanta, they were joined by twenty-one IPC sports, who had also been awarded voting rights at general assemblies following a vote in Atlanta, making a total of ninety-nine votes.

Position	Name
President	Dr Robert Steadward (Canada) *
Vice-President (Policy, Planning & Development)	Dr York Chow (Hong Kong)
Vice-President (Marketing and Communication)	Duncan Wyeth (USA) ^
Vice-President (Games Liaison)	François Terranova (France)
Secretary General	Miguel Sagarra (Spain)
Treasurer	André Auberger (France) *
Technical Officer	Carol Mushett (USA) *
Medical Officer	Dr Michael Riding (Canada)

^ Duncan Wyeth resigned his position in May 1998.
* Elected by acclamation (No other candidate)

It appears the suggestion by the task force made in Atlanta to include the Chairmen of the Sports Science Committee and the Sports Council on the Executive Board was not adopted and IPC continued with a Technical and a Medical Officer. Three of the positions were filled by acclamation as no other candidates stood. In May 1998, Duncan Wyeth (USA) resigned from the position of Vice-President (Marketing and Communication) and Dr Nabil Salem was co-opted into the position until his place was finally ratified at the Eighth General Assembly in Salt Lake City in November 1999. The following individuals were elected by their regions to serve as Regional Representatives:

Region	Name
Africa	Ali Harzallah (Tunisia)
Americas	Jose Luis Campo (Argentina)
East Asia	Dr Yoshihiro Hatsuyama (Japan)
Europe	Hans Lindström (Sweden)
Middle East	Dr Abdulhakim Al-Matar (Saudi Arabia)
South Pacific	George Dunstan (Australia)

Following his election as the new Chairman of the Athletes' Commission, Manfred Kohl from Germany took his place on the Executive Board as the Athlete's Representative. Fred Jansen and Jack Benedick were elected by the Sports Council to be the Summer and Winter Sports Representatives respectively.

	Name
Athletes' Representative	Manfred Kohl (Germany)
Summer Sports Representative	Fred Jansen (Netherlands)
Winter Sports Representative	Jack Benedick (USA)

The newly elected, or in some cases re-elected Presidents of the IOSD's on the third IPC Executive Board were as follows:

IOSD	Name
CP-ISRA	Lina Faria
IBSA	Enrique Sanz
ISMWSF	Bob McCullough
ISOD	Juan Palau Francas
INAS-FID	Fernando Martin Vincente

The third IPC Executive Board actually held twelve meetings during its term of office as well as two general assemblies.

Meeting	Date	Venue
EC 19 (Pt 2)	9th September 1997	Sydney, Australia
EC 20	4th March 1998	Nagano, Japan
EC 21	19th-20th May 1998	Lausanne, Switzerland
EC 22	4th-5th December 1998	Bonn, Germany
EC 23	23rd-24th April 1999	Sydney, Australia
EC 24	4th September 1999	Bonn, Germany
EC 25	18th November 1999	Salt Lake City, USA
GA 8	19th-20th November 1999	Salt Lake City, USA
EC 26	12th-13th May 2000	Cairo, Egypt
EC 27	15th-16th & 26th October 2000	Sydney, Australia
EC 28	9th-10th March 2001	Salt Lake City, USA
EC 29	28th April 2001	Kuala Lumpur, Malaysia
EC 30	5th December 2001	Athens, Greece
GA 9	7th-8th December 2001	Athens, Greece

Although the previously rumoured motion for changes in the Executive Committee structure did not materialise at the 1997 General Assembly the matter was again raised by Sweden at the 1999 General Assembly in Salt Lake City. Sweden, seconded by Iceland, put forward a motion for a new structure to the IPC Executive Board that did not include the IOSD's or the Regional Representatives. This raised many objections at the time. However, the President had already made a statement earlier in the day that the Executive Committee had extensively discussed possible changes to the IPC Executive Committee and Management Committee structure and had made five recommendations as follows:

- That the existing Executive Committee and Management Committee structure be retained for the current and next tenure (2001-2005)

- There was a need to identify and prioritise the important strategies, policies and tasks for IPC for the following six years, and establish relevant commissions to address, develop and implement those policies.
- That the Management Committee and staff should develop a more detailed and revised manual and schedule of delegated authority in order to streamline all operational functions of IPC, with a clear delineation of the roles of all members of the Executive Committee and IPC staff.
- That the above recommendations were to remain under constant review.
- That the IPC actively promote an overall review of the future functions of IPC and to this end a formal IPC seminar/ workshop be held in the Spring of 2001.

The Strategic Planning Congress as the seminar in the last point came to be known was originally scheduled to be held in Phnom Penh, Cambodia in April 2001. However, following severe floods and logistical problems the congress was moved at the last minute to Kuala Lumpur, Malaysia and was held from 25th to 30th April 2001. The congress afforded a unique opportunity for members of the international Paralympic Movement to take part in the process of strategic review and to determine the future direction of the Movement. The congress was split into three themes (Governance, Roles and Responsibilities and Structure) and the final recommendations were as follows:

> **Governance**: The General Assembly should have ownership of the Paralympic Movement and there should be transparency in management with the Executive Board having a balance of representation. There was also a strong consensus that IPC should eventually be solely responsible for the Paralympic Games, with IOSD's concentrating on development and the sports moving towards autonomy.

> **Roles and Responsibilities**: Athletes should play a far greater role in the governance of IPC, two-way communication between IPC, NPC's and the Regions needed strengthening and the sports should have a stronger representation within the IPC and sports decision-making structures.

> **Structure**: It was concluded that a strategic analysis of the IPC structure was needed to more clearly define the roles of the Commissions, to ensure athlete representation was reflected throughout the structures of the Movement and to clarify the position and role of the IPC Headquarters and its staff within the structure.

The IPC Executive Board and Structure 2001–2005

Prior to the 2001 General Assembly in Athens there had been several attempts to both change and circumvent the constitutional rule that no individual could serve more than three terms of office on the IPC Executive Board. All attempts were, however, blocked by the nations and so it was that several individuals including IPC President Bob Steadward, Treasurer André Auberger and Medical Officer Michael Riding became ineligible for re-election. More than three hundred delegates from seventy-five countries, the five IOSD's and twenty-two sports gathered in Athens to elect the new Executive Board.

Position	Name
President	Philip Craven (United Kingdom)
Vice-President (Policy, Planning & Development)	Dr York Chow (Hong Kong) *
Vice-President (Marketing and Communication)	Dr Nabil Salem (Egypt) *
Vice-President (Games Liaison)	François Terranova (France)
Secretary General	Miguel Sagarra (Spain) *
Treasurer	John Teunissen (Netherlands)
Technical Officer	Carol Mushett (USA) *
Medical Officer	Dr Björn Hedman (Sweden)

* Elected by acclamation (No other candidate)

The following individuals were elected by their regions to serve as Regional Representatives. However it should be noted that Dr Abdulhakim Al-Matar (Saudi Arabia) was replaced as Middle East Regional Representative in February 2003 by Dr Hussein Adu Al-Ruz (Jordan) following his election as Regional President for the Middle East. In addition, in April 2004, at their meeting in Arnhem the Executive Committee agreed to change the regional structure from six to five regions with the Middle East Region ceasing to exist and its member nations being included in the Asia Region. This took effect on 1st January 2005, but both Regional Representatives were allowed to keep their position on the Board until the next elections. In order to align the membership of the regional organisations with those of the IOC the NPC's of Kazakhstan, Turkmenistan and Uzbekistan, who were formally members of the Europe Region were transferred to the Asia Region with effect from the same date.

Region	Name
Africa	Rashid Meskouri (Algeria)
Americas	Jose Luis Campo (Argentina)
Asia	Zainal Abu Zarin (Malaysia)
Europe	Dr Bob Price OBE (United Kingdom)
Middle East	Dr Abdulhakim Al-Matar (Saudi Arabia)
Oceania	Greg Hartung (Australia)

At the time of the elections Kjarten Haugen (Norway) was the elected representative of the IPC Athlete's Commission to sit on the Executive Board, but he was later replaced by Ljiljana Ljubisic (Canada) following new elections within the Athletes' Commission. Fred Jansen and Rita van Driel were elected by the Sports Council to be the Summer and Winter Sports Representatives respectively.

	Name
Athletes' Representative	Kjarten Haugen (Norway)
Summer Sports Representative	Fred Jansen (Netherlands)
Winter Sports Representative	Rita van Driel (Netherlands)

The newly elected, or in some cases re-elected Presidents of the IOSD's on the fourth IPC Executive Board were as follows:

IOSD	Name
CP-ISRA	Alan Dickson
IBSA	Enrique Pérez Bazan
ISMWSF	Paul DePace
ISOD	Juan Palau Francas
INAS-FID	Jos Mulder

The fourth IPC Executive Board once again held ten meetings during its term of office. There was also an extraordinary General Assembly held in Cairo in 2004 to vote on a number of key issues regarding the future of IPC and to adopt a new constitution.

Meeting	Date	Venue
EC 31	9th December 2001	Athens, Greece
EC 32	4th-5th March 2002	Salt Lake City, USA
EC 33	11th-12th October 2002	Bonn, Germany
EC 34	4th-6th April 2003	Athens, Greece
EC 35	19th November 2003	Torino, Italy
GA 10	21st-22nd November 2003	Torino, Italy
EC 36	23rd-24th April 2004	Arnhem, Netherlands
EC 37	15th September 2004	Athens, Greece
EC 38	24th November 2004	Cairo, Egypt
GA 11	25th November 2004	Cairo, Egypt
GB 39	9th-10th April 2005	Torino, Italy
GB40	16th November 2005	Beijing, China
GA 12	18th-19th November 2005	Beijing, China

Following on from the Strategic Planning Congress in Kuala Lumpur, this fourth electoral period of IPC saw some major changes take place to the overall governance structure. At the 2001 General Assembly in Athens it was decided to carry out a full strategic review of the IPC structure, which was to be completed by the end of 2002. Due to the expected strong impact of the strategic review upon the work of IPC the Executive Board decided at their meeting in Bonn in January 2002 to suspend the activities of many of its commissions as it was decided that they did not yet have a clear mission statement or mandate. The IPC worked with external consultants, McKinsey and Company, to set specific goals for the organisation's future. The project's Steering Committee identified three main issues to be addressed by IPC. Firstly, to improve the organisation's marginal income base. Secondly, to enhance the service portfolio to IPC's members and thirdly, to clarify roles and responsibilities within the organisation.

Following several years of consultation and planning IPC presented the findings and recommendations of the strategic review to the nations at their tenth General Assembly in Torino in 2003. Here the membership overwhelmingly approved the framework for a new governance structure, which would result in an IPC Governing Board replacing the Executive Committee structure in place at the time. The new Governing Board would be comprised of fourteen members, twelve of which would be elected by the General Assembly. These would be the President, a Vice-President and ten board members. There would also be two ex-officio members – an athlete's representative, elected by the Athlete's Council and the IPC Headquarters CEO. Four Councils were also to be created to represent the different groups of stakeholders with common interests (IOSD's, sports, regions and athletes) that were designed to provide a forum to share their objectives and develop common strategies that would facilitate their development and co-ordinate their activities.

Over the next year a Constitutional Commission developed a new constitution for IPC to take into account the new structure. This was presented to the membership at an Extraordinary General Assembly held in Cairo in November 2004, which was attended by seventy-eight National Paralympic Committees, five IOSD's and eighteen sports. A very clear majority voted in favour of the new constitution and Governing Board structure. In addition it was decided that all persons standing for election to the new Governing Board, which would be elected in 2005, would start with a clean slate and would be eligible for three term of four years. This raises the intriguing possibility that if he stands and is re-elected Dr Nabil Salem of Egypt could possibly serve on the IPC Executive or Governing Board in some capacity for every one of the first seven terms, totalling some twenty-eight years of service.

One final important event that occurred during this term of office was the amalgamation of the International Stoke Mandeville Wheelchair Sports Federation (ISMWSF) and the International Sports Organisation for the Disabled (ISOD), the two original and oldest IOSD's, to form the International Wheelchair and Amputee Sports Federation (IWAS). This amalgamation was many years in the planning and execution, but finally occurred in January 2004 reducing the number of IOSD's in membership with IPC to four.

The IPC Governing Board and Structure 2005–2009

More than three hundred participants attended the largest ever IPC General Assembly in Beijing, China in 2005. Representatives of ninety National Paralympic Committees, the four IOSD's and twenty-four sports gathered to elect IPC's first Governing Board. Sir Philip Craven was the sole candidate for the Presidency and was re-elected by and overwhelming majority, with former Secretary General, Miguel Sagarra, being elected as his Vice-President. In addition to the twelve elected positions and the two ex-officio positions on the Governing Board the new constitution also allowed for the co-option of up to three extra board members to assist the Governing Board in their work. However, so far only Fred Jansen as Chairman of the Sports Council has been co-opted to the Board.

Position	Name
President	Sir Philip Craven (United Kingdom)
Vice President	Miguel Sagarra (Spain)
Member at Large	Masoud Ashrafi (Iran)
Member at Large	Jose Luis Campo (Argentina)
Member at Large	Ann Cody (USA)
Member at Large	Alan Dickson (United Kingdom)
Member at Large	Greg Hartung (Australia)
Member at Large	Patrick Jarvis (Canada)
Member at Large	Karl Vilhelm Nielsen (Denmark)
Member at Large	Nabil Salem (Egypt)
Member at Large	Zainal Abu Zarin (Algeria)
Member at Large	Shen Zhifei (China)
Athletes' Representative	Ljiljana Ljubisic (Canada)
Chief Executive Officer	Xavier Gonzalez (IPC)
Co-opted Member	Fred Jansen (Netherlands)

Meetings held during this latest term of office include the following:

Meeting	Date	Venue
GB 41	20th November 2005	Beijing, China
GB 42	28th January 2006	Bonn, Germany
GB 43	7th-8th March 2006	Torino, Italy
GB 44	22nd-25th June 2006	Lausanne, Switzerland
GB 45	23rd-25th November 2006	Kuala Lumpur, Malaysia
GB 46	22nd-24th April 2007	Beijing, China
GB 47	9th-11th August 2007	Rio de Janiero, Brasil
GB 48	20th-21st November 2007	Seoul, South Korea
GA 13	24th-25th November 2007	Seoul, South Korea
GB 49	8th-9th February 2008	Bonn, Germany
GB50	4th-6th May 2008	Tehran, Iran
GB 51	3rd-4th September 2008	Beijing, China
GB 52	27th-29th March 2009	Colorado Springs, USA
GB 53	26th-28th June 2009	Vancouver, Canada
GA 14	21st-22nd November 2009	Kuala Lumpur, Malaysia

In 2006 IPC published its Strategic Plan to cover the period 2006-2009. The overall vision of the strategic plan is to enable Paralympic athletes to achieve sporting excellence and inspire and excite the world. In order to achieve this vision the strategic plan encompasses five strategic objectives developed in co-operation with the management team and the IPC committees, which must be successfully delivered in order to achieve this mission. These objectives are as follows:

1. To be a **high performing organisation**. The IPC is a high performing democratic sporting organisation that abides by its values and is dedicated to excellence. In order to ensure that this is maintained and improved upon IPC needs to be an efficient organisation with a clear governance structure and concise strategic direction, which supports reliable operations.

2. To facilitate **membership development** in order to ensure that that all IPC member organisations are active, self-sustainable and deliver quality services within their respective roles within the Paralympic Movement. In order to achieve this IPC must ensure that its member organisations have defined roles and responsibilities, are able to sustain their operations and are accountable and effective when delivering their activities.

3. Improve **resource creation** by ensuring IPC has a solid and sustainable human and financial foundation that ensures its long-term viability, which will ensure that IPC is an effective and well-resourced organisation that is able to meet its objectives and the needs of all its members.

4. To ensure Paralympic **Games success** by ensuring that the Games are a viable, sustainable and distinctive sporting experience that inspires and excites the world. This should result in a sporting event with a clear and comprehensive identity with services that are of the highest quality and are sport and athlete focused.

5. To achieve **global recognition** by ensuring that the Paralympic brand is defined and globally recognised, understood and valued, resulting in a brand that has defined attributes and clear messages that is recognised in the sporting environment, instantly understood by the general public and the media and valued by partners.

The structure of IPC has grown and changed beyond all recognition since its creation in 1989, which is a clear reflection of the growth that has occurred in both the Paralympic Movement and the organisation necessary to maintain it. Below is a structural diagram of the current general structure of IPC showing the vast number of individuals and organisations who now have a stake in the running of the movement.

The IPC Governing Board and Structure 2009–2013.

Position	Name
President	Sir Philip Craven (United Kingdom)
Vice President	Greg Hartung (Australia)
Member at Large	Jose Luis Campo (Argentina)
Member at Large	Ann Cody (USA)
Member at Large	Alan Dickson (United Kingdom)
Member at Large	Rita van Driel (Netherlands)
Member at Large	Ali Harzallah (Tunisia)
Member at Large	Hyang-Sook Jang (Korea)

Member at Large	Patrick Jarvis (Canada)
Member at Large	Andrew Parsons (Brasil)
Member at Large	Miguel Sagarra (Spain)
Member at Large	Zainal Abu Zarin (Algeria)
Athletes' Representative	Robert Balk (USA)
Chief Executive Officer	Xavier Gonzalez (IPC)

Meetings held during this term of office include the following:

Meeting	Date	Venue
GB 54	17-18 November 2009	Kuala Lumpur, Malaysia
GB 55	10 March 2010	Whistler, Canada
GB 56	12-14 June 2010	Bonn, Germany
GB 57	10-12 December 2010	Guangzhou, China
GB 58	2-4 April 2011	Antalya, Turkey
GB 59	26 – 28 August 2011	Budapest, Hungary
GB 60	3-4 December 2011	Beijing, China
GA 15	10th-11th December 2011	Beijing, China
GB 61	20th-21st April 2012	Madrid, Spain
GB 62	27 August 2012	London, UK
GB 63	25th-27th Jan 2013	Bonn, Germany
GB 64	7th-9th June 2013	Sao Paulo, Brazil
GB 65	20 – 21 November 2013	Athens, Greece
GA 16	23rd-24th November 2013	Athens, Greece

The 2010–2014 IPC Strategic Plan

The 2010-2014 IPC Strategic Plan identified six strategic goals which they claim will support and contribute to the overall philosophy and vision of the Paralympic Movement:

1. PARALYMPIC GAMES: Ensure successful Paralympic Games for all participants.
2. ATHLETE DEVELOPMENT: Promote opportunities to engage in and grow Paralympic sports.
3. PARALYMPIC BRAND: Build greater understanding and use of the Paralympic brand.
4. FUNDING: Ensure appropriate funding and identify revenue opportunities.
5. ORGANISATIONAL CAPACITY: Enhance efficient structures to ensure the ability to deliver.
6. STRATEGIC PARTNERSHIPS: Leverage partnerships to use synergies and broaden the reach.

The IPC Governing Board and Structure 2013–2017.

Position	Name
President	Sir Philip Craven (GBR)
Vice President	Andrew Parsons (BRA)
Member at Large	Mohamed Alhameli (UAE)
Member at Large	Ann Cody (USA)
Member at Large	Rita van Driel (NED)
Member at Large	Patrick Jarvis (CAN)
Member at Large	Duane Kale (NZL)
Member at Large	Jairus Mogalo (KEN)
Member at Large	Kyung-won Na (KOR)
Member at Large	John Petersson (DEN)
Member at Large	Miguel Sagarra (ESP)
Member at Large	Yasushi Yamawaki (JPN)
Athletes' Representative*	Todd Nicholson (CAN)
Chief Executive Officer**	Xavier Gonzalez (ESP)
Co-opted Member***	Bernard Bourigeaud (FRA)

* ex-officio member with voting right
** ex-officio member without voting right
***co-opted member without voting right

Below is an organogram showing the current organisational structure of the International Paralympic Committee.

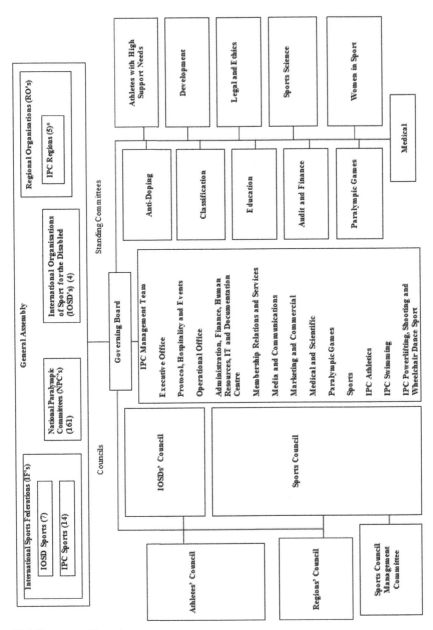

IPC Honorary Board.

In order to assist in the implementation of the vision and mission of the IPC Strategic Plan IPC introduced an Honorary Board in 2006, the main purpose of which is to allow leaders within society the opportunity to support the vision of the Paralympic Movement and to keep sport for persons with a disability high on the global agenda. Members assist the IPC in creating opportunities for raising awareness and funding, through their own network of contacts and spheres of influence. IPC President Sir Philip Craven stated that the enthusiasm and commitment to the Paralympic Movement of the Honorary Board Members was contagious and he hoped that with their help it would be possible to continue to spread the excitement of Paralympic sport around the world. Current board members in order of acceptance of their place on the Board are as follows:

Member	
HRH Princess Margriet	Netherlands
HRH Grand Duchess Maria Teresa	Luxemburg
HRH Crown Princess Victoria	Sweden
HSH Prince Albert	Monaco
Maria Guleghina	Ukraine
James Wolfensohn	Australia
HRH Princess Haya Bint Al Hussein	Dubai
Hassan Ali Bin Ali	Qatar
Thérèse Rein	Australia
HRH Princess Astrid	Belgium

Appendices

Appendix 1: Results of All Summer Olympic Wheelchair Demonstration Events (1984–2004)

Athens 2004 (August 22, 2004)

Men's 1500m wheelchair			Women's 800m wheelchair		
FIGL, Robert	GER	3:10.91	PETITCLERC, Chantal	CAN	1:53.66 OR
MENDOZA, Saul	MEX	3:11.35	STANKOVICH, Eliza	USA	1:53.84
TANA, Rawat	THA	3:11.48	SAUVAGE, Louise	AUS	1:53.92
HOLLONBECK, Scot	USA	3:11.49	ROY, Diane	CAN	1:54.20
FEARNLEY, Kurt	AUS	3:11.60	BLAUWET, Cheri	USA	1:54.22
YASUOKA, Choke	JPN	3:11.75	HUNKELER, Edith	SUI	1:54.68
JEANNOT, Joel	FRA	3:22.14	DAWES, Christie	AUS	1:55.97
ADAMS, Jeff	CAN	DNF	GREY-THOMPSON, Tanni	GBR	1:56.87

Sydney 2000 (September 28, 2000)

Men's 1500m wheelchair			Women's 800m wheelchair		
MENDOZA, Saul	MEX	3:06.75	SAUVAGE, Louise	AUS	1:56.07
ISSORAT, Claude	FRA	3:07.65	TSUCHIDA, Wakako	JPN	1:56.49
FREI, Heinz	GER	3:07.82	HERNANDEZ, Ariadne	MEX	1:56.59

FEARNLEY, Kurt	AUS	3:08.27	GREY-THOMPSON, Tanni	GBR	1:56.86
ADAMS, Jeff	CAN	3:08.95	BECERRA, Cheri	USA	1:57.19
HOLLONBECK, Scot	USA	3:09.15	PETITCLERC, Chantal	CAN	1:57.22
VAN DYK, Ernst	RSA	3:12.35	ANGGRENY, Lily	GER	1:57.63
MACLEAN, John	AUS	DNF	NORDLUND, Madeleine	SWE	1:57.82

Atlanta, 1996

Men's 1500m wheelchair			Women's 800m wheelchair		
ISSORAT, Claude	FRA	3:15.18	SAUVAGE, Louise	AUS	1:54.90
HOLLONBECK, Scot	USA	3:15.30	DRISCOLL, Jean	USA	1:55.19
NIETUSPACH, Franz	SUI	3:16.41	BECERRA, Cheri	USA	1:55.49
COUPRIE, Philippe	FRA	3:16.45	GREY, Tanni	GBR	1:55.55
MENDOZA, Saul	MEX	3:16.58	PETITCLERC, Chantal	CAN	1:55.61
LUNA, Jorge	MEX	3:16.78	SHANNON, Leann	USA	1:55.82
WIGGINS, Paul	AUS	3:16.86	WETTERSTROM, Monica	SWE	1:56.83
HEILVEIL, Jacob	USA	3:16.90	ANGGRENY, Lily	GER	2:05.33

Barcelona, 1992

Men's 1500m wheelchair			Women's 800m wheelchair		
ISSORAT, Claude	FRA	3:13.92 WR	HANSEN, Connie	DEN	1:55.62 WR
NIETUSPACH, Franz	SUI	3:14.07	DRISCOLL, Jean	USA	1:56.56
NOE, Michael	USA	3:14.76	WETTERSTROM, Monica	SWE	1:56.57
BERSET, Jean-Marc	SUI	3:14.95	JANSEN, Jeanette	NED	1:56.71
HOLLONBECK, Scot	USA	3:14.98	CABLE, Candace	USA	1:57.45
LUNA, Jorge	MEX	3.19.01	MAIER, Barbara	GER	1:57.69
ADAMS, Jeffrey	CAN	3:26.06	SODOMA, Deanna	USA	1:57.74
NUNEZ ALCADE, Ricardo	MEX	DNF	GREY, Tanni	GBR	1:57.75

Seoul. 1988

Men's 1500m wheelchair			Women's 800m wheelchair		
BADID, Mustapha	FRA	3:33.51	HEDRICK, Sharon	USA	2:11.49
VAN WINKEL, Paul	BEL	3:33.61	HANSEN, Connie	DEN	2:18.29
BLANCHETTE, Craig	USA	3:34.37	CABLE-BROOKS, Candace	USA	2:18.68
AMAROUCHE, Farid	FRA	3:50.40	LAURIDSEN, Ingrid	DEN	2:28.24
GOLOMBEK, Gregor	FRG	3:51.14	JANSEN, Jeanette	HOL	2:28.56
VIGER, Andre	CAN	DNF	CODY-MORRIS, Ann	USA	2:28.78
FIGL, Robert	FRG	DNF	WETTERSTROM, Monica	SWE	2:30.28
YOO, Hee-Sang	KOR	DNF	KANG, Hyung Soon	KOR	3:16.28

Los Angeles, 1984

Men's 1500m wheelchair			Women's 800m wheelchair		
VAN WINKEL, Paul	BEL	3:58.50	HEDRICK, Sharon	USA	2:15.73
SNOW, Randy	USA	4:00.02	SAKER, Monica	SWE	2:20.73
VIGER, Andre	CAN	4:00.47	CABLE, Candace	USA	2:28.37
FITZGERALD, Mel	CAN	4:00.65	HUNTER, Sacajuwea	USA	2:32.22
GEIDER, Juergen	FRA	4:00.71	ORVEFERS, Anna-Marie	SWE	2:32.49
TROTTER, Peter	AUS	4:00.83	LERITI, Angela	CAN	2:41.43
HANSEN, Rick	CAN	4:02.75	HANSON, Connie	DEN	2:41.53
MARTINSON, Jim	USA	4:21.37	LAURIDSEN, Ingrid	DEN	2:43.06

Appendix 2: Results of All Winter Olympic Demonstration Events (1984–1988)

Sarajevo Winter Olympics 1984 Disabled Skiing Demonstration Event Results.

Saturday 11th February - 35 Gates, 1050m with a 269m drop in altitude

Men's giant slalom for single-leg amputees Class LW2			Men's giant slalom for single-arm amputees Class LW6/8		
Alexander Spitz	FRG	1:08.05	Paul Neukomm	SUI	1:02.19
Reiner Bergman	AUT	1:09.91	Dietmar Schweninger	AUT	1:03.04
David Jamison	USA	1:10.18	Rolf Heinzimann	SUI	1:03.25
Michael Hipp	FRG	1:12.15	Heinz Moser	SUI	1:03.66
Peter Perner	AUT	1:12.32	Reed Robinson	USA	1:04.78
Patrick Knaff	FRA	1:12.55	Sreco Kos	YUG	1:05.32
Chew Philip	CAN	1:12.92	Franc Komar	YUG	1:08.40
Greg Oswald	CAN	1:13.81	Stefan Ahacic	YUG	1:10.57
Ola Rylander	SWE	1:14.94			
Rajko Strzinar	YUG	1:18.69			
Jordi Faurat Prat	ESP	1:24.46			

Men's giant slalom for above-knee amputees Class LW4			Men's giant slalom for double-arm amputees Class LW5/7		
Markus Ramsauer	AUT	1:02.66	Lars Lundstroem	SWE	1:05.09
Josef Meusburger	AUT	1:04.90	Felix Abele	FRG	1:05.91
Bill Latimer	USA	1:05.41	Cato Zahl Pedersen	NOR	1:06.21
Eugen Diethelm	SUI	1:06.04	Niko Mull	FRG	1:06.44
Paul Fournier	SUI	1:07.10	Felix Gisler	SUI	1:08.38

Calgary Winter Olympics 1988 Disabled Skiing Exhibition Event Results

Cross Country (Canmore) Friday 19th February
Men 5km Class B1 (10 Competitors, 9 Countries)

1. Aalien, Hans Anton/ Homb, A. (Guide)	NOR	18.51.2
2. Pettersson, Ake/ Stridh, R. (Guide)	SWE	19.29.7
3. Tveit, Asmund/ Ulvang, K. (Guide)	NOR	19.48.6
4. Young, P/ Knutsen, J. (Guide)	GBR	19.49.3
5. Sulisalo, M/ Ukkonen, E. (Guide)	FIN	19.56.3
6. Novotny, J/ Ward, C. (Guide)	USA	20.45.5
7. Gerard, G/ Bret, S. (Guide)	FRA	21.43.0
8. Walch, E/ Seebacher, P. (Guide)	ITA	22.10.6
9. Höglund, E/ Thor, K. (Guide)	SWE	22.44.1
10. Zhukov, V/ Menchikov, V. (Guide)	URS	24.02.7

Ladies 5km Class B1 (5 Competitors, 3 Countries)

1. Preining, Veronika/ Haberl, S. (Guide)	AUT	22.56.3
2. Pennanen, Kirsti/ Viljaharu (Guide)	FIN	23.00.1
3. Heger, Margaret/ Pucher, M. (Guide)	AUT	26.59.3
4. Grigorjeva, V/ Fjodor, L. (Guide)	URS	27.44.3
5. Campbell, D/ Tidl, H. (Guide)	AUT	29.31.4

Giant Slalom (Canada Olympic Park) Sunday 21st February
Men's Locomotor Disabled Class LW2 (13 Competitors, 8 Countries))

1. Spitz, Alexander	FRG	44.04	37.06	**1.21.10**
2. Mannino, Greg	USA	44.94	37.93	**1.22.87**
3. Berger, Fritz	SUI	45.98	39.62	**1.25.60**
4. Perner, Peter	AUT	46.40	39.26	**1.25.66**
5. Jamison, David	USA	46.33	39.62	**1.25.95**
6. Emerson, Robert	USA	46.99	40.23	**1.27.22**
7. Bergamann, Rainer	AUT	48.99	39.44	**1.28.43**
8. Von Arx, Richard	SUI	47.90	40.56	**1.28.46**
9. Chew, Philip	CAN	49.55	39.53	**1.29.08**
10. Hanse, Karel	HOL	50.04	41.49	**1.31.53**
11. Milton, Michael-John	AUS	51.79	41.28	**1.33.07**
12. Duranceau, Michel	CAN	53.69	39.76	**1.33.45**
13. Amalfitano, Guy	FRA	55.94	41.41	**1.37.35**

Ladies Locomotor Disabled Class LW2 (5 Competitors, 3 Countries)

1. Golden, Diana	USA	47.68	38.73	**1.26.41**
2. Gentile, Catherine	USA	51.42	41.44	**1.32.86**
3. Hill, Martha	USA	53.63	41.24	**1.34.87**
4. Chyzyk, Lynda	CAN	54.05	42.16	**1.36.21**
5. Lopez, Virginie	FRA	59.38	42.48	**1.41.86**

Appendix 3: The Top Ten Overall Medal Winning Nations At the Summer and Winter Paralympic Games.

Summer Games (1960-2012)					Winter Games (1976-2010)				
	G	S	B	Tot		G	S	B	Tot
USA	732	656	678	2066	Norway	134	101	80	315
Great Britain	563	550	539	1652	Germany*	121	108	101	330
Germany*	487	493	466	1446	Austria	102	108	104	314
Canada	386	319	329	1034	USA	96	97	68	261
Australia	359	373	345	1077	Finland	76	48	60	183
France	338	342	329	1009	Russia	55	59	39	153
China	331	259	199	789	Switzerland	49	55	48	152
Netherlands	260	226	204	690	France	47	44	48	139
Poland	255	242	197	694	Canada	36	41	42	119
Sweden	230	223	170	623	Sweden	25	30	40	95

* These totals include medals won by the former Federal Republic of Germany (FRG) and the German Democratic Republic (DDR)

Appendix 4: Top Three Individual Medalists at the Summer and Winter Paralympic Games

Summer Paralympic Games

Trischa Zorn	United States	Swimming	1980-2004	F	37	9	5	51*
Béatrice Hess	France	Swimming	1984-2004	F	20	5	0	25
Jonas Jacobsson	Sweden	Shooting	1980-2012	M	17	4	9	30
Michael Edgson	Canada	Swimming	1984-1992	M	17	3	0	20**

*Many sources claim she actually won 41 gold medals. The discrepancy appears to be in New York in 1984 where many sources claim she actually won 10 gold medals, but not one of these sources lists the ten events the medals are supposed to have been won in. My own research using swimming timetables, results and newspaper coverage of the 1984 Games can only verify 6 gold medals in New York. It is true, however, that many results were missed out of the official results for New York across a number of sports and so if this claim is true she actually equalled or bettered Mark Spitz's feat on no less than four occasions! Although, if she really had won ten gold medals in New York I would have expected the media in the United States, which gave a fair bit of coverage to the Games, to have mentioned this amazing feat.

** The Swimming Canada website (https://www.swimming.ca/michaelEdgsonen) claims that Michael Edgson actually won eighteen gold medals including five in New York 1984. I can only find evidence for four gold medals in New York.

However, as with Trischa Zorn (above) it is possible that the missing gold medal is down to a missing result from the official results.

Winter Paralympic Games

Ragnhild Myklebust	Norway	Biathlon, Cross-country skiing, Ice sledge racing	1988-2002	F	22	3	2	27
Gerd Schoenfelder	Germany	Alpine skiing	1992-2010	M	16	4	2	22
Rolf Heinzmann	Switzerland	Alpine skiing	1980-2002	M	12	2	0	14

Summer and Winter Paralympic Games

Reinhild Moeller	Germany	Alpine skiing, Athletics	1980-2006	F	19	3	1	23
Heinz Frei	Switzerland	Athletics, Cycling, Cross-country skiing	1984-2000	M	14	6	11	31
Frank Höfle	Germany	Biathlon, Cross-country skiing, Cycling	1992-2002	M	14	5	5	24

Appendix 5: Countries Who Have Participated At All....

Summer Paralympic Games (11)	Winter Paralympic Games (12)
Australia	Austria
Austria	Canada
Belgium	Czechoslovakia/ Czech Republic
France	Finland
Federal Republic of Germany/ Germany	Federal Republic of Germany/ Germany
Great Britain	France
Ireland	Great Britain
Italy	Japan
Netherlands	Norway
Sweden	Sweden
United States	Switzerland
	United States

Summer and Winter Paralympic Games (6)
Austria
France
Federal Republic of Germany/ Germany
Great Britain
Sweden
United States

For any Swiss reading this who think they have competed in every summer Paralympic Games I would point out that Switzerland were not represented in Madrid 1992 in the Paralympic Games for the Intellectually Disabled. For any Australians that think they have competed in every winter Paralympic Games I would point out that Ron Finneran, Australia's sole representative at the first winter Paralympic Games in Örnsköldsvik, 1976 was deemed ineligible to compete as (having polio) he did not fit into any of the impairment classifications taking part in those Games i.e. amputees and blind and visually impaired.

Appendix 6: Athletes with a Disability and the Olympic Games.

The following is a list of athletes with disabilities who have competed at the Olympic Games or Olympians who have become disabled and then competed at the Paralympic Games. It also includes a list of deaf/ hearing impaired athletes who have competed at the Olympic Games. It is most likely not a complete list.

Athletes with a disability who have competed at the Olympic Games only

George Eyser (USA) (Gymnastics—1904)
American gymnast George Eyser, who had a wooden leg, competed at the 1904 Summer Olympics, and won three gold medals, two silver and a bronze.

Oliver Halassy (HUN) (Water Polo—1928, 1932, 1936)
Oliver Halassy of Hungary, whose left leg was amputated below the knee, won three medals (two gold and a silver) in water polo in the Olympic Games of 1928, 1932 and 1936.

Karoly Takacs (HUN) (Shooting—1948)
Karoly Takacs, also from Hungary, won gold in shooting at the 1948 Summer Olympics. His right hand had been destroyed by a hand grenade ten years earlier, and he had taught himself to shoot with his left.

Lis Hartel (DEN) (Equestrian Dressage—1952)
Lis Hartel was one of the first women allowed to compete against men in the equestrian dressage. Despite being paralysed below the knees after contracting polio in 1944, when she was 23, Hartel was chosen to represent Denmark in the 1952 Olympic Games in Helsinki. She responded by earning the silver medal.

Harold V. Connolly (USA) (Athletics [Hammer Throw]—1956, 1960, 1964, 1968)

Harold Connolly was Olympic hammer throwing gold medallist at the Melbourne Olympic Games of 1956 , a fact made remarkable by the fact that he had Erbs Palsy, which meant the his left arm was some 4.5 inches shorter than his right arm, far less muscularly developed and his left hand was two-thirds the size of his right hand.

Im Dong-Hyun (KOR) (Archery - 2004, 2008, 2012)

South Korean archer Im Dong-Hyun has 20/200 vision in his left eye and 20/100 vision in his right eye, meaning he is legally blind in his left eye. He won Olympic gold in the team competition in 2004 and 2008, and bronze in 2012.

Athletes with a disability who have competed at the Olympic and Paralympic Games

Neroli Fairhall (NZL) (Archery)

Paralympics - 1980, 1988, 2000
Olympics - 1984
New Zealander Neroli Fairhall was the first paraplegic competitor to compete in the Olympic Games. After competing in the 1980 Summer Paralympics in Arnhem she competed in the Los Angeles Olympic Games in 1984.where she finished 35th in the women's individual event.   Fairhall also won gold when archery was first introduced to the Commonwealth Games in Brisbane in 1982.

Sonia Vettenburg (BEL) (Shooting)

Paralympics – 1984, 1988
Olympics – 1992
Having been a medallist at the 1984 1nd 1988 Paralympic Games Sonia Vettenburg from Belgium finished 37th at the Barcelona Olympic Games in the women's 10 metre air pistol.

Paola Fantato (ITA) (Archery)

Paralympics – 1988, 1992, 1996, 2000, 2004
Olympics – 1996
Paola Fantato of Italy contracted Polio at the age of eight and has been a wheelchair used ever since. She competed in archery at five consecutive Paralympic Games from 1988 to 2004 winning three individual and two team gold medals. In addition she represented Italy in archery the Atlanta Olympic Games where she finished 54th in the individual event and 9th in the team event

Marla Runyan (USA) (Athletics—Middle Distance)

Paralympics – 1992, 1996
Olympics – 2000, 2004
Marla Runyan is an American visually impaired athlete who won multiple medals in a range of track and field events in the 1992 and 1996 Paralympic Games. She then turned her talents to middle distance running and successfully qualified to compete in the Sydney Olympic Games in the 1500m where she finished 8th. She

also finished 9th in a first round heat of the women's 5000m at the Athens Olympic Games of 2004.

Natalia Partyka (POL) (Table Tennis)

Paralympics – 2000, 2004, 2008, 2012

Olympics – 2008, 2012

Natalia Partyka of Poland was born without a right hand or forearm. She first competed in the Paralympic Games at the age of just eleven in Sydney 2000. She has been women's individual champion in her class at the last three Paralympic Games and also represented Poland at the Olympic table tennis events in Beijing 2008 and London 2012.

Natalie du Toit (RSA) (Swimming)

Paralympics – 2004, 2008, 2012

Olympics – 2008

Natalie du Toit is a South African single above the knee amputee who won multiple gold medals at the Paralympic Games between 2004 and 2012. In Beijing 2008 she also qualified to represent South Africa at the Beijing Olympic Games in the 10km Open water Swim, finishing 16th.

Assunta Legnante (ITA) (Athletics—Shot Put)

Paralympics – 2012

Olympics - 2008

Assunte Legnante was born with congenital glaucoma in both eyes. Prior to 2009 she had sufficient sight to compete in non-disabled sport and took part in the Beijing Olympic Games in the women's shot put. However, in 2009 her sight deteriorated dramatically and is now classified as legally blind. She is the current F11 World record holder for shot put, set when she took the gold medal at the London 2012 Paralympic Games.

Oscar Pistorius (RSA) (Athletics)

Paralympics – 2004, 2008, 2012

Olympics – 2012

In London 2012 Oscar Pistorius became the first amputee to run at the Summer Olympic Games, where he competed in the 400m and 4 x 400 relay events.

Athletes who have competed at the Olympic Games, become disabled, and then competed at the Paralympic Games.

Pál Szekeres (HUN)

Olympics – 1988 (Fencing)

Paralympics – 1992, 1996, 2000, 2004, 2008, 2012 (Wheelchair Fencing)

There is at present only one athlete who has won a medal at the Olympics prior to becoming disabled, and has then gone on to win medals at the Paralympics. Hungarian fencer Pál Szekeres won a bronze medal at the 1988 Summer Olympics, then was disabled in a bus accident, and went on to win three gold medals and three bronze in wheelchair fencing at the Paralympics. He currently has the distinction of being the only person ever to have won medals at both the Olympic and Paralympic Games.

Orazio Fagone (ITA) (Winter Sports)

Olympics – 1988, 1992, 1994 (Short Track Speed Skating)
Paralympics – 2006, 2010 (Sledge Hockey)

Orazio Fagone competed for Italy as a short track speed skater in three Olympic Games from 1988 to 1994. At the Lillehammer 1994 Games he was part of the Italian team which won the gold medal in the 5000 metre relay competition. However, Fagone's right leg was amputated after a motorcycle accident in 1997. He has since competed in two winter Paralympic Games in 2006 and 2008 with the Italian sledge hockey team.

Ilke Wyludda (GER)

Olympics – 1992, 1996, 2000 (Athletics – Discus)
Paralympics – 2012 (Athletics – Discus & Shot Put)

Ilke Wyludda from Germany competed in the Olympics from 1992 to 2000 winning the gold medal in women's discuss in Atlanta in 1996. In early January 2011 Wyludda revealed in German newspaper Bild that she had to have her right leg amputated because of Sepsis. She then competed in the London 2012 Paralympic Games in the F57/58 discus and shot put competitions finishing 9th in the discus and 5th in the shot put.

Deaf/ Hearing Impaired Athletes Who Have Competed at the Olympic Games

Although officially not currently part of the Paralympic movement I have included a list of athletes who are either deaf or hearing impaired and have competed at the Olympic Games

Carlo Orlandi (ITA) 1928

Carlo Orlandi was an Italian boxer who competed in the 1928 Olympics in Amsterdam, and was also a deaf-mute. He won the gold medal in the lightweight class.

Donald Gollan (GBR) 1928

UK rower Donald Gollan won a silver medal as a member of the rowing eights in 1928. He was deaf and mute.

Ildikó Újlaky-Rejtő (HUN) 1960—1976

Deaf Hungarian fencer Ildikó Újlaky-Rejtő won two individual medals (a gold and a bronze) and five team medals at the Olympics between 1960 and 1976.

Jeff Float (USA) 1984

Jeff Float swam the third leg for the US in the 4 × 200-meter freestyle relay. He had lost 80% of his hearing in his right ear and 60% in his left ear after contracting viral meningitis at the age of 13 months.

Terence Parkin (RSA) 2000, 2004
Deaf South African swimmer Terence Parkin won a silver medal in the 200-meter breaststroke at the Sydney Olympic Games in 2000 and also participated in 2004 in Athens

Frank Bartolillo (AUS) 2004
Australian Frank Bartolillo is profoundly deaf, and competed in the individual foil event in fencing at the Athens 2004 Olympics.

Chris Colwill (USA) 2008, 2012
Chris Colwill, who has a 65% hearing loss, is a diver from the USA. Colwill is not able to wear his hearing aid when he dives, so he can't hear the whistle that signals to the divers when they can go. Therefore, the referees nod to him in addition to the whistle so that he can recognize the signal.

David Smith (USA) 2012
David Smith was part of the USA volleyball team at the 2012 London Olympics. Smith has been deaf since birth, having 80-90% hearing loss, and has worn hearing aids since he was three years old.

Appendix 7: Upcoming Paralympic Games and Dates

Summer

Rio de Janeiro, Brazil:	7th-18th September 2016
Tokyo, Japan:	25th August–6th September 2020

Winter

Sochi, Russia:	7th–16th March 2014
Pyeonchang, South Korea:	9th–18th March 2018

CPSIA information can be obtained at www.ICGtesting.com
Printed in the USA
BVOW10s0914100315

390951BV00011B/399/P